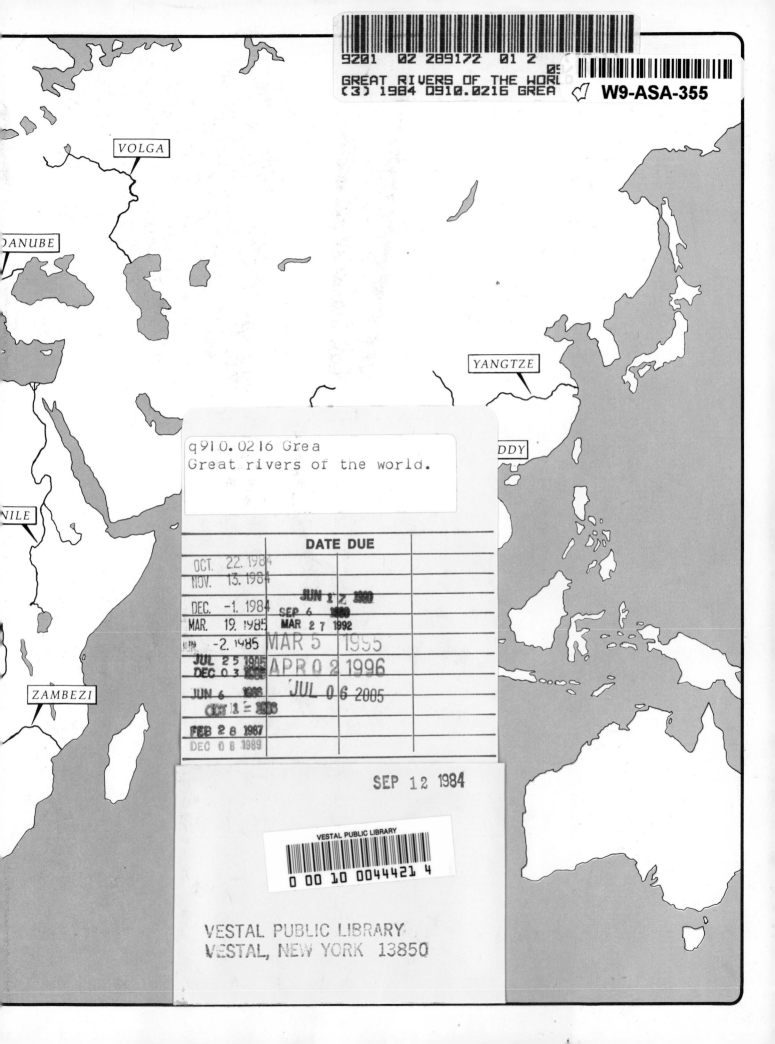

VOLGA

DANUBE

YANGTZE

NILE

DDY

ZAMBEZI

GREAT RIVERS
OF THE WORLD

GREAT RIVERS
OF THE WORLD

EDITED BY ALEXANDER FRATER
PHOTOGRAPHED BY COLIN JONES

Little, Brown and Company   Boston   Toronto

LIBRARY OF CONGRESS CATALOG CARD NO 83-83383

FIRST AMERICAN EDITION

THE MAPS WERE DRAWN BY CONSTANCE AND BRIAN DEAR

PRINTED IN GREAT BRITAIN

CONTENTS

ILLUSTRATIONS

INTRODUCTION

The idea of launching a series based on the world's greatest rivers came about at a small restaurant located near the offices of *The Observer* – the world's oldest Sunday newspaper – and well-patronised by its editorial staff. I was lunching with photographer Colin Jones and talking about possible new stories for the paper's Colour Magazine. We were looking for the kind of subjects we knew our readers liked best – big, expansive features about faraway places, well-written and handsomely illustrated.

How we got on to the subject of rivers I do not recall. I like to think it was due to a ship's siren sounding on the Thames a hundred yards or so from where we sat, but that may have been a trick of the memory. Anyway, suddenly the notion was there, probably reached by a kind of osmosis. We pondered it a while and thought it seemed promising. From a writer's point of view it was very good indeed. A river is a fine literary device. It has a beginning, a middle and an end, and possesses its own narrative flow. A river does much of the writer's work for him. It dictates its own pace and structure, imposes its own order and disciplines. All he need do is follow, record, interpret and describe. Jones said the same thing went for the pictures. He said the prospect of photographing a few rivers sounded fairly interesting.

Back at the office we began making lists. In terms of length, the greatest river of all was the Nile, 6,648 kilometres from source to sea. Though the Amazon was shorter (by just 211 kilometres) it remained the greatest in every other sense, navigable by deep-sea steamers for over 3000 kilometres, carrying twenty-five times more water than the Nile in flood, pouring two and a half million tons of silt into the Atlantic each day; the Amazon diminishes most other rivers, reducing them to the category of storm drains. Next came the Mississippi, last of the earth's trio of 6000-kilometre rivers, followed by the 5494-kilometre Yangtze. They were the top four, and they went to the head of the list.

The world number five turned out to be the Ob, a vast, obscure Siberian stream rising in the Altai mountains and flowing down to the Arctic Sea, but it was never really a runner, not for our purposes. Too much icy wilderness, too few people, nowhere to stay, no one to talk to. The Lena, another Soviet river flowing into the Arctic, was discounted for the same reasons.

The Zaire, or Congo, came next. This was the mighty African waterway of H. M. Stanley, King Leopold of the Belgians, Sir Roger Casement, Joseph Conrad, Graham Greene and V. S. Naipaul, and to ignore that would have been unthinkable. We rejected the Mackenzie, the Niger and the Paraná, and pencilled in the 4000-kilometre Mekong as a standby; we had our eye on certain other Asian rivers which, if we could get to them, would make the Mekong superfluous to our needs. We said yes to the Volga, flowing through the historical and emotional heartland of Russia, no to the St Lawrence, yes to the Zambezi, no to the Madeira, the Brahmaputra and the Indus, yes to the Danube. The Danube, stitching together Germany, Austria and a basket of Warsaw Pact countries, would be our chief European river.

The Tigris and Euphrates we turned down with regret. They passed through the sad battlefields of the Iraqi–Iranian war, and access to them would have been impossible. We said no to Australia's Murray but an emphatic yes to the Ganges. Apart from its extraordinary plethora of mouths, ringing the northern end of the Bay of Bengal like a battery of siege guns, it is not really a great river in the physical sense; its water levels are erratic and numerous stretches are unnavigable. It remains, however, the main religious and spiritual artery of India, so it went straight on to the list, unlike the Colorado, Dnieper and Orinoco, which didn't. The Irrawaddy was put on without hesitation. Rangoon to Mandalay! Those names were imbued with such piquancy that, when speaking them, one could almost taste the spices on the tongue. We said no to the Don and the Limpopo, no to the Rhine (too extensively written-about already) and, finally, yes to the Loire, France's longest and prettiest river. We closed our list there, saying no, with varying degrees of regret, to the Seine, the Susquehanna, the Saguenay, the Shannon and the Severn. We also turned down the Thames. At a mere 336 kilometres, it simply did not qualify.

After that Peter Crookston, then editor of *The Observer Magazine*, and I sat down and tried to match each river with a writer likely to do it justice. To maintain continuity, Colin Jones would take all the pictures. While Crookston made the executive decisions, I looked after the paperwork. My job was to get our people into the relevant country, out to the right river and on to the appropriate boat. I became *The Observer*'s Riverine Comptroller, equipped with a telephone, a telex machine and a *Times Atlas*, surrounded by piles of visa-application forms. We launched ourselves first upon the Amazon, and immediately ran into trouble with the documentation. For some reason the Brazilian Embassy in London were unable to issue the visas. That would be done, they said, by their embassy in Lima, Peru, where Jones and our writer, Ronald Fraser, were calling en route to the Amazon's glacial source in the Andes. But the Lima Embassy denied all knowledge of any visas, and precious days were lost while telexes clattered between London, Lima and various government offices in Brazil. The experience taught us a small but significant lesson. We should take nothing on trust and be prepared for any contingency. Our travellers should leave their return air tickets open-ended and enter into no binding arrangements for dinner parties, speaking engagements, television appearances, jury service, bar mitzvahs or family holidays until they held confirmed reservations for their homeward flights.

The most difficult countries to get into were Zaire, Burma and Mozambique. All three have a profound suspicion of the media. For much of its length the Zambezi flows through two sovereign states, Zambia and Mozambique. Negotiations to arrange access to Mozambique for Jones and writer Nicholas Wollaston were protracted but eventually successful. After completing the Zambian section they were to cross the border at the Mozambique village of Zumbo where, according to Senhor Mota Lopes of the Ministry of Information at Maputo, the capital, they would be met by an official who would furnish them with a guide, visas and the necessary papers. But there was nobody waiting for them at Zumbo. The village, reached by dugout canoe, was virtually deserted. The few people who saw them arrive ran away. Eventually a shopkeeper named Hannibal emerged from the trees and offered them a supper of fish, rice and beans. Then a man called January allowed them to sleep in his small, rat-infested house. Next day Wollaston hitched a lift on a truck and eventually made contact with Senhor Lopes's man 350 miles downstream.

Wollaston also travelled down the Zaire for us, an epic journey from Kisingani to Kinshasa aboard an extraordinary floating township made up of a flotilla of double-decker barges lashed together (and including, among its numerous facilities, a busy shipboard brothel). It took the Zaire authorities two years to approve our applications. From time to time, in response to my entreaties, letters would arrive from His Excellency Matungulu N'Kuman Tavun, Zaire Ambassador at the Court of St James's. They were placatory, amiable and infinitely courteous – *'J'ai l'honneur d'accuser bonne réception de vos deux lettres du 17 septembre . . . Veuillez agréer, Monsieur, l'expression de ma considération distinguée'* – and written on notepaper embossed with a leopard, an olive branch and an object not unlike a banana. But, despite Ambassador Tavun's assurances, there was little sign of movement from Kinshasa. Letters and telexes to the Département de l'Information there went unanswered. Telephone calls were intercepted by a monosyllabic citoyen sitting at the switchboard who, after grunting, sighing and sucking audibly at his teeth, always contrived to cut them off.

It was the British Foreign and Commonwealth Office which finally turned the trick, working away patiently behind the scenes. The British Ambassador in Kinshasa, Mr J. M. O. Snodgrass, even found the time to write to us with practical advice. 'You will need to allow plenty of time, and to be prepared to live roughly,' his letter said. 'For example, you may need to provide your own food for much of the time in the interior.' Mr Snodgrass seemed confident that the Zaire authorities would let us in, and his optimism turned out to be justified. His letter was eventually followed by one from Monsieur Kande Dzambulate, a senior Kinshasa civil servant with the majestic title of 'Le Commissaire d'Etat à l'Information, à la Culture et aux Arts, Membre du Comité Central du M. P. R., Commissaire Politique'. M Dzambulate wrote to say that we could come. *'Je me réjouis du projet du journal* THE OBSERVER *d'inclure le fleuve Zaire dans cette série d'articles,'* he told us gravely. He rejoiced that we were including the Zaire in our series of articles! We, in turn, celebrated by speeding Wollaston and Jones hotfoot to M Dzambulate's river before he could change his mind.

Negotiating entry to Burma proved almost as difficult and, once again, it was the Foreign Office which persuaded the local authorities to allow us on to the Irrawaddy. My thanks are due to Mr Patrick Brooks of the South-East Asian Department who, in conjunction with the British Embassy in Rangoon, was instrumental in obtaining our visas. Mr Brooks remained unperturbed even when I received a telex from the Burmese Ministry of Home and Religious Affairs, two days before we were due to fly to Rangoon, perfunctorily denying all knowledge of our visit. Mr Brooks told me to calm down. That afternoon he called back to say the trip was on again. There had been one or two small misunderstandings. These had now been resolved. 'You can pick up your visas at their London Embassy in Charles Street any time you like,' he said, 'provided it's within the next twenty-four hours. After that they're closing down for the annual Burmese Water Festival.'

Our thanks are due also to Mr Brooks's colleagues at the British Embassy in Rangoon. They entertained us, offered us books and advice, made appointments, arranged for the purchase of our steamer tickets, even delegated one of their Burmese clerks to act as our guide and interpreter. It was he who, shortly before our departure for the river, took me to the Shwedagon Pagoda, the astonishing bullion-plated temple that towers 326 feet over Rangoon (with 5,452 large diamonds glittering in its weather vane) and bade me buy a booklet of gold leaf at a stall that specialised in painstakingly beating the stuff into sheets finer than a bee's wing. Then he urged me up a high, rickety ladder propped against the outside of the Shwedagon and showed me how to lick the leaf and stick it on to the temple's gleaming flanks. Around us other pilgrims were balancing precariously on their own ladders, all licking their costly offerings and helping to gild their temple. It was, I learned, a means of gaining merit, of calling down Buddha's blessings on our journey.

Many people helped us with this series, and we are indebted to Mr K. B. Bala, Counsellor (Press and Culture) at the Indian High Commission in London, who smoothed Geoffrey Moorhouse's passage down the Ganges; to Mr Konayessi, of the Egyptian Embassy in London, who personally supervised the arrangements for Norman Lewis on the Nile; to Ms Eileen Houlder of Lindblad Travel, Inc., for generously offering Paul Theroux a free passage down the Yangtze; and to Colm Foy of the Mozambique and Angola Information Centre in London, who arranged for Nicholas Wollaston to negotiate the Mozambique end of the Zambezi. And my special thanks are due to Mr Hans Wörndl, UK manager of the DER Travel Service, for using his impressive list of contacts on either side of the Iron Curtain to get Bruce Chatwin on to the Volga and Piers Paul Read down the Danube; the latter, which flows through a bewildering succession of East European borders, is a bureaucratic nightmare. Mr Wörndl, invariably helpful and good humoured, took the whole thing in his stride. If he had problems, we certainly never heard about them.

Our thanks are also due to the writers who made these journeys, often suffering discomfort, occasionally even a degree of hardship. And, finally, to Colin Jones who, having completed these assignments, has now, as far as I can judge, travelled down more great rivers than any man alive. His pictures speak for themselves, reflecting the extraordinary range of places and people he saw. He did the Yangtze mostly in the rain, sharing a cabin with twenty Chinese (unlike Theroux, whose stateroom was aboard a luxury yacht that once belonged to Chairman Mao), who all got up at 5 a.m. when the ship's loudspeakers began playing 'The East is Red'. 'We entered the Gorges at four in the morning, in pouring rain,' he recalls. 'The light was terrible – f8 at a fortnight. The place seemed to have an almost mystical significance for the Chinese. They stood on deck, applauding like a theatre audience. The authorities there were very good about letting me take pictures. At one point we steamed past the whole Chinese navy, but nobody told me to put my cameras away. In Russia, though, it was *nyet* all the time. Our boat seemed to travel the most interesting stretches of the Volga at night, and, when we moored, it was always in some rural reach, well away from the centres of population.'

On the Amazon the launch he and Ronald Fraser had hired broke down and, for the better part of a day, they drifted helplessly down the huge, silent river, past thickly jungled banks where nobody lived. Then he hired a plane to take some aerial shots, ordered the door removed and, 5000 feet over the river, nearly fell out. His best pictures, he thinks, were of the Loire, though he hated everything about the region. 'The châteaux looked as though they'd been brought in from Disneyland, and the restaurants were too pretentious for words. I went into a very posh one for lunch one day and ordered the *plat du jour*. It cost a fortune and turned out to be offal.'

He liked the dignity and courtesy of the Burmese, and was beguiled by the lovely Burmese light. 'But the Ganges light is even better. It's more spectacular, with the most amazing reds and greens. All the tropical rivers left me short of sleep; if you wanted good pictures you had to be in position before dawn so that you could get the marvellously soft, rich, radiant light of sunrise. By breakfast it's all over. Then the light gets hard, the shadows harsh; the effect is like a hammer. Oddly enough, that early-morning and late-afternoon light in the tropics reminds me of England. In England we live in the greatest photographic light of all. There's a marvellous translucent quality to it that's almost unique. Funny, eh? You spend your career working all over the world and you finally come back to that corny old platitude – there's no place like home.'

ALEXANDER FRATER

THE YANGTZE

PAUL THEROUX

*T*he main paradox (there are many others: we are dealing with China, population one billion) is that there is no Yangtze river. The name is unknown to most Chinese, who call it Ta Jiang, 'Great River', or Chang Jiang, 'Long River', unless they live above Chongqing – there, the swift silt-filled waters are referred to as Chin-sha Jiang, 'The River of Gold Sand'. That is only a misnomer now. As recently as fifty years ago, in the winter months when the level dropped, the Chinese squatted at its edge and panned for gold, sluicing the mud and gathering gold dust. European travellers reported seeing washerwomen wearing thick gold bangles, made of the metal that had been carried from where the river – let us call it the Yangtze – rises in Tibet.

But it has more moods than names. 'I am careful to give the date of each day's notes,' Archibald Little wrote in *Through the Yangtse Gorges* (1887). 'The river varies so wonderfully at different seasons that any description must be carefully understood only to apply to the day upon which it is written.' Captain Little was overwhelmed by it; he compared it to the Mississippi and the Amazon; he said it was indescribable. It has in many stretches a violent magnificence. It is subject to murderous floods, and its winter levels create rapids of such turbulence that the river captain steers his ship through the foam and travels down the tongue of the rapid, praying that no junk will lie in his path, as it is impossible for him to stop or reverse. But it is not all so dramatic. Its four divisions are like four separate rivers: above Chongqing, it is mythic and still associated with gold and landslides; the Upper River (Chongqing-Yichang) is the wildest – here are the gorges and the landscape of China's Walter Scottish classic, *The Romance of the Three Kingdoms*; the Middle River (Yichang-Wuhan) is serene and a mile wide; the Lower River (Wuhan-Shanghai) is slow and sticky yellow and populous.

I sailed 1,500 miles downstream, from Chongqing to Shanghai. Every mile of it was different; but there were 2,000 miles I did not see. It crosses twelve provinces or regions, 700 rivers are joined to it – all Yangtze statistics are hopelessly huge and

13

ungraspable; they obscure rather than clarify. And since words can have a greater precision than numbers, one day I asked a Chinese ship captain if he thought the river had a distinct personality.

He said, 'The mood of the river changes according to season. It changes every day. It is not easy. Navigating the river is always a struggle against nature. And there is only one way to pilot a ship well.' He explained, 'It is necessary to see the river as an enemy.'

Later, a man told me that in the course of one afternoon, he had counted nine human corpses bobbing hideously down the river.

The Yangtze is China's main artery, its major waterway, the source of many of its myths, the scene of much of its history. On its banks are some of its greatest cities. It is the fountainhead of superstition; it provides income and food to half the population. It is one of the most dangerous rivers in the world, in some places one of the dirtiest, in others one of the most spectacular. The Chinese drink it and bathe in it and wash clothes in it and shit in it. It represents both life and death. It is a wellspring, a sewer and a tomb; depthless in the gorges, puddle-shallow at its rapids. The Chinese say if you haven't been up the Great River, you haven't been anywhere.

*T*hey also say that in the winter, on the river, the days are so dark that when the sun comes out the dogs bark at it. Chongqing was dark at nine in the morning, when I took the rattling tin tram on the cog railway that leads down the black crags which are Chongqing's ramparts, down the sooty cliffs, past the tenements and billboards ('Flying Pigeon Bicycles', 'Seagull Watches', 'Parrot Accordions') to the landing stage. A thick sulphurous fog lay over the city, a Coketown of six million. The fog had muffled the morning noises and given the city an air of frightening solemnity. It also stank like poison. Dr Ringrose, who was from Leeds, sniffed and said, 'That is the smell of my childhood.'

There were thirty-three of us, including Ringrose. The others were American, most of them millionaires, many of them multi-millionaires. 'If you have two or three million,' one of them told me in the dreary city of Wanxian, 'you're not a millionaire – you're just getting by.' Another enlarged on this. 'How rich is rich? Twenty-five million,' she said crisply. 'If you have twenty-five you're all right.' But Lurabelle Laughlin, from Pasadena, had inherited $50 million. Her husband Harry told me this. He said Lurabelle could buy and sell every person on board our ship. He wasn't being malicious, only factual. 'And I'm not too badly off myself,' he said. 'My mother inherited the Standard Oil of California fortune.'

It was I, not they, who brought up the subject of money. I was the only freeloader on this trip. The rest had paid an average of about £5,000 (including the airfare) to take this Lindblad 'Yangtze River Cruise'. The tour and the Pan American airfare were given to me free of charge through *The Observer*, and though I withheld this information from my fellow passengers (no one is more irritating to the paying passenger than the person getting a free ride), I gladly acknowledge the assistance of Lindblad Inc. It would be cheating not to do so, especially as it was one of the grandest trips I have ever made. Tour companies take all the headaches out of travel: no standing in line for tickets, everything arranged, all meals planned, all entertainments fixed. You sit back, put your feet up and let China wash over you. The guided tour is, in many ways, the opposite of travel; and it frequently attracts sedentary types, who would rather be carried through China than read about it.

'I hate walking,' Mrs Ver Bryck told me. Mrs Ver Bryck, another oil heiress, was seventy and a chain-smoker, and she hailed from Incline, Nevada. 'I never walk. I've been everywhere and didn't have to walk. I pay so I don't have to walk. And stairs are my bugbear! But you look like a walker, Paul. Are you going to walk and do all that crappy-ola?'

I cherish the memory of Ami Ver Bryck and Lurabelle Laughlin walking from the tramway at Chongqing across the muddy paving on the foreshore, with hundreds of Chinese, in baggy blue suits, watching in utter silence. Lurabelle's mink coat was golden, made from thirty-five creatures of the 'tourmaline' variety; Ami's was a rich glossy mahogany. And here was Bea Brantman, also in mink. 'This is my football coat!' she cried. 'I wear it to all the games!' Bea and her husband, who was known to everyone as Big Bob, had eleven children. Big Bob said, 'I guess they'd put me in jail for that in China! Watch out, Bea, it's kind of slippery here. It looks more like an ocean than a river. You can't even see the other side.'

It was a good companionable crowd, and though it seems a contradiction to say so, these millionaires represented a cross-section of American society. Half had been to China before and knew their way around Inner Mongolia. The rest were novices and called Mao 'Mayo', and confused Thailand with Taiwan and Fuji with Fiji. They were as tenacious and practical as the Chinese, and just as ethnocentric, but much funnier and better at cards.

We boarded *Tung Fang Hong* ('The East is Red') *Number 39*, and were soon underway. Because of the construction of locks and a dam at Yichang, we would travel downriver in two ships: the MS *Kun Lun* awaited us just below Yichang. *Number 39* and the *Kun Lun* were the same size, built to carry 900 people. But they had been specially chartered by Lindblad. There were, as I say, only thirty-three of us, and a crew of 102. No hardships for us, and it seemed at times as if, though we were travelling through the very heart of the country, China was elsewhere.

'The Blue Danube Waltz' was playing on the ship's loudspeakers as *Number 39* swung between the sampans and the fishing smacks and the burdened ferries. The captain greeted us in the lounge and told us the current was moving at two metres per second and added, 'As your captain, I am responsible for your safety, so please don't worry about it.'

Captain Liu was sixty. He had a narrow, flat-backed head and bristly hair and a seeping wound in his left eye and large spaces between his teeth. He had always worked on the river. His father had been a tracker on a junk, rowing and towing junks upstream. Captain Liu himself had started out as a steward, serving food on a Chinese river boat, at the age of fifteen. 'I was the "boy" as they say in English, but I worked my way up to captain. I never went to school. You can't learn about this river in a school. You can only learn it by being on the bridge.'

This is true; and not much has been written about the Yangtze. But before I left London I had been given a list of twenty-eight landmarks on the Upper River, patiently typed by Captain A. R. Williamson, who spent nearly thirty years sailing up and down the river.

Captain Williamson is ninety, living in vigorous retirement in Hove, and is one of the historians of the river. I was lucky in meeting him and lucky to have a detailed list of things to look out for – towns, cliffs, pagodas, rapids and shrines. It was Captain Williamson's list that convinced me that, though a great deal has changed in China ('China,' Premier Deng had promised, 'will be a modern power by the year 2000'), little on the Yangtze has altered. The cities are bigger and filthier, the rapids have been dynamited, there are more ships; but the river today is essentially the river Captain Williamson travelled on in 1920, and Archibald Little sailed on in 1886, and the Abbé David botanised on in the 1860s, and Italian missionaries proselytised on in the seventeenth and eighteenth centuries. The river and the ways of many of the river dwellers are as old as China. There is a painting in the Shanghai Museum of junks and sampans on a river, by Zhang Zheduan. Those vessels have the same sails, masts, rigging, rudders and oars as ones I saw on the Yangtze the other day. But it is a Sung Dynasty painting, 1,000 years old.

A half hour below Chongqing, Captain Williamson's notes said, was a large Buddha in a shrine at the top of a long flight of steps. The niche was there, and the steps; but the Buddha was gone. In Captain Williamson's day, all upbound junks fired strings of firecrackers on passing the Buddha, 'in gratitude for safe passage'. Veneration has become political in China: there were no firecrackers, though there were dozens of passing junks.

Mottled hills appeared in the mist on both sides of the river, and here, just above Changshou, the river narrowed to about seventy-five feet. The ship slowed to negotiate this rocky bottleneck and gave me time to study the hills. Abbé David saw fortifications on the tops of these hills. In his *Diaries* is a wonderful account of his Yangtze trip. He wrote, 'These are refuges in times of trouble for the country people, where they can go with their possessions and be safe from the depredations of rebels and brigands.' Banditry was widespread on the Yangtze from the earliest times, and the Twenties and Thirties of this century were especially terrible, as warlords' armies fought their way towards Chongqing; there was no peace on the river until 1949, when a brooding bureaucracy with parrot slogans took over.

Now, every inch of these hills was farmland: it is the agricultural overstrain of China. On the steepest slopes were terraces of vegetables. How was it possible to water the gardens on these cliff-faces? I looked closely and saw a man climbing up the hillside, carrying two buckets on a yoke. He tipped them into a ditch and, without pausing further, started down the hill. No one is idle on the Yangtze. In the loneliest bends of the river are solitary men breaking rock and smashing it into gravel. You might think they would sit down and rest (who is watching?), or soak their feet in the shallows. It is killing work. But they go on hammering, and the sound I associate with these hidden stretches of the Upper River is the sound of hammers and chisels, a sound like the sweetest chimes.

I n 1937, Captain Williamson saw only the city walls of Changshou from the river. Today there are no city walls, and Changshou (the name means 'Long Life') is one of the nightmare cities of the river. It burst through its old walls and sprawled across the banks, blackening three hillsides with chimneys and factories and blocks of workers' flats. 'Looks like Pittsburgh,' someone said. But Chongqing had looked like Pittsburgh, and so did six others downstream. Yellow froth streamed from pipes and posterns, and drained into the river with white muck and oil and the suds of treated sewage and beautifully coloured poison. And on a bluff below the town, there was an old and untroubled pagoda, still symmetrical, looking as if it had been carved from a piece of laundry soap. These pagodas have a purpose. They are always found near towns and cities and, even now in unspiritual China, serve a spiritual function, controlling the *feng-shui* ('wind-water') of a place: they balance the female influences of the *yin* ('darkness') and the male influence of the *yang* ('light'). The Chinese say they no longer believe in such superstitious malarkey, but the visible fact is that most pagodas survived the Cultural Revolution. Anything that a fanatical Red Guard left intact must be regarded as worthy, if not sacred. The pagodas on the Yangtze bluffs remain pretty much as they always were.

It was near Changshou, about noon on that first day, that I saw a junk being steered to the bank, and the sail lowered, and five men leaping on to the shore with tow-lines around their waists. They ran ahead, then jerked like dogs on a leash, and immediately began towing the junk against the current. These are trackers. They are mentioned by the earliest travellers on the Yangtze. They strain, leaning forward, and almost imperceptibly the sixty-foot junk begins to move upstream. There is no level towpath. The trackers are rock-climbers: they scamper from boulder to boulder, moving higher until the boulders give out, and then dropping down, pulling and climbing until there is a reach on the river when the junk can sail again. The only difference – but it is a fairly large one – between trackers long ago and trackers today is that they are no longer whipped. 'Often our men have to climb or jump like monkeys,' wrote a Yangtze traveller, in the middle of the last century, of his trackers, 'and their backs are lashed by the two chiefs, to urge them to work at critical moments. This new spectacle at first revolts and angers us, but when we see that the men do not complain about the lashings we realise that it is the custom of the country, justified by the exceptional difficulties along the route.' Captain Little saw a tracker chief strip his clothes off, jump into the river, then roll himself in sand until he looked half-human, like a gritty ape; then he did a demon dance, and howled, and whipped the trackers, who – scared out of their wits – willingly pulled a junk off a sand-bank.

The trackers sing or chant. There are garbled versions of what they say. Some travellers have them grunting and groaning, others are more specific and report the trackers yelling, '*Chor! Chor!*' – slang for '*Shang-chia*' or 'Put your shoulder to it.' I asked a boatman what the trackers were chanting. He said they cried out '*Hai tzo! Hai tzo!*' over and over again, which means 'Number! Number!' in Szechuanese, and is uttered by trackers and oarsmen alike.

'When we institute the Four Modernisations,' he added – this man was one of the two per cent who are members of the Chinese Communist Party – 'there will be no more junks or trackers.'

But from the look of it, the junks and this antediluvian labour will be on the river for some time to come. Stare for five minutes at any point on the Yangtze and you will see a junk, sailing upstream with its ragged, ribbed sail; or being towed by yelling, tethered men; or slipping downstream with a skinny man clinging to its rudder. There are many newfangled ships and boats on the river, but I should say that the Yangtze is a river of junks and sampans, fuelled by human sweat. Still, there is nothing lovelier than a junk with a following wind (the wind blows upstream, from east to west – a piece of great meteorological luck and a shaper of Chinese history), sailing so well that the clumsy vessel looks as light as a waterbird paddling and foraging in the muddy current.

That image is welcome, because there is little bird-life on the Yangtze – indeed, China itself is no place for an ornithologist. The eminent bird-man Roger Tony Peterson, editor of the twenty-two Peterson Field Guides, was recently on the Yangtze. A friend asked him whether he had done any bird-watching, and Mr Peterson's response was something like, 'You must be joking.'

It is hard to say if the absence of trees is the reason for the scarceness of birds; or is it the use of powerful insecticides, or the plain hunger of the people who seem to kill anything that moves? Apart from a few kites and hawks, and some feeble sparrows, the only wild ground-dwelling creature I saw in China was a rat, and in twenty-two trips on the Yangtze a Lindblad guide told me he had only seen one wild thing, a small snake. No wonder the Chinese stared at mink coats and alligator handbags! Abbé David saw very few birds on the Yangtze in the 1860s and, as a naturalist, he was looking hard for them. He put it down to the wilful destruction of animals by the Chinese, and his reflection on this has proven to be prophetic: 'A selfish and blind preoccupation with material interests has caused us to reduce this cosmos, so marvellous to him with eyes to see it, to a hard matter-of-fact place. Soon the horse and the pig on the one hand and wheat and potatoes on the other will replace hundreds of thousands of animals and plants given us by God.'

Down the Yangtze the awful prediction has been fulfilled. You expect this river trip to be an experience of the past – and it is. But it is also a glimpse of the future. In 100 years or so, under a cold uncolonised moon, what we call the civilised world will all look like China, muddy and senile: no trees, no birds, short of fuel and metal and meat, but plenty of pushcarts, cobblestones, ditch-diggers and wooden inventions. Nine hundred million farmers splashing through puddles.

Forget rocket-ships, super-technology, moving sidewalks and all the rubbishy hope in science fiction. No one will ever go to Mars and live. We are stuck with this mildly poisoned earth and its smoky air. We are in for hunger and hard work, the highest stage of poverty – no starvation, but crudeness everywhere, clumsy art, simple language, bad books, brutal laws, plain vegetables and clothes of one colour. It will be damp and dull, like this. It will be monochrome and crowded – how could it be different? There will be no star wars or galactic empire and no more money to waste on the loony nationalism in space programmes. Our grandchildren will probably live in a version of China. On the dark brown banks of the Yangtze the future has already arrived.

Sixty-five miles below Chongqing, at Fuling, I was joined at the rail by one of the passengers, a stockbroker. We talked about the price of gold and the delinquent bullion market as, on the shore, small tent camps of Chinese sifted gravel and lugged it in buckets to waiting sampans. We passed gardens and talked about land deals and Washington real estate. The bare hills provided inspiration for further investment. 'Timber,' he said. 'This is a very good time to buy timber. What you want is a well-managed company, with a good product and a good record.'

There was a commune on the next hill: vegetables, a factory, chimneys, huts, a brickworks. We watched it pass. 'The American stock market is vastly under-rated. There are a lot of real bargains. And with Reagan as President –' The dinner-gong rang and, for the fiftieth time, I reminded myself not to assault any Republican on board.

We were soon at Fengdu. Abbé David: 'Very pretty because of its pagodas, towers and the green hills around it.' Captain Williamson: 'One hill is said to be haunted.' Nothing had been torn down, but a certain amount had been added: it was a sullen agglomeration of scorched factories and workers' flats under a weeping corona of smog.

'It certainly looks haunted to me,' I said to the Political Commissar on our ship. The Political Commissar is the labour relations man. If there is slackness in the galley or the engine room on a Chinese ship, the Political Commissar reminds the workers of their duties. Ours was Comrade Sun; he had been working on the river since 1950 ('Just after Liberation'), when he was seventeen. He knew the hills and temples of Fengdu very well.

No, he said, it was not haunted.

'There are no ghosts,' says a Chinese pamphlet entitled STORIES ABOUT NOT BEING AFRAID OF GHOSTS. 'Belief in ghosts is a backward idea, a superstition and a sign of cowardice. This is a matter of common sense today among the people. But while there are no demons . . . there are many things which resemble them – imperialism, reactionaries, difficulties and obstacles in work, for example.' Comrade Sun was a member of the Party: he agreed with this pamphlet. We talked about river superstitions. It was not easy. He did not want to give me the idea that people today were silly enough to believe any of this stuff. But I pestered him for frights and beliefs.

'There was an old belief,' he said, 'that if a fish jumped out of the water on to the deck of a ship you could not eat it. Fish often jumped on to the junks. They still do, when they're swimming upstream. Such fish were regarded as demons.'

'Did they throw the fish back?' I asked.

'No. They had to take it ashore. Dig a hole. Then bury it.'

'What do they do now?'

'Eat them!'

I had read of another belief of the junk sailors, that when the wind died, they stood on the deck and whistled, to call the wind, so that they would not have to go ashore and tow the boat. Whistling up a wind may have been a practice among old British sailors – the idea occurs in *Macbeth*. It struck me as a weird and attractive superstition.

Comrade Sun said yes, long ago it was believed that if you whistled, the wind would rise. Then he smiled. 'I don't think it does any good at all.'

That evening our ship, *Number 39*, anchored below the remote town of Shibao Block (Shih Pao Chai, or 'Precious Stone Castle'). This is one of the most unusual, and probably least spoilt places in China. It is a perfect butte, 100 feet high, which once had a monastery on top and now has a bare temple. The way to the top is up a staircase in an eleven-storey red pavilion built against the perpendicular side of the rock. Amazingly, it remains just as it was described by travellers 100 years ago, and the view from the top is a reminder that there are towns in China with no factories, little mechanisation, and only the oldest methods of ploughing and planting. The town at the base of the rock is a labyrinth of slimy alleys and muddy streets, and cobblestone passageways that look like the wynds of Edinburgh. And shops: carpenters, bakers, weavers of funeral wreaths, fruitsellers. Just outside the town an old man led a blindfolded buffalo around in circles, trampling mud to soften it for the making of bricks and roof tiles.

I had brought a snapshot to Shibao Block. It was one of Captain Williamson's and it showed the town through the simple eye of a box camera in 1927. The townsfolk were interested. They called the mayor, Comrade Lu, and examined the snapshot. They found it very odd. It was clearly their town, and yet one house was not where it should be. This snapshot was the past: they had never seen an old picture of the town. The mayor asked to be photographed holding the picture.

'Please take his picture,' the interpreter said. 'He is a big potato.'

He meant it as the highest praise.

Nearly the whole town of Shibao Block saw us off: silent faces staring at Howard Buhse's red golfer's cap and Ira Weinstein's foot-long telephoto lens and Lurabelle's mink and Jerry McCarthy's whirring cine camera and old Mr Chase's tape-recorder (he recorded everything, even the sound of the ship's engines) and the pinks and blues of the ladies' $350 'ultra-suede' dresses ('They're drip-dry!') and my yellow suede shoes. We were bizarre. There was not a sound, not a murmur from the hundreds of people on the shore.

There were more watchers downstream at Wanxian, a city more nightmarish than Chongqing – mud, rain, black streets, broken windows, smoke, and every housefront wearing a film of soot. It was once a city of great beauty, and famous for its perfectly poised *feng-shui*. But the bluffs and hills that were praised are now covered with factories, the most shocking a silk filiature plant, where 1,300 women and girls were losing their health in the dim light, making silk thread from soaked cocoons. It was a sweat shop, all these women sacrificed to the manufacture of hideously patterned silk in garish colours. They worked quickly, silently, with ruined hands, to the racket of the jolting looms.

In the days that followed, we passed through the gorges. Many people come to the Yangtze for the gorges alone: they excite themselves on these marvels and skip the rest of the river. The gorges are wonderful, and it is almost impossible to exaggerate their splendour; but the river is long and complicated, and much greater than its gorges, just as the Thames is more than what lies between Westminster and Greenwich.

The great gorges lie below Bai De ('White King City'), the lesser gorges just above Yichang. Bai De was as poisonous-looking as any of the other cities, but as soon as we left it the mountains rose – enormous limestone cliffs on each side of the river. There is no shore: the sheer cliffs plunge straight into the water. They were formed at the dawn of the world, when the vast inland sea in western China began to drain east and wear the mountains away. But limestone is a curious substance. It occurs in blocks, it has cracks and corners; and so the flow zigzagged, controlled by the stone, and made right angles in the river. Looking ahead through the gorges you see no exit, only the end of what looks like a blind canyon.

There are graffiti on the gorges. Some of them are political ('Mankind unite to Smash Capitalism'), or poetic ('Bamboos, flowers and rain purify the traveller'), while other scribbled characters explain that this is Wind Box Gorge, and those holes are where General Meng Liang made a ladder to scale the heights and smash the Shu army on top in the second century AD. The wind blows fiercely through the gorges, as it does in New York between skyscrapers; and it is a good thing, too, because the junks can sail upstream – there is little room here for trackers. Every rock and cliff has a name, 'The Seated Woman and the Pouncing Lion', 'The Fairy Princess', and – less lyrically – 'The Ox-Liver and Horse-Lung Gorge' (the organs are boulder-formations, high on the cliff-face). The Yangtze is a river of precise nomenclature. Only simple, wild places, like the volcanic hills of south-west Uganda, are full of nameless topography; naming is one of the features of Chinese civilisation and settlement. I asked the pilot of our ship if it was so, that every rock in the Yangtze had a name. He said yes.

'What is the name of that one?' I asked quickly, pointing out of the window.

'That is Pearl Number Three. Over there is Pearl Number Two. We shall be coming to Pearl Number One in a few minutes.' He had not hesitated. And what was interesting was that these rocks looked rather insignificant to me.

One of the millionaires said, 'These gorges come up to expectations. Very few things do. The Taj Mahal did. The pyramids didn't. But these gorges!'

We passed Wushan. There was a funeral procession making its way through the empty streets, beating drums and gongs, and at the front of the procession three people in white shrouds – white is the Chinese colour of mourning – and others carrying round paper wreaths, like archery targets. And now we were in the longest gorge, twenty-five miles of cliffs and peaks, and beneath them rain-spattered junks battling the current.

At one time, this part of the Yangtze was filled with rapids. Captain Williamson's list of landmarks noted all of them. They were still in the river, breaking ships apart in 1937. But the worst have been dynamited away. The most notorious was the Hsin Lung Tan, a low-level rapid caused by a terrific landslide in 1896. It was wild water, eighty-feet wide, but blasting opened it to 400 feet, and deepened it. Thirty years ago, only the smallest boats could travel on the river during the winter months; now it is navigable by even the largest ships throughout the year.

Our ship drew in below Yellow Cat Gorge, at a place called Dou Shan Tuo ('Steep Hill Village'). We walked to the road and took a bus to the top of the hill. Looking across the river at the pinnacles called 'The Three Daggers', and at the sun pouring honey into the deep cliffs, one of the passengers said with gusto, 'What a place for a condominium!'

*T*he MS *Kun Lun* is by any standards a luxurious ship. She is popularly known as 'Mao's yacht' because in the Fifties and early Sixties she was used to take visiting dignitaries up and down the Yangtze. Any number of prominent Albanians can boast that they slept in one of *Kun Lun*'s sumptuously carpeted suites and danced in the lounge or got stewed to the gills in the sixty-feet wide club room. The idea for this fancy ship was Jiang Qing's – Chairman Mao's third wife and now the celebrated political criminal of the Gang of Four. She had the guts of a river ship torn out and she redecorated it in the style of Waldorf Astoria Ming – art deco and lotus blossoms – and did not stint on the curtains or the blue bathtubs. The Gregorys (Fred and Merial) had a rat in their room, but never mind – Raymond Barre of France once slept in their suite.

The chief feature of this wilderness of antimacassars is space: wide passageways, large cabins, huge lounges, and sofas on which seven can sit comfortably and catch up on the *Peking*

Review or listen to *News About Britain* or *The Book Programme* on the World Service of the BBC – there are two gigantic 'Spring Thunder' brand shortwave radios on board. You hardly notice the grand piano, the bar is so big. For this reason, the *Kun Lun* was 'criticised' during the Cultural Revolution; she was turned over to the people and more or less raped. Cots and bunks were crammed into the suites, and for four years the proletariat used her as an ordinary river ship. When the Lindblads found her a few years ago she was in mothballs. Mr Lindblad made a deal with the China Travel Service: he would fix her up, restore her to her original splendour if he was allowed to use her for tours. The scheme was agreed upon, and now the *Kun Lun* is afloat once again, as great an anachronism, as large a contradiction, as could possibly be found in the People's Republic.

We transferred from *Number 39* to the *Kun Lun*. We were on the Middle River now, and there were no complaints. Or rather, not many. I did hear a shrill drunken voice moan one evening, 'I hate Chinese food! Once a month, maybe. Not more than that. But every damned day? I can't eat the stuff. I have to drink vodka. Anyway, vodka's good for you, but Chinese food makes me sick!' And another night, Mrs Ver Bryck looked at me and said, unprovoked and unbidden, 'Of course I'm happier than you are. I've got more money than you!'

We stayed two days at Wuhan. The river had become wider, the banks lower and flatter; but the cities had grown more interesting. We watched a thyroidectomy at a hospital at Wuchang, the patient anaesthetised by four acupuncture needles in her hands, and a little voltage (Mr Clark: 'Is that AC or DC?'); and in the early morning I prowled the streets of Hankow and noted that free markets had sprung up – until this year, such improvisatory capitalism was forbidden. There were also card players on the pavement. Although gambling is severely punished in China, they looked to me as if they were gambling, playing a card game called 'Aiming High'. At six o'clock one morning I saw my first Chinese beggar, and on the next corner a trio of child acrobats balancing plates on their heads and doing hand-stands, and then passing the hat. New Hankow looked something like old Hankow.

And all over the river, people were fishing, some with hooks and lines, others with circular weighted nets, or curtains of nets which they trailed behind their sampans, or the complicated tent-like nets in bamboo frames that Abbé David saw raised and lowered at Shashi. They caught tiny fish – sardine-sized, and they kept even the minnows. More modern methods might have emptied the Yangtze of all its fish, but Comrade Sun had told me that some men still fished with trained cormorants and otters.

The river had widened again: on this stretch of the river I was seldom able to see the far bank, and we sailed to Jiujiang in a heated mist, glad for a night at the nearby hill station of Lushan. ('The road is very twisty,' Mr Chen said, 'but we have a good driver and he will not go bananas'.) In both Jiujiang and Lushan, people could be seen fighting for cinema tickets. The same films were playing in both places, *The Great Dictator* and *City Lights*, starring China's favourite actor, Cha-Li Zhou Bi-lin.

On our way to Nanjing, I talked to the *Kun Lun*'s captain. Like Captain Liu of *Number 39*, he had worked his way up to captain, from steward, by on-the-job training, and had never gone to naval college. 'There is no reason for a man to remain a steward his whole life. I tell my men – "Work hard and there will be promotions for you." '

I asked him what the difficulties were in navigating on the Yangtze. 'Two main ones,' he said. 'From December to March, the water is very low and the channel is narrow. This makes things difficult, because there is so much other traffic on the river. The second is the weather. There is fog and mist from October to April, and sometimes it is impossible to see what lies ahead. Radar is often no help. To avoid getting into an accident, some nights we anchor until the weather clears.'

I said that it seemed that very little had changed on the Yangtze. People fished in the old way; they sailed and rowed and towed wooden junks; they watered their fields carrying buckets on yokes; and right back there at Jiujiang, women were washing clothes, clubbing bundles of laundry and thrashing it in the muddy water. They crossed the river in rusty ferries and still drowned by the score when the river was in flood.

The captain reminded me of the Four Modernisations and said that with the smashing of the Gang of Four, things would improve. How ironic, I thought: the leader of the Gang of Four had probably sat in this very cabin; she was certainly responsible for its décor.

'Before Liberation, this river was different. The foreigners were very careless. They ran rampant. The Chinese people hated and feared them, because they had a reputation for not stopping for a junk or a sampan, or they might swamp a small boat in their wake. It made them unpopular. The gun-boats were the worst of all. The foreigners were disliked for the way they used the river – Japanese, French, Italian, English, American. But things are different now.'

And then, to stem his harangue, I asked him about the river's personality. He said – he was smiling and blowing smoke out of his nostrils – 'It is necessary to see the river as an enemy . . .'

We went ashore at Nanjing. The Gang of Four trial had started. We were encouraged to watch it, by the China Travel Service guides: it reminded me of Hate Week in *1984*, and the defendants looked sick and crazy after four years in prison. I ended up playing gin rummy with Harry Laughlin, who said he was dying to get back to Pasadena.

At the Nanjing quays, the Yangtze was flowing to Shanghai. There, some things had changed. A new slogan was DOWN WITH THE FOUR BIGS, and one of the 'Bigs' was big character posters. These posters, all over Shanghai, had been whitewashed and scraped and almost obliterated, although NEVER FORGET CLASS STRUGGLE was cheerfully translated for Big Bob Brantman and UP WITH THE EIGHT ANTIS ('Anti-Bourgeois, Anti-Intellectual, Anti-Western' etc) explained to Norma Weinstein. Now children in school were being taught the Five Loves ('Love Work, Love Science, Love Public Property . . .') and these were listed along with billboards advertising glue and bicycles and sewing machines. On the Upper River, tethered men were screaming '*Hai tzo!*' and pulling junks against the current and sleeping in mud huts and yanking fish out of the throats of cormorants. But here in Shanghai, not far from Shanghai Mansions (formerly 'Broadway Mansions'), boys were posing for pictures wearing trilby hats and sunglasses and one – the only one I saw in China – a blue necktie.

When James Joyce searched for a form for *Finnegans Wake* he came up with the image of a river, and both ended and began 'A way a lone a last a loved a long the riverrun . . .' The river, which lends its shape to works as diverse as *Huckleberry Finn* and Eliot's *The Dry Salvages*, wonderfully illustrates the flow of history and its relentless passions. The Yangtze is China: seeing it, you are prepared for everything else. It seems to contain the whole of Chinese culture, the ineradicable past and the convulsed and sometimes contradictory present, 'by a

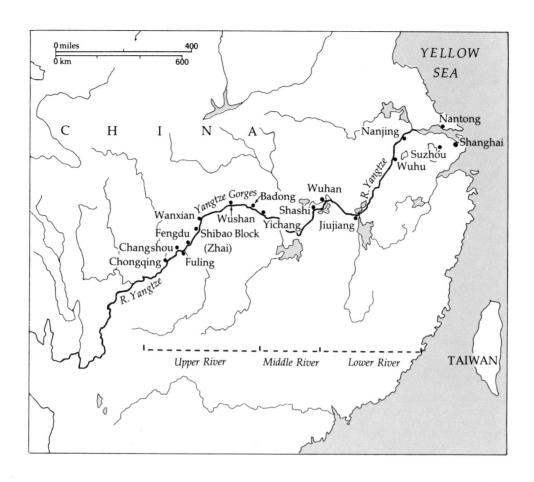

1. The Gorges, the Yangtze's crowning glory. There is hardly any shore to speak of; often the great limestone cliffs plunge straight into the river.
2. It takes the traveller several days to pass through the Gorges, occasionally seeing settlements like this one.
3. The Gorges are not entirely pristine and unspoiled. There are industrial centres too.
4. At one of the townships in the Gorges vehicles queue for the ferry.
5. The wind blows fiercely through the Gorges, and junks with a stiff breeze behind them can sail upstream. Periodically, though, oars have to be used as well.
6. At Chongqing the landing stage is reached by a rattling tin tram. The city is often assailed by thick sulphurous fogs.
7. Near Yichang crowded tenements look over a vast concrete river bank.

6

7

commodius vicus of recirculation'. As for the future, there was another billboard in Shanghai, saying in Chinese and English, ADVERTISING SPACE FOR SALE. That was, appropriately, at the Mouth of the Yangtze.

THE VOLGA

BRUCE CHATWIN

O n the MV *Maxim Gorky*, a cruise-boat belonging to Intourist, we spent ten September days sailing smoothly down the Volga; through the Volga-Don Canal, and on down the Don to Rostov. The days were clear and the nights were cold. All the other passengers were Germans. Some had been Panzer officers who had wasted their youth in Siberian labour camps, and were revisiting the scene of lost battles. Others had been pilots whose planes had failed to crash. Then there were the war widows – moist-eyed women clinging to the remains of prettiness, who, forty-one years earlier, had waved and waved as the trains drew out for the Russian front; and who, now, when you asked why they had come to the Volga, would bow their heads and say, *'Mein Mann ist tot in Stalingrad.'*

Also on board was the Prussian Junker, Von F – a proud ex-aviator with the planed-off skull of Bismarck and a stump of an arm on which he balanced his Leica. His fate, in peacetime, was to be a water-engineer; and he would be up at dawn, pacing the deck in a dark green loden coat, and gazing bleakly at the locks through which we passed. His views on the technical achievements of the Soviet Union were summed up in the words 'East minus West equals Zero.' He had fought for the Fascists in Spain. Yet nothing could be more agreeable, on our rare walks ashore, than to pace through the steppe grass beside this stringy and optimistic man, while he aired his encyclopaedic knowledge of Russia, or the migration of barbarian hordes. From time to time, he would point to a bump on the horizon and say 'Tumulus!' – and once, when we had come to a slight depression in the middle of a level plain, he stopped and said, conspiratorially, 'I believe this is a fortification from the Second World War.'

Every morning, at eight precisely, a peremptory voice would sound over the loud-speaker, *'Meine Damen und Herren . . .'* and announce the events of the day. These began with a programme of gymnastics on the sun-deck – which, to my knowledge, no one attended. Then there might be a lecture on the turbulent and revolutionary history of the Volga region. Or a visit to a riverside town. Or to one of the hydroelectric schemes which have turned this Mother-of-all-the-Rivers into a chain of sluggish inland seas the colour of molasses.

We went aboard the *Maxim Gorky*, after dark, at Kazan. The ship's band was playing a

26

medley of melancholy Russian favourites. A woman in peasant costume offered us the customary bread and salt; and the captain, whose deep blue eyes were set in a face composed of horizontals, went about squeezing everyone's hand. The river port lay on a reach of the Kazanka river, a short distance from the Admiralty, where Catherine the Great once landed from her state galley – after almost being drowned. Beyond a mole, we could see the lights of tugboats towing barges up the Volga. After supper, a paddlesteamer with a raking funnel tied up in the berth ahead. Her cabins were freshly varnished, and there were swagged lace curtains in her saloon.

I asked the captain how old was such a vessel.

'Eighty years,' he said. 'Perhaps even one hundred.'

She was the ordinary passenger boat from Moscow to Astrakhan on the Volga Delta – a journey which took ten days. The stopover at Kazan lasted half an hour. Then a boy slipped her mooring rope from the bollard; her paddles frothed the water, and she eased back into the night – a survivor of the Ancien Régime, reminding one of the stiff-black-skirted ladies sometimes to be seen manoeuvring through the foyer of the Moscow Conservatoire.

Chekhov took a Volga cruise for his honeymoon in 1901. His wife was Olga Knipper, the actress for whom he wrote *The Cherry Orchard*. He was, however, already suffering from consumption, and his doctors had ordered a 'koumiss cure'. Koumiss is fermented mare's milk, the staple of all steppe nomads and remedy for every kind of sickness. The 'noble mare-milkers' appear in literature as early as the *Iliad*, and it was nice to think of Chekhov, on his paddlesteamer, scribbling notes for a new short story, and sipping a drink known to Homer.

Kazan is the capital of the Tartar Autonomous Republic, and lies about 500 miles due east of Moscow at a point where the Volga, after meandering through the cities of northern Muscovy, takes a right-angled bend towards the Caspian. There are two Kazans. One is the Russian city, with its kremlin and cathedrals, founded in 1553 by Ivan the Terrible after a victory which finally rid Russia of the so-called 'Tartar-yoke'. The other Kazan, punctuated here and there by minarets, is the Muslim town to which the Tartars were banished, and where they have remained. Tartars number nearly half the population, speak Tartar as their first language, and are the descendants of Batu's Horde.

For the purpose of Russian history, the words 'Tartar' and Mongol are synonymous. The Tartar horsemen who appeared on the fringe of Europe in the thirteenth century were thought to be the legions of Gog and Magog, sent by Antichrist to announce the End of the World. As such, they generated the same kind of fear as the hydrogen bomb. Russia bore the brunt of their attack. In fact, so long as the Tartar empire survived, the Russian Grand Dukes were sub-vassals of the Great Khan in Peking – and this, together with a folk memory of whistling arrows, piles of skulls, and every kind of humiliation, may account for a certain paranoia the Russians have always shown towards the slant-eyed peoples of Inner Asia.

The Volga is the nomadic frontier of Modern Europe, just as the Rhine-and-Danube was the barbarian frontier of the Roman empire. Once Ivan crossed the Volga, he set Russia on her course of eastward expansion, which would roll on and on until the Tsar's colonists met the Americans at Russian river in northern California.

I went ashore before breakfast. Hydrofoils skimmed by and, in the flowerbed beside the boat terminal, a solitary mongrel sat chewing verbena. Through a mishmash of telegraph wires I caught sight of the Peter-and-Paul Cathedral which, at this hazy hour of the morning, resembled the pagoda of an imaginary Cathay. The terminal building was deserted; but in the square behind, sweepers were sweeping the night's fall of leaves; the stench of cheap gasoline hung in your nostrils; and a woman in a scarf of aniline roses was unshuttering the front of her kvass bar – in front of which a queue had formed.

Kvass is a beer brewed from rye flour, but I did not want it for breakfast. I wanted koumiss, and had been told I could get it. 'Koumiss, *nyet!*' the woman said. Was there anywhere, I persisted, that did sell koumiss? 'Koumiss, *nyet!*' she repeated. 'Koumiss, *nyet!*' bellowed a Tartar in a black hat and black padded jacket. He had been standing behind me.

Plainly, the mares weren't giving milk at this season, and plainly I should have known it. So I went back to the quay where another, northbound steamer had docked. Families with bundles were shuffling up the gang-plank. Soldiers in top-boots were striding about as if they had saddles between their legs. Then a slender young man stepped ashore carrying a single stalk of pampas grass.

At eleven we went into town. Across the street from the university, the bus pulled up in front of a reckless adventure in stucco, its façade encumbered with naked figures, and its windows painted with peacocks and peonies. This, the guide confessed, had been the house of a millionaire. It was now a technical bookshop.

By contrast, apart from the odd hammer and sickle, there was nothing in the sombre, neo-classical university building to distinguish it from any minor college in the American Midwest. Students strolled about with satchels, or sunned themselves in a small memorial garden. The entrance hall, however, was lined with sad-faced academics, and we were made to wear grey felt overshoes in case we damaged the parquet flooring.

Upstairs we were shown the lecture room where Lenin studied law before being booted out for taking part in a student strike – a room of bare benches, a blackboard, a white tiled stove, and green shades around the gas lights.

In his Kazan days, of course, Lenin had not yet assumed the name of that other, Siberian, river, the Lena. He was Vladimir Ilyich Ulyanov – a boy with red hair and an excessively determined lower lip, who, with his mother and sisters, had come here from his native Simbirsk. Only a year before, his elder brother, Alexander, had been executed in St Petersburg for making a bomb to kill the Tsar. The Ulyanovs' house is a cosy timber building, painted treacly brown, and situated in a hilly suburb once known as 'Russian Switzerland'. On hearing of his brother's death, young Vladimir is supposed to have said, icily: 'That means we shall have to find another way.' And in the half-basement, you are shown a scullery, hardly more than a cubby-hole, where, feet up on the stove, he first dipped into *Das Kapital*.

Another Kazan student who left before his time was Count Leo Tolstoy. He was here for five and a half years in the 1840s, studying Oriental languages, law, history and philosophy. Already, at the age of eighteen, he was keeping a diary of his thoughts and 'Rules of Life': 'Keep away from women' . . . 'Kill desire by work . . .' But, in the end, he decided his professors had nothing to teach him, and ordered the coachman to drive to Yasnaya Polyana. 'Men of genius,' he wrote only twelve years later, 'are incapable of studying when they are young, because they unconsciously feel that they must learn everything differently from the mass.'

On leaving the Ulyanov house, the Germans went back to the *Maxim Gorky* for lunch.

We gave them the slip and went to the Maxim Gorky Museum, a whitewashed building on a corner, next to a playground with cardboard figures of athletes. Across the street, people with wooden shovels were pitching a pile of potatoes into a cellar. Inside, two motherly women brooded over an immense display of photographs and memorabilia associated with this now almost deified novelist. His desk was awash with knickknacks; and along with his suits, there was a pair of Samoyed reindeer-skin leggings.

Gorky – Alexei Maximovich Peshkov as he was then – came here as a blushing boy from Nizhni Novgorod (now Gorky) in 1884. He, too, had hoped to enter the university, but the authorities turned him down as being too young, ignorant and poor. Instead, he had to educate himself in tawdry lodgings, in flophouses, in a brothel, on the wharves along the river, or in the cellar of the bakery where he earned himself a wage. These were his *Universities* – the title of the second volume of his autobiography. His friends were amateur revolutionaries and professional tramps. At the end of one winter, he shot himself – but the bullet pierced his lung and not his heart. The river called him, to the South; to the freer air of the Cossack steppe; to what, later, he called his 'Sky-Blue Life'. He left Kazan by boat: 'The ice on the Volga had only just broken up. From upstream floated porous grey ice-floes, bobbing up and down in the muddy water. The boat overtook them, scraping against her sides and shattering into sharp crystalline flakes. . . . The sun was blinding. . . .' For three years he lived as a hobo. Then he published his first short story in a Tiflis newspaper. A map in the museum charted the zigzag course of his wanderings – and then we looked at the photographs: the successful young 'peasant' author, in an embroidered shirt, reading to a gathering of bourgeois intellectuals; the villa in Capri, dated 1908; or with his new friend, now definitively known as Lenin, who would insist on going to the beach in a bowler. Then New York; then another villa, in Taormina; and then back to Moscow in the Twenties. The last pictures, taken in his hideous art nouveau house on Kachalova Street, just before his death (by poisoning?) in 1936, show a kind old man at the end of his tether.

The streets of Kazan bore the imprint of a vanished mercantile vitality. Yards once stacked with barrels of fish-oil or bitumen now lay overgrown with burdocks and thistles. Yet the little log houses, with their net curtains, their samovars, their currant bushes, their African violets in the window, and the streams of blue woodsmoke spiralling from their tin chimneys – all reaffirmed the dignity of the individual and the resilience of peasant Russia. Somewhere on these streets was the 'house of comfort' where Tolstoy lost his virginity; and where, once the act was over, he sat on the whore's bed, and broke down and blubbed like a baby. This is the subject of his story, *A Holy Night*.

Strolling into the yard behind a church, I found a nun feeding bread to her pigeons. Another nun was watering the geraniums. They smiled and asked me to come for the service, tomorrow. I smiled back, and said I should not be in Kazan. We tried to lunch at the Kazan Restaurant, but only got as far as its grandiloquent gilded entrance. '*Nyet!*' said the black-tied waiter. He was expecting a delegation. So instead we had cabbage soup and fried eggs in a noisy white-tiled café, presided over by a powerful Tartar woman, who couldn't stop laughing. Her head was wrapped in the kind of white cloth superstructure you sometimes see in Persian miniatures.

The lanes of Tartar-town were muddy but, on some of the houses, the door and shutters were a lovely shade of blue. By the door of the mosque sat an old pair of shoes. The interior was dingy, and the evening sunlight, squeezing through a coloured glass window, made blotches of red on the carpet. An old man in an astrakhan cap was kneeling to Mecca, to say his prayers. On top of the minaret, a golden crescent glinted over this, the northernmost extension of Islam, on the latitude of Edinburgh.

After dark, at a Friendship Meeting, we saw a slender Tartar girl craning her neck to watch the foreigners. She had glossy black hair, rosy cheeks, and slanting grey-green eyes. The dancing seemed to excite her, but a look of horror passed over her face when the Germans played musical chairs.

*T*he *Maxim Gorky* sailed through the night, down the Kuybyshev Reservoir and past the mouth of the Kama river. By dawn, we were approaching Ulyanovsk. On the way we must have passed the ancient city of Bolgar where, in the tenth century, an Arab traveller called Ibn Fādlan awoke one morning to see some sleek ships at anchor in the river. These were the Vikings. 'Never,' he wrote, 'had I seen a people of more perfect physique. They were tall as date-palms, and reddish in colour. They wear neither coats nor mantle, but each man carries a cape which covers one half of his body, leaving one hand free. Their swords are Frankish in pattern, broad, flat and fluted. Each man has tattooed upon him trees, figures and the like, from the fingers to the neck.' At the approach of winter, one of the Viking chieftains died, and his companions decided to bury him, in a ship mound, on the bank of the river. Such is Ibn Fādlan's description: the ship carved with dragons, four posts of birch; the frost-blackened body sewn up in its clothes; a faithful dog sacrificed, and then the man's horses. Finally, the slave woman, who was to be buried as well, made love to each of the companions. 'Tell your master,' they said, 'I did this out of love for him.' On the Friday afternoon, the companions held her up three times over the ship's rail. 'Look!' she cried out. 'I see my master in Paradise, and Paradise is beautiful and green, and with him are the men and young boys. He calls me. Let me join him!' – whereupon an old She-Giant, the hag they called the 'Angel of Death', took the woman's bracelets from her wrists. The companions drowned her cries by beating on their shields. Six men made love to her again; and as she lay back exhausted, the 'Angel of Death' slipped a cord around her neck, and a dagger between her ribs.

Approaching Ulyanovsk, the cliffs along the Volga were dotted with summerhouses, each set in its orchard of tart green apples and painted a different, bright, peasant colour. Ulyanovsk is Lenin's home town – which, until it was renamed in 1924, was the sleepy provincial capital of Simbirsk. People used to call it 'The Place of the Winds'. The bus zigzagged uphill from the waterfront and came to a wide street lined with poplars and timber houses. This was Ulitza Moskovskaya where the school inspector Ilya Nikolaevich Ulyanov lived with his severe and beautiful wife, Maria Alexandrovna Blank. She was a devout Lutheran of Volga-German descent; and in her orderly house – with its bentwood chairs, its painted floors, antimacassars, flounced net curtains, piano, wallpaper of daisies, and map of Russia on the dining-room wall – you felt the puritanical, not to say pedagogic, atmosphere of Lenin's own quarters in the Moscow Kremlin.

Edmund Wilson, who came here in 1935 to take notes for his book, *To the Finland Station*, wrote that there was little to remind the traveller he'd ever set foot outside Concord or Boston.

A few doors up, I'd seen a shuttered Lutheran church. The place reminded me, rather, of Ohio.

Photos of the school inspector showed a pleasant, open-faced man with a bald dome, side-whiskers and the elevated cheekbones of his Astrakhan Tartar forebears. Alexander, by contrast, took after his mother – a moody-looking boy, with a shock of black hair, flaring nostrils and a fall-away chin. But in the lip of young Vladimir you got a taste of the Earth-Shaker. . . .

Threading through the cramped bedrooms, the guide pointed to the children's paper boats, their hoop, the nurse's sewing machine, and a drawing, by Lenin's sister, of Dutch windmills – windmills, perhaps, of the Volga-Dutch colony downstream. All the cot-frames had spotless, white, plumped-up pillows. In Alexander's room we saw his chemistry test-tubes, and the gold medal he pawned in St Petersburg to buy the nitric acid for the bomb. He was, at the time, studying marine isopods at the School of Biology.

The Ulyanovs were a literary family and, as she gestured to the bookcase, with its sets of Goethe and Heine, Zola and Victor Hugo, the guide said that Maria Alexandrovna had spoken nine languages – 'including German', she added, smiling at the Germans.

'She *was* German,' I said.

The guide froze and said, 'NO!' in English.

'And up the road,' I said, 'that's her Lutheran church.'

The guide shook her head and murmured, '*Nyet!*' – and the German ladies turned on me, and frowned. Obviously, from either standpoint, I had uttered a heresy.

In 1887, when Vladimir Ulyanov was in the seventh grade, the headmaster of the Simbirsk *gimnaziye* was Fedor Kerensky, whose son, another Alexander, would grow up to be an emotional young lawyer with a mission to save his country – 'that ass Kerensky', who removed the Tsar, and was in turn removed by Lenin. In the classroom where Lenin studied there was a black desk with a bunch of crimson asters on it. At least once in his or her school career, every pupil has the right to sit at *that* desk.

Downstairs in the entrance hung a huge canvas of Lenin, in his student's greatcoat, contemplating the break-up of the Volga ice. The image of Russia as a river or a slow-moving ship is one that occurs again and again in her music, literature and painting. 'The Song of the Volga Boatmen' inspired perhaps the most politically effective picture of the nineteenth century – Ilya Repin's 'Barge Haulers on the Volga' – which shows a gang of peasants heaving a ship against the current. The laden ship is returning from a mysterious eastern land, whence will come a saviour to redeem a suffering people.

After lunch, I strolled about The Crown – the old aristocratic quarter of Simbirsk, now shaved of its mansions and churches and replaced by acres and acres of Karl Marx Garden, tarmac, and the offices of the local Soviet. At the edge of the tarmac, I crossed a bridge of rickety timbers and ambled downhill through the Park Druzby Narodov – a wilderness of decaying summerhouses and gardens gone to seed. Thistles choked the path, and the leaves of the brambles were red. There was a smell of potato tops burning on a bonfire. Below, the river dissolved into the haze. I peered through a scrap-metal fence and saw an old man pottering round his cabbages in the last of the summer sunshine.

On the waterfront I went aboard one of the shore stations, a kind of houseboat, painted the ice-floe green of the Winter Palace, where in Tsarist days travellers would eat, rest, or have

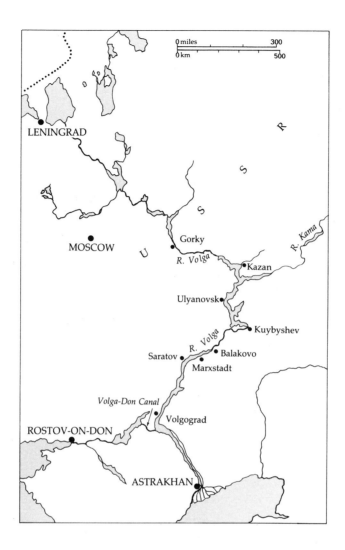

Captions for the following photographs:

1. Volgograd's massive statue, The Motherland, appears to be warning the West never to attempt a crossing of the Volga.
2. Watched by a trio of bystanders, fishermen ponder the size of their catch.
3. An honour guard of cadets slow-march through Fallen Heroes Square, where the Eternal Flame burns.
4. This family saloon, appropriately, is receiving a tender wash not far from the Togliatti automobile plant, the largest car factory in Russia.
5. Near Rostov-on-Don an old fisherman, well-wrapped against the autumn chill, suns himself in an inflatable rubber dinghy.
6. Tied up near Kazan, a pair of tugboat men play dominoes in the hazy autumn sunshine.
7. The first leaves are beginning to turn in this solitary and tranquil spot beside the river.
8. An extraordinary Tsarist boat house, beached in a backwater, is as ornate as a small palace.
9. Volgograd, once known as Stalingrad, rises in layers along the European bank of the river.

3

4

5

6

a brief affair between steamers in one of the cabins upstairs. On a bench by the boarded-up kiosk, a man without fingers was munching a bun. He eyed me suspiciously, having heard that there were Germans about. When I said I was English, his metallic teeth lit up and he started explaining how many Germans he'd shot in the war: 'Boom! Da! . . . Boom! Da! . . . Boom! Da! . . .' – slicing the sky with his fingerless fists and getting so excited I was afraid he'd forget I wasn't German, and I'd end up in the oil slick. I said goodbye and he pressed a fist into my outstretched hand.

One of the Intourist guides was an agitated young man who spoke perfect French and wore a white shirt printed with Cossack sabres. He said that few sturgeon were caught nowadays in this part of the river: for caviare one had to go to Astrakhan. For some reason he knew all about Lenin's visit to London for the Second International, and even about Lenin's English friends Edward and Constance Garnett. I said I had known their son David, a small boy at the time, who used to keep in his wallet Lenin's bus ticket from Tottenham Court Road to their house in Putney. '*Mais c'est une rélique précieuse,*' he said.

The rum merchant at our table on the *Maxim Gorky* would wait, frantic with concentration, in the hope of ambushing all the butter pats. Sometimes, if he saw us faltering over the main course, he would raise his fork in the air; say 'Please?'; and prong the lumps of pork from our plates. He had fought at the battle of Stalingrad. Out of a company of 133, he was one of seven survivors. He shared his cabin with a schoolmaster, an impetuous ballroom dancer, perennially bronzed, whose transplant of hair seedlings resembled a young rice paddy. He had been the observer on a Stuka. He had, at one time or other, bombed several of the places on our route, and was returning in the spirit of *Kameradschaft*.

Not far from Kuybyshev, we moored alongside a fuelling barge around ten o'clock. There were gas flares along the horizon. The night was warm. On the barge's deck a young man, in gumboots and shirt open to the navel, sat sprawled on a chair while an old woman who could have been his grandmother tugged at the rubber fuel pipe, then screwed in the nozzle. The barge itself was a Constructivist masterpiece, cobbled together by dockyard welders and painted grey and red. In the stern, some babies' nappies were hanging out to dry on the same clothesline as half a dozen carp. And what a life went on below! No sooner had we tied up than a party of girls swarmed out of the cabin, invaded the *Maxim Gorky*, and began to dance. One of our crew, a boy with a neat sandy moustache, had rigged up a tape-recorder on the aft deck; and they were all soon jigging away to some rather off-beat disco music. The boy was terribly concerned to give the girls a good time; kept ordering people to dance with each other; and, with perfect manners and not a hint of condescension, made a point of dancing with the ugliest of the bunch. She was, it must be said, vast. For twenty minutes she revolved on her axis, slowly, like a stone statue on a pedestal, while he capered round and round, laughing, singing and kicking. Then the fuel-pipe woman shouted; the girls poured back over the rail; everyone waved, and we slunk back into the night.

In my cabin I had a copy of *War and Peace*. I turned to Chapter Twenty and reread the account of old Count Rostov dancing the 'Daniel Cooper' with Marya Dmitrievna: (*le terrible dragon*): 'The count danced well and knew it. But his partner could not and did not want to dance well. Her enormous figure stood erect, her powerful arms hanging down (she had handed her reticule to the countess), and only her stern but handsome face really joined in the dance. . . .'

Wrapped in his loden, Von F was up at sunrise to inspect the three locks that mark the end of the Kuybyshev Reservoir. 'Remarkable,' he said, alluding to the 600 kilometres of inland sea that backs up nearly all the way to Gorky. 'But,' he waved at the walls of the lock-basin, 'this concrete is cracked.'

It was perishing. The sun was a ball on the horizon. The last lock-gates parted and we advanced into a path of golden light. Beyond, the Volga had shrunk to the proportions of a river. On the west bank were a sandy beach and a line of poplars: on the east, a string of fishermen's shanties and boats hauled clear of the water. We rounded a bend and saw the Zhiguli hills, the only hills hereabouts, once the refuge of bandits and revolutionaries. Their slopes were clothed in birch and pine, and their names: the Brave Man's Tumulus, the Maiden's Mountain, the Twin Brothers . . .

From Zhiguli island we then drove to Togliatti, the largest automobile factory of the Soviet Union. Togliatti is named after the former head of the Italian Communist Party; yet the factory owes its existence to the leading Italian capitalist of his generation, Giovanni Agnelli. Agnelli, I was once told, sat out most of one Moscow winter, in the Metropol Hotel, watching executives from every great car corporation come and go – and, eventually, by his presence, winning the contract for Fiat.

An expanse of glass and concrete stretched away over a naked plain. But the aim of our rather arduous bus journey was not to visit the factory but to establish where, on the horizon, it ended. Once this point was reached we turned back. Meanwhile, the guide bombarded us with statistics. The average winter temperature was −18° Centigrade. Cars streamed off the production line at an average of 2,500 a day. The average age of the workers was twenty-seven. The average number of marriages was 5,000 a year. Almost every couple had an apartment and a car, and there were very few divorces.

In a car park by the Volga we came across a wedding couple. The bride was in white, the bridegroom in a red sash. They seemed shy and embarrassed; and the Germans, having at last found something human in Togliatti, proceeded to treat them as an exhibit in the zoo. Pressed to the balustrade by amateur photographers, the pair edged away towards their car. They had thrown red roses into the scummy water, and one of these had snagged on a rock.

When I woke next morning the trees were gone and we were sailing through the steppe – a lion-coloured country of stubble and withered grass. There were fiery bushes in the ravines, but not a cow or a cottage, only a line of telegraph wires. I sat on deck, turning the pages of Pushkin's *Journey to Erzerum*: 'The transition from Europe to Asia is more perceptible with every hour; the forests disappear; the hills level out; the grass grows thicker . . . you see birds unknown in European forests; eagles perch on the hillocks that line the main road, as if on guard, staring disdainfully at the traveller. Over the pastures herds of indomitable mares wander proudly. . .'

For reasons of Soviet security the locks were unmarked on the map of the Volga that had been pinned to the ship's noticeboard. As a result, the reservoirs and rivers resembled a string of inexplicable sausages. Again and again, the tour leader warned against taking photos, and spoke of armed guards and other bogeymen who would pounce on anyone seen flashing a camera. The lock before Balakovo was a particularly impressive specimen with a road-and-rail bridge running over it, and a gigantic orange mosaic – of a Hermes-like figure, presumably representing 'Progress'. Von F was itching to sneak a shot, and had his camera hidden up his sleeve. Yet apart from the women who worked the machinery, the lock looked deserted except for a gang of spindly boys who catapulted pebbles that bounced on to our sky-blue deck.

It was a Sunday. The sun was shining: picnickers waved from the bank, and wheezy launches chugged up and down the river, loaded to the gunwale with trippers. At three, we went ashore at Djevuschkin Ostrov, Maiden's island, where a Khan of the Golden Horde once kept his harem. Before that, however, the island had been the home of Amazons. The Amazons had the practice of making love to their male prisoners, and then killing them. Sometimes, the prisoners put up a fight, but one young man agreed, willingly, to be killed – if they would grant him one favour in return. 'Yes,' they said. 'I must be killed by the ugliest among you,' he said – and, of course, got off the island. This story was told by Svetlana, an Intourist girl with a wonderful curling lip and green come-hither eyes.

I struck inland along a path that led through stands of red-stemmed nettles. The wormwood gave off a bitter smell underfoot. Aspens rustled, and the willows blew white in the breeze. The young willow shoots were covered with bloom, like the bloom on purple grapes. A pair of ducks flew off a weedy pond. Then there were more willows, and more water, and then the blue distance and sky. Crossing a patch of bog, I thought, 'This is the moment in a Turgenev sketch when the narrator and his dog are crossing a patch of bog, and a woodcock flies up at their feet.' I took a step or two forward – and up flew the woodcock! There should also have been, if this *were* a Turgenev sketch, the distant sound of singing and, after that, the sight of an apple-cheeked peasant girl hurrying to a tryst with her lover. I walked another 100 yards or so, and heard first the singing and then saw a white peasant headscarf through the trees. I approached, but the woman went on blackberrying. She was not young. She had hennaed hair and false teeth. I offered her the mushrooms I'd collected, and she said, '*Nyet!*'

Back at the boat station, another Winter Palace in miniature, the guardian had caught a small, sad-faced sturgeon, and our deckhands were tremendously excited at the prospect of fish stew. One carried a cauldron, another a knife and, while the cauldron was boiling, the fishmen and an officer played billiards in the lower-deck saloon. Osip Mandelstam says, 'The hard-headed knocking together of billiard balls is just as pleasant to men as the clicking of ivory knitting needles to women.' I, for one, could think of far worse places to be holed up in – a routine of Russian novels, fishing, chess, and billiards – interrupted by an occasional visit from the *Maxim Gorky* to remind one that this was 1982, not 1882.

Monday, 27 September, was a blustery morning that began with a lecture on the inland waterways of the Soviet Union. Two nights earlier, I had seen a small sailing yacht beating upstream. If only one could get permission, how adventurous it would be to sail from the Black to the White Sea! In Kazan, which we had left only four days earlier at the height of an Indian summer, it was now four degrees below.

Next day, we stayed on the boat. From time to time a smudge of smokestacks and apartment blocks moved across the horizon. One of the towns was Marxstadt, formerly Baronsk, and capital of the Soviet Republic of the Volga Germans. 'And where are those Germans now?' asked a lady from Bonn, her neck reddening with indignation as she gazed at the thin line of shore. 'Gone,' I said. 'Dead!' she said. 'Or in Central Asia. That is what I heard.'

Later in the afternoon we cruised close inshore along cliffs whose strata were striped in layers of black and white. Over the loudspeaker, a deep bass voice sang the song of the Cossack rebel Stenka Rasin. We saw a flock of black and white sheep on a bare hill. Suddenly, in the middle of nowhere, there was a MIG fighter perched on a pedestal.

Stepan (or Stenka) Razin, the son of a landowner on the Lower Don, believed that the Cossack custom of sharing plunder should form the basis of all government. He believed that these levelling practices should be applied to the Tsardom of Russia itself. The Tsar, at the time, happened to be Peter the Great. At Astrakhan, Razin captured a Persian princess who became his mistress and whom he dumped in the Volga to thank her, the river, for the gold and jewels she had given him. At Tsaritsyn, he murdered the governor, one Turgenev, possibly a forebear of the novelist. Abandoned by his followers, he was defeated at Simbirsk and beheaded in Moscow. In Soviet hagiography he is a 'proto-communist'.

W e arrived at dawn at Volgograd. The city once known as Stalingrad is a city of stucco and marble where Soviet veterans are for ever photographing one another in front of war memorials. Rebuilt in the 'Third Roman' style of the Forties and Fifties, it rises in layers along the European bank of the Volga; and from the flight of monumental steps leading down to the port, you can look back, past a pair of Doric propylaea, past another Doric temple which serves as an ice-cream shop, across some sandy islands, to a scrubby Asiatic waste with the promise of deserts beyond.

At ten, to the sound of spine-tingling music, we, the passengers of the *Maxim Gorky*, assembled in Fallen Heroes Square as a delegation of penitent Germans to add a basket of gladioli and carnations to the heaps of red flowers already piled up that morning around the Eternal Flame. On the side of the red granite obelisk were reflected the Christmas trees of the garden, and the façade of the Intourist Hotel, built on the site of Field-Marshal Paulus's bunker. A squad of cadets came forward at a slow march, the boys in khaki, the girls in white plastic sandals with white tulle pompoms behind their ears. Everyone stood to attention. The rum merchant and the schoolmaster, both survivors of the battle, performed the ceremony. Their cheeks were wet with tears; and the war widows, who, for days, had been bracing themselves for this ordeal, tightened their fingers round their handbags, sniffed into handkerchiefs, or simply looked lost and miserable.

Suddenly, there was a minor uproar. Behind us was a party of ex-soldiers from the Soviet 62nd Army, who had come from the Asiatic Republics. Their guide was showing them a photo of Paulus's surrender; and they, hearing German spoken nearby, seeing the 'enemy' inadvertently trampling on a grass verge, and thinking this some kind of sacrilege, began to murmur among themselves. Then a bull-faced man shoved forward and told them to clear off. The ladies, looking now more miserable than ever, shifted hastily back on to the concrete path. '*Most* interesting,' said Von F, as he swept past on his way to the bus.

Once the war was over, someone suggested leaving the ruins of Stalingrad *as they were* – a perpetual memorial to the defeat of Fascism. But Stalin took exception to the idea that 'his' city should remain a pile of rubble, and ordered it to be rebuilt the way it was, and more so. He did, however, leave one ruin intact – a shell-shattered mill-building on the downward slope to the river. Now marooned in acres of concrete plaza, the mill lies between a model bayonet, some 200 feet high and still in scaffolding, and a structure the shape and size of a cooling-tower where visitors (by previous appointment) can view a mosaic panorama of the battle. I stood on the plaza and felt I could almost chuck a stone into the river – yet, despite Hitler's hysterical screaming, despite the tanks and planes and men, the Germans could never reach it. The Russians fought to the slogan, 'There is no place for us behind!' It was probably as simple as that.

All around were elderly men and women, some missing an arm or a leg, and all aglow with medals in the sunshine. Then I caught sight of Von F, striding furiously around a selection of Soviet armaments lined up on display. 'No thanks to the Americans!' he said, lowering his voice. 'It was American tanks, not these, that saved them . . . and, of course, Paulus!'

'How?'

'Good Prussian soldier!' he said. 'Continued to obey orders . . . even when those orders were mad!'

In an earlier discussion, I asked Von F why Hitler hadn't gone straight for Moscow in the summer of '41. 'Fault of Mussolini,' he answered flatly. 'The invasion of Russia was planned for the spring. Then Mussolini made a mess in Greece and Germany had to help. It was too late in the year for Moscow. Hitler refused to make the mistake of Napoleon in 1812.'

Mamayev Kurgan is a hill in a northern suburb where the Tartar Khan Mamay once pitched his royal yurt and where, to celebrate the twenty-fifth anniversary of Stalingrad, the Soviets have built a monumental complex to the Fallen Dead. During the battle, whoever held the hill held Stalingrad; and though the Germans took the water-tower on the summit, Marshal Zhukov's men hung on to the eastern flank. When they cleared the site, an average of 825 bullets and bits of shrapnel were found on each square metre. Leonid Brezhnev opened Mamayev Kurgan with the words, 'Stones have longer lives than people. . .' The monuments, however, were made of ferro-concrete – and Von F, for one, didn't rate their chances of longevity all that high.

The first thing we saw from the bus was the gigantic statue of The Motherland, striding into the haze and waving a sword instead of the Tricolour – for, plainly, she owes her inspiration to Delacroix's 'Liberty Leading the People to the Barricades.' From Lenin Avenue we then set off for the hilltop – but what an obstacle course lay in between! Like pilgrims to, say, Rome or Mecca or Benares, visitors to Mamayev Kurgan are obliged to progress round a sequence of shrines – Fallen Heroes Square, the Hall of Valour and many more – before arriving at the feet of The Motherland. And there are no short cuts! 'Kurgan' is a Turco-Tartar word meaning 'hill', 'mound' or 'grave' – and Mamayev Kurgan, with its grave, its temples and the 'sacred way', reminded me of the great temple complexes of ancient Asia. In this same steppe region a Turkic tribe, known as the Polovsty, used to set stone statues over their burial kurgans – and these, known as *kameneye babas*, served as a memorial for the dead, and a warning to tomb robbers.

I could hardly help feeling that 'The Motherland' represented Asia, warning the West never to try and cross the Volga, never to set foot in the heartland. The atmosphere was eerie, and religious; all too easy to scoff at; but the crowds, with their rapt and reverential expressions, were no scoffing matter. I followed a lame old woman into the Pantheon. Her down-at-heel shoes had been slit at the toes to relieve the pressure on her bunions. She shuffled forward, in a raincoat, on the arm of a younger companion. She had tried to make herself a little festive by wearing a red scarf shot with tinsel. Her cheeks were caked with white powder, and streaming with tears. As she crossed the Court of Sorrows, her raincoat flapped open – to show a white blouse covered in medals.

At three, in the city planetarium, we watched a film of the battle, put together from German and Soviet newsreels and adorned with Cosmic overtones. The film was supposed to be violently anti-German, and the Germans had been warned not to attend if they felt squeamish. It could have been much worse. It never once stooped to mockery or satire; and in the heartrending shots of wounded German prisoners, you felt that the film-makers, at least, were not glorifying the Soviet victory, rather showing the utter futility of war. That night, as we headed for the Volga-Don Canal, I sat at the bar beside one of the Panzer officers who sadly contemplated a double Georgian brandy and said: 'For us Germans this has been a hard day.'

*T*he journey was ending. It was a sunny, silvery morning as we sailed into Rostov-on-Don. In the shallows a team of fishermen were drawing in a seine net. An old man sunned himself in an inflatable rubber-dinghy. Tugboats tooted, and a crane un-loaded crates from an ocean-going ship. There were old brick warehouses on the waterfront; and, behind, the city rising in terraces to the onion-domed cathedral on the hill. Along the esplanade, beds of soviet-coloured salvias were waiting to be nipped by the first autumn frost. The ship's band played 'Shortenin' Bread' as we docked. Meanwhile, onshore, a troupe of Cossack dancers, none older than twelve, had tumbled out of a bus and were putting on a rival entertainment. Two boys held up a banner which said 'Friendship' in any number of languages from Latvian to Portuguese; and the girls, like drum-majorettes in their shakos and scarlet jackets, flicked their legs about amid the flurrying leaves. A hundred yards away there was a statue of Maxim Gorky.

Rostov was a city of shady, tree-lined avenues shamelessly given over to private commerce. Police and policewomen sauntered round the street markets with an air of amused condescension while Armenians haggled with Russians, Cossacks haggled with Armenians, and wallets bulged with roubles as the piles of aubergines, persimmons and secondhand furniture, little by little, diminished. An old babushka gave me a bunch of bergamot and I went away sniffing it.

Someone pointed to a slit-eyed woman with a shopping bag and asked, 'What are all these North Vietnamese doing here?' 'They're not Vietnamese,' I said. 'They're Kalmucks. They're the locals.' The Kalmucks live across the river in their own republic. They were the last Mongolian people to ride over into Europe and they settled there. Even now, they are Lamaists. One Kalmuck boy looked very racy, with a sweep of shiny black hair, and a monkey chained to the pillion of his motor-bike.

I went to the museum and caught a whiff of goat's grease floating off the churns and ladles in a reconstructed Cossack cottage. In the section devoted to 1812 hung a portrait of V. F. Orlov Denisov, the regimental commander whom Tolstoy fictionalised, with a lisp, in *War and Peace*. There was also an English print, entitled 'Foxy Napoleon – Tally Ho!' and the following verse:

Hark, I hear the cry Cossack
They have got the scent of me
I must take to my heels at once
They are close to my brush.

After dark, on our last night in Russia, I strolled downhill, through the old merchants' quarter, and saw a crystal chandelier alight in an upstairs room. The walls were covered with faded red plush and there was a gilt-framed canvas, of mountains and a river. I stood under a street lamp, and tried to imagine the tenant of the room. On the pavement, little girls in white socks were playing hopscotch. Two sailors, their caps thrust back on their heads, came out of a shooting-alley and sat down on the kerb to share their last cigarette. Then an old lady, in a grey headscarf, came to the window. She looked at me. I waved. She smiled, waved back, and drew the curtain.

At the foot of the steps I passed Maxim Gorky, staring from his pedestal, across the gently flowing Don, towards the plains of Asia.

THE IRRAWADDY

ALEXANDER FRATER

O n the road to Mandalay your shock absorbers self-destruct. Though it is tar-sealed and kept in a reasonable state of repair, many stretches seem to have been graded by plough, and only heavy-duty vehicles are likely to survive the 700-mile journey from Rangoon. There are actually two roads – the direct route from the capital, which follows the railway line, and the meandering indirect route shadowing the course of the Irrawaddy river. We chose the latter. Having come to Burma to sail down the Irrawaddy from Mandalay to Rangoon we wished, before taking passage aboard our steamer, to get the measure of the river at the points where, unexpectedly, the road sneaked on up it and, for a mile or two, careered precariously along its crumbling banks.

Our hired Toyota van, with two drivers and a mechanic, left Rangoon at dawn, pushing impatiently through the antique Vauxhalls and Rileys that, lovingly maintained, still clatter through the broad boulevards of the unkempt, down-at-heel capital. On the outskirts of town we halted at a crowded roadside shrine. Our drivers, bearing flowers and sweetly scented ropes of jasmine, shouldered through the congregation of praying truckers and, with heads bent over clasped hands, called down blessings upon our journey. It was growing warm in the back of the van, and the drivers' observances took some time. Propped sleepily against a drum of gasoline I watched the sun touch the gilded flanks of the Shwedagon, the greatest pagoda in Burma. Started during the Buddha's lifetime and containing, in its vaults, eight hairs plucked from his head, it soared flamelike 326 feet above the city, clad with thousands and thousands of thick, foot-square plates of solid bullion. Much of the country's gold reserves were stuck up there, topped by a weather vane studded with 6,835 precious stones, 5,452 of them diamonds. Yet this stupendous structure was surrounded by a metropolis whose city fathers were unable to find the paint and plaster needed to mask the decay over which, helplessly, they presided. Rangoon, once the smartest city in South-East Asia, was now one of the sleaziest and, not for the first time, I found myself pondering the paradoxes and contradictions that constitute Burma's uniquely idiosyncratic brand of socialism.

There was, for example, her notorious bureaucracy. Our brief fifty-minute flight from

Bangkok two days earlier had been spent filling in forms. There were visa forms, immigration forms, customs forms and currency forms but, on touching down at Rangoon's Mingaladon airport and trooping into the hot little terminal, more forms confronted us. You wish to use your American Express card in Burma? Fill in a form. You have a camera, a pocket calculator? Fill in a form. You are wearing a wristwatch? Fill in a form. You are – what's this – *a journalist*? Fill in a form, fill in a form! But the appropriate form could not be found. The official attending to me, his forehead seamed with worry, began a search. 'Where are journalists' forms?' he cried to a colleague. The colleague said, 'Journalists' forms over there, on shelf!' The shelf was examined. 'No, no,' he cried. 'Shelf empty, journalists' forms all gone!' Shaking his head abstractedly, he considered calling up the Ministry of Home and Religious Affairs for guidance; but then, in a sudden demonstration of the instinctive ingenuity all Burmese display when taking on the system, he amended an existing form and, with a faint, conspiratorial smile, let me into his country.

I had imagined that bureaucracy would haunt me for the duration of my visit, but I was wrong. Instead, we were received everywhere with a tolerance and courtesy that is characteristically Burmese. At Rangoon's echoing Strand Hotel, where cheeky Wandsworth barmaids once brought Kipling pink gins and today you can get succulent lobster thermidor for less than a pound, the elderly room boys attended us like courtiers. And when we called at the Inland Waterways Board to book our passage from Mandalay, it was the managing director himself who elected to make the arrangements. A trim old mariner with an ascetic's eyes, he ran the largest fleet of river steamers on earth – 600 ships dispersed around the country, carrying 1.36 million tons of freight and 14 million passengers annually. We were, he said, the first foreigners to make the Mandalay-to-Rangoon run for many years, and he was anxious that we understood what lay ahead. 'I must warn you,' he said, with an apologetic bob of the head, 'that the water is now very low and we are gravely compromised by sandbars. There is, I am afraid, a strong chance that you will run aground. Refloating your ship may take some time and I strongly urge you to include plenty of books in your luggage.'

Our drivers returned and, spiritually refreshed, took the Toyota down the road to Prome. Prome stands on the Irrawaddy – unlike Rangoon, which is served by a tributary – and it was there that I caught my first glimpse of that broad and stately waterway. It came curving sleekly in from the north, gliding past the little bluff on which the town stands, lying low between lofty cinnamon banks and mirroring the pale, hot season sky above. We lunched off noodles and foaming mugs of fresh sugarcane juice. Our driver had drunk tainted water and contracted gastro-enteritis and now, sitting groaning at the wheel, took us through the arid, baking plains of central Burma at very high speed. The Irrawaddy, I soon saw, was a built-up area, its banks crowded with villages, townships and settlements while, only a few miles away on either side, there was desolation, empty of people or human points of reference. If an astronaut passed overhead in the evening, when the lamps were lit, the 1,300-mile course of the river would be marked out for him in lights, a curving, radiant line reaching from China to the Bay of Bengal.

We arrived in Mandalay at night, after two days on the road. Mandalay, for me, was one of the most romantic names on the map. I had long regarded it as a place where the citizens lived in pavilions of sandalwood and put up uncut rubies as collateral for the purchase of their elephants. But the streets smelt of gamey sun-dried fish and were full of blaring transistors and kamikaze cyclists, many of them monks, who tried to cut us up. The nation's religious and cultural centre and the last of her royal capitals, it's a young city. Built in 1857 by King Mindon and laid out on a modern grid system, the town's centrepiece is a great mile-long walled and moated enclosure which once contained the palace, a sumptuous building decorated by Venetian craftsmen. It was the Japanese HQ during their World War Two occupation and before General Slim and the 14th Army turned the tables in 1945 and drove the enemy down the Irrawaddy and out of Burma, the palace was destroyed by bombing. The Burmese have never forgiven us for that 'act of vandalism' and Britons discussing it with them are advised to approach the subject with discretion. As for Kipling, the man whose poem conferred a kind of immortality on Mandalay (though he never bothered to visit the place), his reputation there today stands even lower than that of the Allied forces.

Above the ruins towers a 775-foot plug of rock called Mandalay Hill. Three covered stairways ascend to the summit which, since they pass holy places and pilgrims prostrated in prayer, must be climbed in bare feet. The view from the top is very fine. On the eastern horizon are the hazy indigo battlements of the Shan hills, allegedly still governed by rebel warlords and, immediately below, Mandalay itself, looking like a great park with temples scattered about it as profusely as bus shelters. The glittering sweep of the Irrawaddy forms its western boundary, its surface dotted with craft bustling around the shoals and sand-banks, leaving wakes like snatches of Arabic script. This is the true hub of the river, which flows from a glacier inside Burma's border with China, a couple of chill alpine streams merging at a great rock basin called the Confluence and then running south through dense jungle, past Myitkyina and Bhamo, a smuggling centre only fifty miles from the Chinese border. Steamers ply between Bhamo and Mandalay all the year round, negotiating en route two defiles where the river narrows and quickens. One is of interest because it passes the mines which produce the world's finest rubies, the other because it is spectacular and, on occasion, very dangerous. Here the Irrawaddy, a mere 300 feet wide, runs turbulently between towering cliffs lined with wild beehives. Close to the entrance stands a large rock, shaped like a parrot's head and painted green and red; it is this the steamer captain consults first. If the water touches the tip of the beak it means a fast, difficult ride ahead. If the beak is submerged he steers for the bank and waits for the level to recede. Then, racing down the defile, he heads for a sheer wall of rock at the end with a tiny pagoda stuck, limpetlike, near the top. At the last moment he puts his helm hard over and skids out of the defile and back into the broad, placid waters of the orthodox river. Now, along the banks, there are duck, geese and waterfowl and, inland, barking deer, sambhur, bison, rhino, elephants, tigers, leopards and many kinds of bear. A day later he docks at Mandalay. The next stage is the mainline run down to Rangoon, the longest section of all, and it was that, the following morning, on which we planned to travel.

The Inland Water Transport Board is located at the end of 26th Road. Dusty trees straggled along the stone embankment and we looked down at the line of ships moored by the muddy shore far below. Both sidewalk and embankment were broken by the small earthquakes that regularly rattle the town. The Mandalay quakes are rarely serious, just brisk tremors that rearrange the paving stones and leave the trees tilted at interesting angles. A man emerged from the Transport Board's warehouse-like offices. His bearing was military, his gaze direct, his shirt and skirtlike *longyi* neatly pressed, his English fluent and idiomatic. He shook hands and said his name was Maung Maung Lay, but that we were to call him David. 'I'm the Board's Marine Officer here at Mandalay,' he said, 'and I've been delegated to come with you on the steamer tomorrow as far as Prome, three days' sailing. At Prome you will catch another ship for the final leg down to Rangoon. I was a steamer captain on the Irrawaddy myself, so I hope I can make some sense of the river for you. That's your vessel down there. You want to come and look her over?'

She was a creek steamer, small, double-decked, iron-hulled, built for service in the tortuous tidal waterways of the delta. Her presence on the Blue Riband run between the nation's two main cities was due to a recent management decision to use their few remaining paddle steamers, Clyde-built monsters able to take a thousand passengers on decks like tennis courts and once the glory of the fleet, for freight. 'This is a T-Class vessel,' said David, 'given to us by the Japanese in 1947 and still going strong. She can carry sixty tons of cargo and up to four hundred deck passengers, and she's powered by Kelvin diesels with automatic transmission. Her great advantage on the Irrawaddy, specially at this time of year, is that, unladen, she draws only four feet six inches. Even so, there's still a strong chance that we'll run aground somewhere. She arrived this morning from Prome and, on the way up, got stuck twice.'

She was called *Tainnyo*, or *Dark Clouds*, and passengers were already claiming sleeping space on the upper deck, laying out their mats, food and possessions on either side of a high metal grille. 'That's the panic barrier,' David remarked, 'to stop people rushing from side to side and turning the ship over. They do that when storms blow up, and we've lost half a dozen of these T-Classes that way. The trouble is, they roll badly even in a one-foot swell.'

'When is the storm season?' I asked.

'You can get some quite interesting storms about now.'

There was a simple cabin on the upper deck, built over the bows to catch the breeze and intended for travelling monks. For a small surcharge we could have access to it as well: it contained a table and chairs, four wooden sleeping platforms without mattresses, a wash basin and a lavatory made of teak. The bathroom was walled off, and it all seemed very satisfactory.

We were due to sail at 5.30 in the morning, and arranged to meet on board half an hour beforehand. Then, having visited the black market for a few last-minute provisions – pillows, rum, a Thermos flask, a couple of pineapples – I went to bed early, pondering the extent to which the old Glasgow-owned Irrawaddy Flotilla Company seemed to have been forgotten by today's Burmese. In its day it was also the greatest river fleet on earth and the forerunner of the present outfit. Its celebrated flagships, the Siam-Class steamers – then the largest river craft ever built – were able to accommodate 4,200 passengers on deck and forty more in opulent staterooms. Over 320 feet long, their massive triple expansion engines raced them *against* the current from Rangoon to Mandalay, with barges carrying 2,000 tons of freight lashed to their sides, a full day faster than our old T-Class boat, unencumbered by cargo flats, would bring us downstream to Rangoon. The ships were Clyde-built, the crews riverwise Indians from the maritime port of Chittagong, the masters and officers mostly Scottish. Old photographs show them with beards combed and moustaches waxed, brass buttons glittering, sitting with ramrod backs before giant paddle boxes emblazoned with huge, gilded coats of arms. Their social standing in Burma was so unassailable that one Mandalay shop sported a sign saying 'Silk Mercer to the King and Queen of Burma and the Captains of the Steamers'.

At five o'clock in the morning we reported to the Mandalay Shore to begin our 600-mile journey. Down on the river the ships were tricked out in lights and brilliant on the dark water. Two vessels, moored side by side, were preparing to sail, and both were thronged with shouting, shoving people; the air reeked of diesel oil, sweat and anxiety. I asked a corpulent, turtle-faced old monk in an orange robe which ship was bound for Prome. He glowered, then yelped and menaced me with his staff, almost driving me on to the horns of a pair of wild-eyed water buffalo tethered amidships. I scrambled aboard the next steamer and made my way forward. In the bows a figure knelt beside a great teak wheel, praying in a soft, rapid voice, asking that good fortune be attendant upon the coming voyage. An iron vase was fixed to the prow – standard issue on all Irrawaddy steamers – in which had been placed a bouquet of gaudy leaves and freshly picked flowers. The man rose from the deck, sprinkled them with water then, tenderly, rearranged them. Behind him, a companion leant sleepily on the wheel, chewing betel, his teeth black, lips crimson. 'Is this ship going to Prome?' I asked.

He nodded.

'You're the captain?'

He pointed to the man attending to his flowers. 'Him captain, mister. Me pilot.'

I thanked him and, pushing through the heaving, clamouring crowd, made my way to the forward cabin on the upper deck. David sat magisterially at the table, preparing to dispense miniature cups of green tea. He accepted a cigarette, touching the inside of his right wrist with the fingertips of his left hand, the formal Burmese gesture of thanks. 'We have finished loading and will cast off any moment now,' he said. 'The first few miles are difficult, due to the number of wrecks around Mandalay. Over there, under the far bank, there are ninety-six. Downstream there are many more, several hundred in this stretch of river alone. They are buoyed, of course, but still a hazard to shipping.'

Those sunken vessels, I knew, were nothing less than the mortal remains of the Irrawaddy Flotilla Company. As the Japanese advanced in 1942 the steamers hurried to Mandalay where, the Allies had decreed, a stand would be made. But when it became clear that the city would fall the Company manager, Mr John Morton, went down to the river with his senior assistants one evening and, working by lamplight, sank the lot. The hulls were thin as sixpences and they used Bren guns, firing bursts from close range just below the water line; slowly the craft settled to the bottom – the great Siam-Class paddlers, the express vessels, the creek steamers, even the pusher tugs and buoying launches. But now I had heard that plans were afoot to raise some of the wrecks and rebuild them. 'It's true,' David confirmed. 'And such thinking is *very* Burmese. If you can't afford new ships, then dig up the old ones and put them back to work. Improvise! Improvise! That is our watchword. In Mandalay, you know, we have craftsmen who build Land-Rovers from 7-Up tins.'

The telegraph jangled and the siren gave a stentorian roar. On the prow the flowers trembled as our twin diesels pushed us slowly out into the stream. It was 5.20 a.m. and Kipling's dawn, coming up out of China, turned the eastern sky pink and made the river as lustrous as dark silk. Mandalay was a city sparkling with dew and full of early morning shadows. High on the hill the gilded pavilions began to glitter and flash. We hissed through the water, staying well clear of the black-flagged bamboo buoys marking the graves of the old steamers and bending like reeds in the current. The river was calm, ample and almost a mile wide, proceeding unhurriedly beneath the ten spans of the Sagaing Bridge, erected in 1931 and still the only bridge across the Irrawaddy – which did not take kindly to this technological interference. All ten spans were supposed to be navigable but, within a decade, eight had been irretrievably silted up and, though the remaining two were kept open – just – there was a price to pay: the Flotilla Company had to chop the tops off its funnels and even then, at high water in August, the captains often went under with whitened knuckles and quickened pulse. Today only one arch is in use and we waltzed through it, saluting a train passing overhead with a long, singing blast of the siren.

We passed Sagaing, a progression of rounded hills crowded with pagodas and once the royal capital. Ava – the fabled City of Gems – and Amarapura, other royal capitals, were only a few miles upstream; Pagan and Prome, more royal capitals, lay downstream. All, including the very last, Mandalay, were built on the banks of the Irrawaddy. The Burmese kings cherished their river. They processed up and down it in crimson barges shaded by giant silken awnings, their courtiers fawning about the Golden Feet of the royal personage, while their generals and scholars made war and taught the scriptures along its length, and their subjects traded down every mile of it. It was, and is, the artery which nourishes the nation and, without it, the nation would perish.

The jewel-encrusted Sagaing pagodas caught the early light and exploded on the dark hills like fireworks as, with engines geared down, we nosed into a tiny dock – an old cargo flat moored to the bank – to load potatoes and bundles of monks' begging bowls, Sagaing's major manufactured product. We were carrying 240 passengers and sixty tons of cargo: onions, rice, livestock, cheroot wrappers, bales of wet and dry tea leaves and polished teak veneer for temple facings. David, the old riverine mariner, did a few sums in his head and announced that our draught was just over five feet.

We went forward to visit the skipper. He stood contemplatively in the bows with folded arms, reading the water ahead like a musical score. It was flecked with eddies, and the diameter of each indicated the depth beneath: thus a twelve-inch eddy meant the bottom was only four feet away, a five foot diameter signalled a comfortable twenty feet. The pilot sat on a small bench behind the wheel, his bare feet resting on the spokes, one hand clasping a truncheon-sized cheroot, the other a tin bowl in which to catch his volcanic discharge of ash and sparks. There was little conversation between the two men. 'They are listening to the sound of the bow wave,' David explained in a low voice. 'When it grows soft, it means the water is getting shallow. When it vanishes altogether, you're in trouble. And he is using his feet on the wheel because the steering on these old T-Class ships is so heavy you need the full power of your leg and thigh muscles.'

We were motoring past a bamboo raft about an acre in size. A thatched hut stood in the centre and, before it, a woman squatted by a fire, preparing breakfast. Two men sat and smoked in the sun nearby, a small girl knelt at the edge, dipped her hands in the river and washed her face. 'Teak,' said David. 'Under the bamboo hundreds of logs are chained together, and they're drifting down to the sea for export. You also see plenty of jar rafts – bamboo platforms floating on thousands of tall clay cooking jars. The trouble with them is that they have a four-foot draught and, when they go aground, the jars break.'

The Irrawaddy was beginning to bustle. Old country craft, laden with cargo and driven by ancient, thumping engines, lumbered by, drawing veils of blue fumes behind; a massive pusher tug shoved a barge of crude oil up to Mandalay; a local ferry cut diagonally through the traffic carrying a lorry and two oxen and, all over the place, there were fishing skiffs running before the breeze with patched sails billowing like the wings of exotic butterflies. The breeze was fitful but at any moment could grow into a wind which, howling out of nowhere, would clout us like a twelve-inch shell. These high-sided steamers could be turned right over by the impact, so skippers had to keep an eye constantly peeled for tell-tale spirals of dust approaching across country. If you spotted one the rule was simple and inflexible: ring up full speed, run for the nearest bank and get your passengers ashore as fast as they could be urged to jump. There had been an incident only two weeks before. The ship survived, but the wind had gone on to rip the roof off the Mandalay Fire Station.

It was growing hot. The light had lost its early limpid radiance and become flat, white and hard. At the stern there was a food stall, run by a handsome woman with fine eyes and a teasing smile. We drank tea, ate delicious little sweet cakes – kept tied, with a plastic bag of sugar, to the ceiling, out of the way of the ants – and tried a savoury snack of wet green tea leaves, salted and mixed with nuts. From a splendid antique dresser of oiled teak, worth its weight in rubies at a London auction house, the manageress sold soft drinks, green bananas and single cigarettes. The temperature in our cabin was 105 degrees Fahrenheit and climbing. On the decks the passengers sprawled listlessly, most sleeping, a few reading the comic books available for hire from the food stall, but all sitting up when, as regularly as a country bus, we stopped to load and unload people and cargo. If there was no landing stage the captain simply beached the ship, driving it hard up on to the mud beneath the bank; at once, regiments of women, with trays of cheroots, sweetmeats, fruit and roasted chickens balanced on their heads, clambered aboard like pirates, yelling for custom as they came.

In the early afternoon we steamed past the confluence with Burma's second great river, the Chindwin, which empties into the Irrawaddy through not one, but several, giant mouths, and then at sunset, miles from anywhere, we ran aground. I was sitting on the roof at the time, watching for the dolphins that often chase the steamers hereabouts when, all at once, there was a sustained grinding noise from below. The engines stopped and the *Dark Clouds* began listing from side to side as the deck passengers began moving anxiously about. I looked around for marker buoys but couldn't see any. There are 8,000 of them between Rangoon and Mandalay but, on this stretch, they were conspicuous by their absence. Clearly, they had been pinched by someone ashore who needed bamboo for a new house – a permanent hazard on the river. I recalled that grounded ships often remained stuck for several months, and that the masters were obliged to remain aboard until their vessels had been refloated. (The skipper who put one of King Mindon's little Italian sternwheelers on a sand-bank was beheaded on his own foredeck.) But our man, prodding at the bottom with a cane, seemed calm enough. He ordered the engines full astern and the steamer trembled violently as a cloud of frothing water, the colour of bitter chocolate, streamed away past her bows. Then he rang up full ahead and, with her plates grinding like iron teeth, the ship inched forward. Backwards and forwards we went, painstakingly digging our own trench and, within half an hour, the skipper got us out of there. It was a performance of consummate skill and, under way again, we proceeded cautiously through a long, long stretch of shallows with hardly any bow wave audible and those tell-tale whorls ahead only the size of dinner plates.

46

I returned to the cabin and, though we kept hitting bottom hard enough to spill a criminal amount of Mandalay Rum, we bounced clear each time and, as darkness fell, arrived at the little town of Pokokku and tied up for the night beside an old cargo flat. Since all the berths had been claimed and no space remained on deck, we took our sleeping bags ashore and laid them out in the flat. Consignments of coolie hats and sacks of onions surrounded us, above us was a perch on which a magnificent fighting cock sat, its plumage lustrous in the dim light of our kerosene lantern. Three hours later, however, its tiny, wild mind sensed a false dawn and, with terrific energy, it began to crow. Awoken from bad dreams and a heavy, rum-induced sleep, I jumped up and clouted it repeatedly with my pillow, sending it spinning round and round on its pole, wings flapping, squawking furiously, until a small boy slipped in and, giving me a deeply aggrieved look, bore it away as tenderly as a puppy.

We sailed before dawn, pulling out into the deserted gunmetal river and making for the ancient capital of Pagan where, at 7 a.m., we ran up on to the sandy beach to discharge passengers. The ship did not dally at Pagan, but it didn't matter. We had called there in the Toyota and now, running downstream, saw again the 5,000 temples stretching for twenty miles along the foreshore like a setting for some stupendous Asian opera. The Burmese claim there were once 13,000 pagodas here, and that the missing ones had succumbed to earthquakes, pillaging armies and the ferocious climate. Some were exquisite miniatures, the size of wedding cakes, and these have been carried away to decorate gardens in Frankfurt, Tokyo and certain lordly estates in the Home Counties. But those 5,000 remain and it takes two hours to sail, in Spithead-review style, past a unique perspective of stupas, domes and cupolas, some soaring hundreds of feet into the shimmering air. Though it is inhabited today by farmers and makers of lacquerware, Pagan remains the spiritual heart of Burma. The country's first king, Anawrahta, transporting the sacred scriptures on the backs of thirty-two white elephants, was enthroned here in the eleventh century. It remained the royal capital for nearly two hundred and fifty years, only falling when an eccentric monarch named Narathihapate, 'the swallower of 300 dishes of curry daily', murdered an embassy sent by Kublai Khan and, fearing retribution, abandoned the city and fled away down the Irrawaddy. Pagan never regained its old eminence and was destined, down the years, to become the most fabulous ghost town on earth.

The last pagoda vanished around a bend and the *Dark Clouds* steamed on cautiously, still wary of the shallows, though David was confident we would complete the day's run without further mishaps. 'The current is faster now and we should be able to jump any sandbars we hit. But on this river, of course, you can never be sure. It changes its configuration all the time, every hour, every day. You might have a fifty-foot channel over there at dawn. But by dusk it will be gone, silted up, and a new one will have opened up on the other side of the river. That is why our pilots concentrate on only one section, maybe fifty or sixty miles, and why that particular section is always handed down from father to son. Between Mandalay and Prome we use no fewer than seven pilots and, at every stop, you will hear villagers advising them of changes since they last passed by. The Irrawaddy engages anyone who sails on her in a running battle of wits. Our buoying launches are going up and down all the time, banging bamboo marker buoys along the new channels with wooden mallets. The skippers suffer from frustration and nervous troubles, and are the only masters allowed to have their wives along with them for solace.'

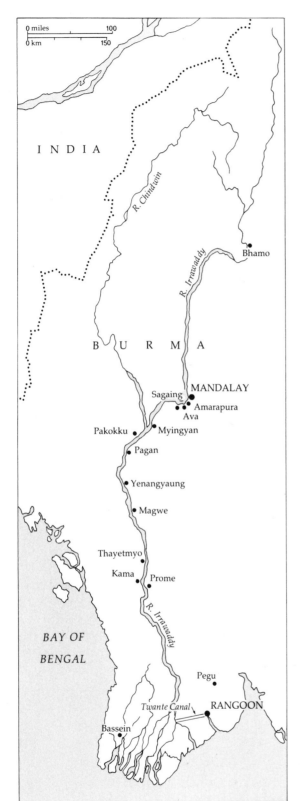

Captions for the following photographs:

1. A Burmese farmer, his wife and children laded aboard the family conveyance, prepares to cross the Irrawaddy on market day.
2. Yenangyaung, a small port in the lee of biscuit-coloured cliffs. It was here, centuries ago, that the Burmese first struck oil, the wells being traditionally owned by the same twenty-four families.
3. Pagan, once the royal capital, remains Burma's spiritual heart. There used to be 13,000 pagodas here and many of the remaining 5,000 are in a state of neglect and disrepair.
4. At each stop women pedlars clamber aboard to sell provisions to the ferry passengers. As well as the wares on display here, whole chickens and giant cigars are available.
5. Villagers prepare to board a miniature ferry on the Rangoon river for a night out in the capital.
6. A violent tropical storm at Kama. Dust clouds whirl about the banks and the pagoda bells ring wildly in the wind.
7. A pair of monks clasping orange sunshades descend the bank to board the ferry.

David was in high spirits. He rigged up a portable cassette player, powered by a couple of old car batteries, and put on a selection of his favourite tapes, including one by a performing monk who had gone to the top of the Burmese hit parade with a recorded anthology of sermons, songs, homilies and jokes. But, while still enjoying his royalties and his new star status, the monk had been murdered by five men who had tied him to a tree and driven a jeep into him. His tape, though I listened closely, wasn't exactly my cup of tea, and neither were the orthodox Burmese pop songs we heard, though one did rather take my fancy for the pain which the female vocalist managed to convey. Her anguish had a kind of epic Wagnerian resonance and, when I asked David what she was singing, he said, ' "Mummy, My Car Has Broken Down".' Ordinary Burmese girls don't own cars, so this one clearly had to be the daughter of either a drug smuggler or a black marketeer. David shrugged. 'Well, I can't deny that both activities go on, even aboard the steamers, though most of the drugs go down the Salween river, which is close to the Golden Triangle. The contraband we most commonly get on the Irrawaddy are towels and painted enamelware from China, raw jade from Kachin and, from India, coming first down the Chindwin, talcum powder, bed linen, gents' neckties and machine tools.'

Lunch was terrible, a chicken curry consisting of blackened fragments of beak, crop and claw. Afterwards, at a dusty halt marked only by a lone tree where we paused to take aboard consignments of cradles and crimson ceremonial drums, David spotted a woman ashore selling two hands of bananas and a solitary egg. 'An egg! An egg!' he cried, leaping from the deck to secure it. He returned, beaming, and promised that we should have it, scrambled, for breakfast.

A blistering afternoon wind, heavy with sand from the plains and picking up more from the lip of the eastern bank, roared across the ship, the grains pattering against the superstructure like hail. The river was a strange milky blue, glittering with heat and, unable to sleep, I leafed through a copy of the Inland Waterways Handbook, noting that it was forbidden to load dynamite from junks in the rain, and that a surcharge had to be paid for the carriage of gold, feathers and books. Later, as the sun began to wane, we paused at Yenangyaung, a small port in the lee of shadowy, biscuit-coloured cliffs. All day we had been steaming past isolated industrial complexes producing chemicals, concrete, fertiliser and oil and, in most cases, paid for by foreign governments and run by expatriate engineers. We had seen the lonely clubhouses built on bluffs overlooking the river where, in the evenings, they gathered to vent their spleen on the Third World and talk wistfully, over cold gin, of California, Adelaide and the skiing around St Moritz. But it was here at Yenangyaung, centuries ago, that the Burmese first struck oil. The wells, operated by hand, were traditionally owned by the same twenty-four families, who sold their crude up and down the river for preserving wood and lighting lamps. In 1795 a young army officer named Captain Michael Symes, on his way upstream to re-establish British diplomatic relations with the Golden Feet, called at Yenangyaung and was shown a cupful. Symes was astonished. He had never seen oil before but he noted its possibilities and sent urgent despatches back to HQ in India, insisting that this strange combustible stuff had a significant future. The despatches were given a cursory reading then filed.

At Yenangyaung, moored beside a trio of ancient teak country boats with high, brassbound rudder posts, we had a swim. It was like plunging into warm bouillon and, while the *Dark Clouds* loaded straw mats, tamarind seeds, kapok and wrought-iron plant stands, I soaped myself beside a small raft dressed with bunting like a ship-of-the-line. It carried a life-sized golden Buddha destined for some village temple upstream, and it surveyed my ablutions with a faint, derisory smile. But then, as I began shampooing my dirt-encrusted scalp and singing aloud, an eddy swung its little conveyance about and, sharply, it turned its back on me.

Under way again, we drank neat rum and watched the dusk turn the river into the colour of lemons. Trees had begun to appear on either side, misty blue hills loomed out of the eastern horizon. 'There used to be monkeys playing along those banks,' said David, 'but the army shot and ate them all. We lost a ship hereabouts several years ago – a T-Class steamer, just like this one. It was caught in a flooded chaung, and that is one of the most terrible things that can happen on the Irrawaddy. It's when a cloud burst causes a flash flood in a dried-up stream bed which carries everything before it – trees, animals, even people. Only last year a visiting dance troupe was performing for a village in a dry creek bed when the water caught them. Everyone was washed into the river and, days later, we were still picking up the bodies of the dancers in their bright silks. Along the length of the river there are thousands of these chaungs and every one is a potential menace. It makes a roaring noise when in spate, and that is something a master must always listen for because, if it strikes his ship broadside on, there is nothing he can do. The T-Class we lost was steaming at night. It caught him at 4 a.m. and that ship vanished entirely. We knew where it went down and we even went looking for it with metal detectors, but it was buried under thousands of tons of sand and there wasn't a trace of it.'

Darkness fell with the speed of a blind being drawn and the skipper switched on his spotlight, a shimmering blade of radiance that flickered along the banks and hunted across the black water for the reflecting tin discs nailed to the buoys. It picked up giant moths, gaudy as humming birds, and flights of flying foxes barnstorming low across the surface. The Flotilla Company steamers' lights were so large they needed twin motors to rotate them and, though the *Dark Clouds* boasted nothing so sophisticated, her beam safely picked out our route and, in between, touched small groups of crystal-studded pagodas on the bank, making them flicker like summer lightning.

Talk of the chaungs had made David morose. He spoke of a great flood when, since there was no real estate for burials, the dead were wrapped in mats and launched upon the river, bobbing corpses through which he had to navigate his side-paddler. But then the rum did the trick and, with a cool breeze filling the cabin, he brightened and played 'Bad Moon Rising' very loudly on his cassette machine. We docked at Magwe and after a dinner ashore prepared by a mad-eyed, bare-chested cook who muttered and sweated into our fish soup, we returned aboard, unrolled our sleeping bags and prepared for bed. But the ship's cockroaches were massing to meet us. They seemed, to my unhappy eye, as large as lobsters and, wheeling like cavalry, they mounted charge after charge across the deck. David laughed. 'The Thais *eat* those,' he said, scornfully, while I took a silent bet that, in their time, they had also eaten a few Thais. When we had climbed on to our berths, the cockroaches sent in their alpine divisions, trained for combat at altitude, and I awoke several times to find them bivouacked on my face and doing route marches up and down my legs. Later, squadrons of mosquitoes came banking in off the river to lend air support with some tactical strike work. When the false dawn filled the cabin with murky light they all went away – followed by a plump rat which wandered off through a hole in the bulkhead.

That afternoon we picked up a wheezing, overweight army colonel who made his way into the cabin and commandeered the best chair. His starched uniform was stained with sweat and he was clearly out of sorts. After exchanging ages, a routine courtesy between strangers, he announced that much of Burma was burning down. It was the heat. As a result, he had to visit all the townships on this sector of the river to check their hoses, tell them about procedures and give them drills. He spent an entire day preparing the citizens of one *dorp* for the eventuality of fire, and what happened a week later? It was burnt to the ground. An estimated 300 died, including a batch of prisoners locked in the gaol. He shook his head and sighed windily. 'They are hopeless, hopeless!' We put him ashore at Thayetmyo where, in 1883, the British had built a fort and a very good golf course, then sailed on, passing one of the antique Clyde-built side-paddlers with massive boilers and steam-driven rudder which, in their heyday, had been the flagships of the Inland Water Transport fleet. David had commanded several in his time and watched affectionately as it laboured upstream, hauling two flats of cement. The captain, reclining in a chair on the flying bridge, lifted a tea cup in salute while his great seven-bladed teak wheels thundered away inside their paddle boxes. The countryside was changing, the sandy wilderness giving way to low green hills, fields of millet and plantations of toddy palms. We saw wild flowers and, close to the water, a country boat slipway hidden in a grove of blossoming plum trees. And, wherever one looked, there were the ubiquitous pagodas. Some were crumbling, indicating lazy monks and shiftless congregations, but most were lovingly tended and a credit to their villages.

The first part of our voyage was almost over. That evening we would disembark in Prome and wait for a ship to take us on to Rangoon. The *Dark Clouds*, after discharging cargo, would turn and, with David aboard, head back for Mandalay. But three hours out of Prome, while taking on onions and charcoal at the village of Kama, we struck a storm. All at once the sky turned black and raindrops came whanging down like dumdums. 'Ah, the mango rains have come,' said David, relishing the sudden chill, but this was no seasonal shower to put the bloom on the fruit. A ferocious wind suddenly sprang up and the skipper shouted at the slim, fine-boned women loading the cargo to quit the ship. Clouds of dust whirled about us as, with engines full ahead, we ran for open water, the pilot complaining loudly that he had sand in his eyes and couldn't see. Canoes and country boats slipped past in the murk, making for the bank while, on the weathered hills above, the pagoda bells were wild and clamorous. The *Dark Clouds*, listing heavily, plunged and yawed among the hissing, foam-capped waves. David called the captain a dolt and yelled down to him to get to the bank too. He needed no urging and hit it at such speed that he buried his bow deeply in streaming red earth. Then, abruptly as it had come, the storm receded, leaving behind it the washed pink skies of evening.

We made good time to Prome. A following breeze sat behind us and the water was full of bounce and energy. David, who had become our friend, talked with a particular intensity about his relationship with the river. He had run away to it as a child, signing up as a ship's boy, and when, soon afterwards, his elder brother drowned in it, his mother's dislike of the Irrawaddy, already considerable, became implacable. His wife had gone into labour aboard one of David's own steamers and their first son, after a difficult delivery in the forward cabin, was still-born. Lots of babies, he added, were lost off the ships; carelessly positioned by their parents at night, they rolled under the guard rail while they slept. 'In an emergency,' he said, 'we must cope by ourselves because these vessels are not equipped with radio. If something goes wrong, it can be two or three days before help arrives.'

Prome at dusk looked homely and welcoming but, having said our goodbyes, we found ourselves trekking through muddy streets filled with bony, growling dogs and the jangle of bicycle bells. At the People's Hotel a wedding was in progress. Music blared and grinning drunks shook our hands as we made our way upstairs to small, squalid, windowless cubicles with graffiti-covered walls and unwashed concrete floors. Aboard the ship my feet had begun to swell. David had diagnosed cockroach bites and, now the size and circumference of pink footballs, they were starting to ache; also, a fever was coming on. I showered beneath a rusting pipe, noting that when the bathroom had been whitewashed an empty bottle standing on a small corner shelf had been whitewashed too, leaving the bit of wall behind it untouched.

Our mentor for the final stage appeared at the hotel shortly before breakfast. Ko Kyaw Win was a thin, silent, watchful man and, while we tucked into sweet coffee and slices of pineapple, he chose bread with a dollop of strawberry jam and a lightly poached egg on top. We had planned to swim in the Heavy Industries Pool but it had been drained so, passing up offers of visits to the Japanese Rubber Ball Factory and the Mazda assembly plant, we called at the Shwesandaw pagoda, reached by electric lift – all rides were free that day, paid for by a local businessman who hoped to gain merit – and notable for relays of priests reading the scriptures into a battery of microphones which dispersed their tinny, chanting voices all over town. Then, since Ko Kyaw Win had put a buoying launch at our disposal, we bathed in the Irrawaddy, attended by the master – highly strung and jumpy after a spell deciphering the course of the lower river – and his gentle, reassuring wife. They pressed tea upon us, together with sweetmeats, movie magazines, small savoury snacks wrapped in leaves, even mugs of palm toddy. The surface was glassy, the current treacherous; and the bottom felt like warm porridge.

We were chased home, not much refreshed, by yet another storm and, after browsing through the black market and discovering that a bottle of whisky, brought down snake-infested jungle trails from Thailand on a smuggler's back, cost only slightly more than at my London off-licence, we checked out of the hotel and made our way to the riverside to board the *Taing Kyo Saung*, or *Patriot*. She was a T-Class too, but her cabin had been spruced up and the floor dusted with anti-cockroach powder. It worked a treat, but my enlarged feet left prints in it the size of rhino spoor.

We sailed soon after dawn. The captain, a balding old man wearing broken spectacles, brought us fresh fruit and tea in his best pot. Such courtesies are routine in Burma and he withdrew shyly, nonplussed by our thanks. Moments later we were under way with the promise, after two hours' hard steaming, of one of the wonders of the river to come. Ghautama Hill is a 300-foot-high cliff extending for one and a half miles and, cut into its entire length, are hundreds of images of the Buddha. Some are done in relief, others are busts inhabiting niches, many are painted and gilded. At the time of the kings this was known as Tax Point and ships were obliged to pay a toll before being allowed to proceed. Prome was, for centuries, a royal seat, and the statues had been commissioned by devout local monarchs.

The first day's run was quiet. At the stops we swam, noting that the current was more vigorous than ever. Entering lower Burma, the river now seemed to feel the distant tug of the sea. We tied up for the night beneath a deserted, lofty mud-bank rearing high above the ship. Darkness brought a heavy silence, broken only by the murmur of the captain saying his prayers below. At 9 p.m., shortly before the lights went out, I idly shone my torch along the bank and found it turned into a public gallery, the packed rows of spectators rising from the water's edge to the crest, all watching intently as we scrubbed our teeth and prepared for bed. They were mortified at being caught and, turning as one, fled up the bank as though running from a tidal wave. We were now in the area of Burma that is alleged to breed the world's largest mosquito and when they arrived and began bleeding me, sleep became difficult. I rose, lit a candle and settled down to work on my notes, but fleas began dancing on the page so I closed the book and gave up.

Daylight brought changes. The river now flowed majestically between high, commanding banks, the pilot doing a sedate slalom around the sandbars. The countryside looked lush and prosperous; even the bamboo groves had a special sheen to them, and there were flights of mallard all over the place. And, with Rangoon just over the horizon, the people had changed too. Gone were the earnest and inflexible courtesies of the upper river. The villagers who met the boat now cracked cheeky jokes and showed a bit of swank. In the afternoon an old scholar joined us. He was bound for the city and wore, in the buttonholes of his white silk shirt, rubies the size of chick peas. He had been specially appointed, he said, by the Minister of Home and Religious Affairs to collect and collate classical Buddhist texts. It was an immense undertaking, and he now spent his life moving from one ecclesiastical library to the next. He sipped tea, impassively, while abeam of us 100 yards of river bank suddenly split off and fell into the water. Perhaps 1,000 tons of earth vanished beneath the boiling surface, but it was such a commonplace happening that our friend didn't even give it a second glance; each year whole villages vanished, victims of erosion. We had heard the rumbles and seen the splashes of collapsing banks all the way down as the river steadily devoured the countryside and flushed it away to the Bay of Bengal.

That evening the sun sank without its customary flourish, slipping unnoted behind massing banks of cumulus. The rains were clearly imminent, and not a moment too soon. After dark there were fireworks. Burma, as the colonel had claimed, was burning all right, and the eastern sky flickered with red light. Was it crops? Stubble? Villages? We asked the pilot who shrugged, neither knowing nor caring, and, moments later, the first heavy shower swept across the river. Soon afterwards we left the Irrawaddy, turning left into the Twante Canal, an artificial cut that links it with the Rangoon tributary. Our great waterway now lay astern, preparing to enter the vast, creek-veined tidal swamp that is her delta. We motored on through the rain, our spotlight flickering as the skipper picked up his tin markers, passing lumbering country boats while we headed for home at a speed befitting an express steamer concluding a mainline run.

The golden finger of the Shwedagon Pagoda, lit and eerie, stood on the horizon and, eventually, the lights of the city shone blearily through the murk. We docked at 4 a.m. and, clambering into a 1947 Buick taxi with a leaking roof, I glanced back at the old ship to say goodbye and realised that I couldn't see her. Well, truth to tell, I wasn't going to lose any sleep over that. I was glad to be off the river. My feet still hurt, the fever persisted and I had lost a stone in weight. But now, weeks later and back in London, I keep seeing, in my mind's eye, a terrific opaline sweep of water backed by a lovely early morning sky and, all at once, I feel a sustained and oddly acute sense of loss.

THE MISSISSIPPI

LIBBY PURVES

Descending through the haze to St Louis Airport, the river seems a wide and reassuringly primitive rut through the geometry of the modern American city. Too broad and erratic for a freeway, it swirls and boils under its bridges, accepting the assault of the swift Missouri, widening, escaping the bounds of its last lock and dam before the sea. 'Alla way from th' mountains of Minnesota to th' Gulf of Mexico,' said the fat cab driver, with satisfaction. 'Longest inna world. Twice as long as the United Kingdom of England, see?'

It is a river to dream of. The most reluctant school reader of a condensed *Huckleberry Finn* has the Mississippi somewhere in his mind: a glittering trail through state after state, thrashing with paddlewheelers but hospitable to rafts and runaways; dimming at night to the stars in the water and the gleam of a candle from a cabin in the trees. A river to run away on, a highway from austere mountains to wicked seaports, down through the heart of America. The Father of the Waters.

June is high river season; great branches and tiny twigs flung down from the Missouri accumulate in solid rafts upstream of the tethered boats. Wood clogged the mooring-lines of the *Sergeant Floyd* museum, a retired workboat resembling a scout hut on a barge. Wood pressed in the five-knot current against the curlicued replica of the *Robert E. Lee*; and aboard a floating McDonald's hamburger house, men with long poles worked to disperse the threatening branches. 'There'll be more down, and more. Storms comin' tonight.' Storms coming. The sky had been slaty grey all afternoon, the heat oppressive. Forked lightning began to streak the sky at dusk like a crack in hell; claps of deafening thunder followed, and a hot gale of wind. Soon the river vanished in the blowing rain, and the unreasonable fury of mid-continental weather was upon us.

'We have a tornado watch,' said the TV newsreader unemotionally. The hotel closed the rooftop pool, and the storm raged on across the indifferent city.

Through early summer, these rains swell the rivers. The Upper Mississippi and Missouri between them have four thousand miles to grow before they meet violently above

55

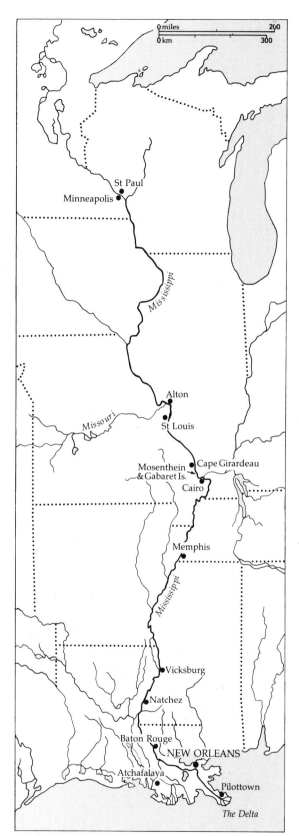

Captions for the following photographs:

1. A bayou channel, lined with quays and dwellings like a suburban street.
2. Mississippi sightseers enjoy the sunshine aboard a vessel shaped like a small sternwheeler.
3. New Orleans musicians serenade an empty street.
4. Bayou fishing boats.
5. An oil installation set in the brackish bayou country where sea and river slowly mix.
6. A red, white and blue riverside water tower, patriotically starred and striped.

6

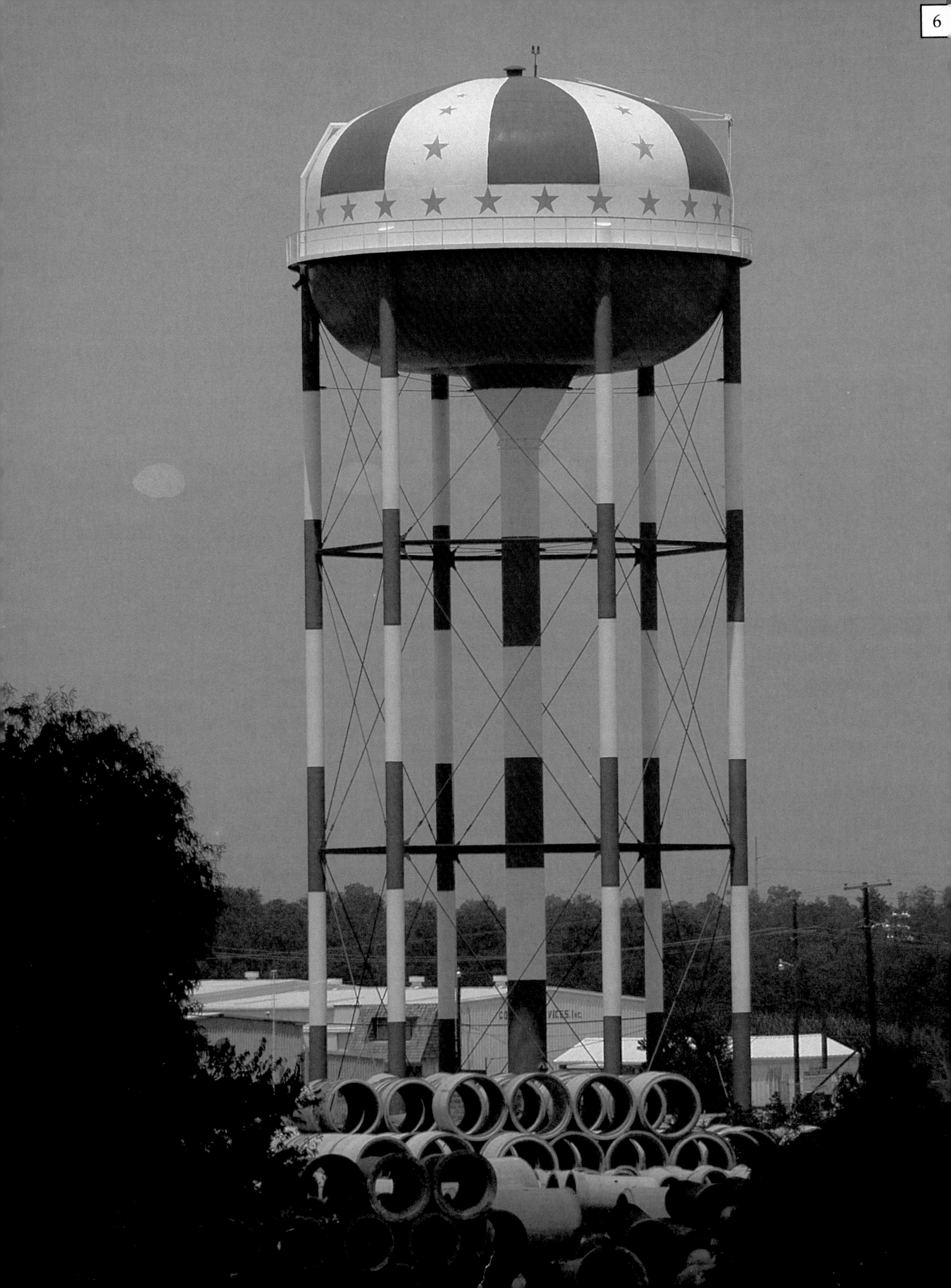

St Louis; their waters together hurtle on until the clear Ohio joins them at Cairo for the last nine hundred and fifty miles to the sea. Above St Louis, it is a lock-and-dam river, descending four hundred and twenty feet in the six hundred and seventy miles from Minneapolis. At the last of the river locks, by the dusty town of Alton, Illinois, I watched a heavy green barge drop in the far chamber with its fellows; outside, two upstream towboats waited patiently. 'Terrible dam' lock, that twenty-six,' said tow captains to me later. 'Small. You have to break up your tow and put it together again.'

The gigantic Mississippi tows consist of twenty-five, thirty, sometimes over fifty barges lashed in a square, a fleet of matchboxes pushed from behind by a stumpy, square-bowed towboat. One tow can carry as much as five hundred railway freight cars; but the delay of the locks exacts the price of time.

The towing company that was to pick me up near Cairo and take me into the south had a barge depot in the city, and I walked upstream to find it. AMERICAN COMMERCIAL TERMINAL. Outside, a huge grey-and-yellow robot rested beside a coaltip; beyond the offices, a long finger of conveyor-belt ran towards the pontoons.

'Coom in,' said the general superintendent, with no Midwestern twang. He comes from Barnsley. Until 1974 Cyril Gough worked in Britain; but repeated missions to service a nine-mile conveyor belt in Kentucky led him at last to move. He has a son building a lead mine in the Ozarks, a daughter in the Missouri Concert Ballet, a growing affection for St Louis despite the poor rose-growing conditions; and, spread around us on the river bank, an engineer's dream of logic and completeness.

Coal trains, 110 cars long, come in from the vast red opencast mines of Wyoming, rattling through the Badlands, to reach St Louis. 'Gateway, see. No more locks.' He leaned across the slide projector, views of the Mississippi rippling on his light shirt. 'Train gets here, coal gets thawed in winter, then the clever bit.' Each carriage tips right over, in mechanical hands, emptying its load without the wheels leaving the track. Pushing buttons, nine men can unload and stockpile a train in three hours. 'Twelve, with me and the foremen.' We walked out through the strange desolation of a robot industry, through a field of purple thistles, and along the steel catwalk over the muddy river. Beneath us, an island of driftwood had formed, mingled with rubbish. 'Look,' said Cyril. 'Balls, kids' toys, bottles, tyres. You find a body in it, now and then.' Across the river the grim sky gave little light to the deep, wooded beauties of Mosenthein and Gabaret islands; a new storm was breaking. When it eased, a procession ('Moolah Shriners') banged and marched past. I packed for the early flight to Memphis, Tennessee, to await orders from the towboat.

At the airport a man was buying a copy of *Guns and Ammo*. Special feature, 'Backup Guns For Marauding Bears'. He put it in his plastic briefcase and hurried to the departure gate. The Old West still feeds dreams. And the Old South, too; my paper informed me that there is a hotel in Atlanta where you can get twenty-five bucks off your bill when you book by saying 'Scarlett sent me.' Burying my Mark Twain deep in my case, I was fearful of being sucked in to some Huckleberry, steamboatin', romantic legend, and losing the real Mississippi in its toils. The towboat I would ride from Memphis was real enough; meanwhile, I could admire from the air the mad, meandering ditch through the chequerboard fields of Arkansas and Tennessee. 'The crookedest river in the world,' said Twain; vast horseshoes curved around, sometimes less than a mile across the neck, wasting time. Not that the river is unaware of this lack of logic;

frequently it has suddenly and savagely shortened its course, cutting across these fragile necks of land, throwing river towns out into the country, drowning fields.

Memphis lies on a tremendous bluff on the east bank of the river, built by the hot dust whirling in down the centuries on the prevailing westerly winds, and losing momentum over the wide cold river. I sat under Highway 55 bridge to contemplate it, and a black truck driver abandoned his vehicle on the road above to sit beside me on the grass. His name was Eddie, and he would have preferred a fishing trip to a day on the Memphis freeways with a load of crispy snacks. 'You goin' on a towboat? Lucky. You git fishin'. Only doan' eat catfish nor bass till mebbe thirty miles down from here. Till then, tastes of castor oil.' He gazed lovingly at the water, sighed, and threw his cigarette into it. A moment later, the lorry roared into life, and I walked up alone to my motel.

The boat store lay just down the bluff. Commercial towboats don't stop; except for fuel. They pick up, and loose and exchange their barges out in midstream or holding gently against the current, near the bank. They are provisioned and watered and brought crew-changes by little chugging storeboats, based at scores of boat services along the banks. Dean Cochrane, standing amid racks of shampoo, magazines and cigarettes in the Economy Boat Store office, delivered news of the towboat *Spartan*. 'Two hunnerd miles north of here, outa Cairo.' You pronounce it Kay-Ro. 'Later'n we thought. Be here twelve noon tomorrow, put y'on then.' I reckoned to check afresh in the morning, in case some furious current from the Ohio should hurry *Spartan* on and past me. Towboats don't stop.

Meanwhile, I could risk an interlude of romance. Memphis is still the biggest spot cotton market anywhere, but the old King-Cotton empires have crumbled, and it is displaced in the river-cargo charts by grain and coal and petrochemicals, iron and sand and stone. But when cotton was sovereign, and its wealth flourished heavily on the backs of the slaves and their barely free children, Memphis mattered; its history is of visionary freedoms, of black schools burned, of hope and oppression. Here Martin Luther King was murdered, at the Lorraine Hotel. I needed to go to Beale Street, spiritual headquarters of black America, and at least salute the place where all the pain and all the faith were distilled into the Blues. In the noonday heat, at last, I found it. Sad and derelict, closed to traffic; dusty and littered with broken bricks and glass. A tombstone row of dead shops glared: COHEN'S LOAN OFFICE. NATHAN NOVICK MUSICAL INSTRUMENTS. NATHAN'S LOANS. BARBER SHOP. LIPPMAN'S LOANS. I walked reluctantly through the rubble, and not one trumpet wailed a greeting.

Next day they sent word: the *Spartan* was approaching. I was ready to go. Down at the boat store, the radio crackled with constant river chat. I sat in a seedy lounge with the *Memphis Press-Scimitar*, until the door opened, a head jerked, and I was hustled on to the storeboat along with a case of milk and a box of cucumbers. Nose to the current, the hutlike boat edged out past a tiny rocking launch with old inner-tubes for lifebelts, adorned with the rebel flag and NEW ORLEANS OR BUST. A log hit us sharply amidships, and we came alongside *Spartan* with a clang. Boxes, bags, and passenger were thrown aboard, and the Memphis bridges grew rapidly smaller astern. I was, at last, on the great conveyor-belt to the south.

Spartan is a biggish towboat and brand new. She is just under 136 feet long, 47 feet wide; an uncompromising rectangle. High 'towknees' rising from the bow proclaim her a pushing boat: what America calls a towboat, as opposed to a tugboat (which tows). Her engines have 6,400 horsepower; her crew of ten include two pilots qualified to take steering-watches day and night on the main river. One pilot is also captain. *Spartan* can push an average load, say twenty-five barges, at over twelve miles an hour, plus current if it is downstream. I looked around and climbed diffidently to the bridge.

Captain Daniel L. Phelps – correctly, Cap'n Dan – is a startlingly handsome bearded Southern gentleman, dark and tanned and saturnine, revealing Indian blood in every line. Pilot Arthur McGrew – Cap'n Arthur – in contrast to Dan and his young crew in shorts, is grave and nearing retirement, and affects the adult dignity of grey trousers and striped braces. Both made me meticulously welcome in their smart new pilot house, offered Cona coffee and Diet Pepsi, and ensured that the boxed lavatory in the corner was tactfully veiled in its camouflage doors. A pilot cannot desert his steering-bars for more than a second.

Growing accustomed to the new rapid movement of the banks past the windows, I looked ahead at the iron acres of barges. We were pushing twenty-four, a mixed cargo. A row of four grain, and a blank space; behind, one coal, two chemicals, one corn, one empty; then three coal, one grain, one empty; then four coal and three grain; closest to our towknees, three coal, one grain, one chemical. Wire hawsers fanned out from the towboat to the barges; more lay between the rafted barges themselves, ratchet-tightened wires making up one stiff load. Altogether our flock measured 1,000 feet by 155 feet, excluding *Spartan* herself; a smallish tow. Empties have been known to travel in seventies. Captain Arthur eased the bars to port for a wide left-hand bend, and the captain, off-watch, filled his Dangerous Dan mug and climbed on to the pilot-house roof to sleep in the sun.

Towboats don't stop. Time is money. But we did, half an hour later. It took nearly fifteen minutes and a lot of black smoke before the load was tucked snugly into the bank, held gently on the engines astern. 'Smoked out,' said Dan crossly, returning from the roof. 'Why?' The radio had ordered a halt to pick up a barge which hadn't been ready at Memphis; it was wanted that night, empty, at Helena seventy miles downstream. 'Must be desperate.' By the cool green bank we lingered two expensive hours; Dan sleeping, Arthur keeping watch and talking.

'Born 'n bred on this river. Used to swim and row and raft it as a boy; worked on it for ever. Never th' same two days. Sometimes can't see the tow for rain; sometimes so low the channel's hardly there.'

A coastguard crackled in on the radio, calling a fellow. 'We have a raft. Two men, one woman, there appears t' be a little boy.'

'They have lifejackets, I presoom?'

'They do. Cain't see lights.'

'Ask Exxon, will they be a problem past there?'

'A raft? Logs with a tent on? You mean like Huck Finn?' I was incredulous.

'Yeah,' said McGrew. 'That's who they're tryin' t' be.' River pilots are indulgent to the great tradition of small boats rafting down the river to adventure; but towmen dread the vulnerability of small craft. ('Appears t' be a little boy,' had had a distinct edge to it, even over the radio.) It had taken us a long time to slow to a halt; on the bending Mississippi 'you cain't see ten minutes ahead.'

We waited two hours there, until a barge appeared in custody of a small towboat, and the deckhands moved forward through the iron alleys between the barges to hitch it in. 'Tonight at Helena,' said Dan, 'she'll go, next two empties move up, put the new one in behind 'em.' He sketched his iron chequerboard to remind himself, and *Spartan* moved off down-river.

Round Cow and Cat islands; through crossings and cut offs; past the sad late town of Commerce, deserted by the river in 1874 and withered to a mere name. I read Dan's personal river notebook, charts glued into a book and webbed around by private observations.

'Memphis Gage 15-21 in bend at Josie Henry.'

'Horseshoe to Kangaroo real close 10.11.78.'

'One way. WATE HERE.'

'All wet at Battleaxe Pt 4.10.77.'

The point of the WATE HERE notes became obvious. Downstream takes priority over upstream traffic; a tow coming up round a corner offers politely to wait for your southbound juggernaut, and you murmur politely back, 'Thank you, Cap'n. I 'preciate it.' Through the nights and the days the words ''preciate it' crackle up and down the Mississippi, a password of the trade. I settled in the corner with the Adventures of Tommy Towboater in *Waterway Journal*; the sun set in orange glory behind the Diamond Woods; the river became a sheet of brass. A deckhand walked across the distant barges ahead, lifting up each navigation light to show the pilot it was burning. Another lit the brazier rubbish-bin to a dim glow in the evening. It was a clear and perfect night. ' 'Preciate it,' murmured Captain Dan to some invisible friend round the corner, and I went to my bunk to rest.

I came back up at midnight. In the glow of the depth-sounder numerals – deep forties in this high river – Dan played his searchlight restlessly on the spans of a bridge. 'Threadin' a needle.' He threaded it, bugs whirling in hundreds in the white beams of light. The boat from the Helena depot appeared under the clear stars, deckhands moved with flashlights among the barge wires; *Spartan* took on her new charges. Dan wrote in the log: AT HELENA D/P CHEM 90 – MTY. SHIFT 2 B-I-T; P/U MEAL LOAD. The empty chemical barge deposited, the two empties in the tow moved forward; the meal barge added. Courteous thanks to the attending towboat, and a slow kick ahead on the engines. In the darkness, as Cap'n Arthur took over, Cap'n Dan paused to explain his edginess at the bridge.

'See, bridges are the worst, with a load and down the current. We always wondered why they had t' put the bridges where there's a bend. Turns out it's because on bends the channel never changes. OK. But it's – psychologically – more difficult for us.' Arthur grunted assent in the gloom. In early days, Dan nearly hit the Vicksburg Bridge. 'It is the worst on the river. It sits right on the bend. You see it – you're through it. No time t' think. That one time, I did miss it. Close. I vomited, here, in the garbage can.'

Arthur roared with laughter. Dan smiled briefly with him, and went below to his exercise machine and his sleep. In the night we crossed the state border into Mississippi, and at six the sun was up in a blaze of gold astern. Mile 589. The miles, on the chart, count down to the point ninety miles below New Orleans, the Head of the Passes, where the river divides into a bunch of thin outlets to the sea. The South proper was opening around us; hidden river towns, green lush islands, odd twisting tributaries haunted by alligators. We threaded the Greenville Bridge, on its bend, with a nine-knot spurt of current underneath us. Then I lay on the pilot-house roof under the smoky Stars and Stripes, breathed in the sour mealy smell of the grain barges, and thought about this life.

A towboat may work half a mile from land, but it is essentially as isolated as a deepwater ship. For thirty days or more the crew do not step on land; ten men are mewed up together, sleeping never more than five hours, relieved only momentarily by the contact of the storeboat. In general there are no women; on *Spartan*, as it happens, there is one. She rules the airy galley, next to the engine room, a motherly figure in tortoiseshell glasses and grey curls. Over a solid lunch of catfish and hushpuppies and cherry pie, Dan introduced her as Evelyn, and made her sit down and talk. 'It's ma first trip. Ma twenty-first day.' Evelyn is from Carrollton, Kentucky, where running off to be a towboat cook still counts as raffish. At the Wesleyan Church, 'ma minister did not want me t' come.' She herself had haunting fears, race memories of rude steamboating roustabouts. But when her job at a factory gave her allergies, Evelyn summoned the pioneer spirit. 'I got eight grandchildren. I've been a mother and a grandmother and a housewife. Nothin' like this' – she indicated the silently eating deck-hands, the passing shore, the throbbing engine – 'ever happened t' me'. When the call-up came she hustled through the spring cleaning, told her husband, and caught the first aeroplane of her life. The fearful rickety Memphis taxi added to the terror; at the boat store she hesitated 't' go into that lounge with the boys all there'. But the boys muted their talk and made her welcome, 'like a new family over again'; and now Evelyn spends her days cleaning the stove, feeding her crew, and reading the Bible as the green shore changes alongside in the sun. A life of more unqualified innocence would be hard to devise.

'An' the captain,' she confided towards evening, 'treats me like his own mom.' Half an hour later I had proof of it. Summoned by an urgent shout on the intercom, I ran to the pilot house to find them standing side by side, gazing at the Tennessee shore. 'Red deer,' said Dan softly. And the two watched the deer touched by the sunset, for a long moment. Arthur steered placidly on. 'Like his own mom,' said Evelyn, descending. 'She's a great lady, she is,' said Dan.

An isolated and a secret life.

In *Waterways Journal* the editor wrote a poem:

> To the riverman's dismay
> The evidence is plain
> While darn few know a towboat
> Most people know a train

Everyone, he complains, knows the legends of the railroad

> . . . But talk about the river
> And towboats workin' there
>   They'll say right off 'A tugboat!'
> Much worse, they just don't care.

Politically – towboat subsidies are nothing to railroad support – and emotionally, rivermen carry a load of public indifference. Carl, the lead deckhand, is from small-town West Missouri, and 'always guessed it'd be kinda fun to ride the river'. One day he wants to be a pilot. But back home they neither believe his stories nor understand the words. 'It's another world. They think a towboat is like a tugboat, they don't even think we push cargo to the coast.'

We pushed it ever south under clearing skies. Evelyn gave me her recipe for hushpuppies. Blackbirds dropped on to the barges, drawn by the grainy smell. Cap'n Arthur discovered that my next leg southward would be on the cruise steamboat *Mississippi Queen*, and dismissed it as 'Miss'ippi Monster, I call it. I remember steamboats, and *her* paddlewheel's all set wrong.' I was sorry when we rounded the Yazoo river cut off, and Captain Dan came up early to psych himself up for the Vicksburg Bridge. A storeboat was waiting below it to jump me ashore.

Round Delta Point a deep romantic chasm opens. The green valley is spanned by a bridge, right on the bend as promised. Dan steered for the centre pier. 'My palms sweat.' He wiped them on a paper towel. Trusting the cross-current, he steered the load hard at the pier. Mine sweated too; there is not one leg of Vicksburg Bridge without a scar of a collision. But the current pushed us clear and under, Dan whirled round to give me a kiss and a clap on the shoulder, and a tiny hut of a storeboat nuzzled alongside. I jumped, and watched *Spartan* pull away.

The storeboat was musty, a floating corner shop full of shaving cream and stag-mags, cigarettes and soap and sweets. It nosed to the jetty, and stopped by CHANNEL FUELLING SERVICES. I felt as though a door had slammed on a spirited piano sonata; the river flowed by regardless, and me not on it.

CFS smelt of disinfectant and gleamed with softball trophies. A taxi took a long time coming. 'Rush hour?' I tried, conversationally. The fuellers gazed at me like some St Louis smoothie. 'Ain't *no* rush hour, in Vicksburg,' they said. When it came, the cool black girl driver expanded on the theme. 'Y'ain't in the city now. We got a rule: 'f we get a call in our zone, even if we got one passenger, we haveta pick up tha other.' So between the boat store and the town we zigzagged precipitously through steep suburban streets, picking up and dropping stout ladies with shopping bags, pausing on crazy sloping streets of wooden shacks, each with a grizzled black patriarch in a rocking chair on the porch; each swarming with children and flowers. *Scarlett sent me.* Past giant Baptist chapels and a grand old antebellum courthouse; to the Downtowner Motel, where my intention of staying three whole nights was met with frank disbelief.

In the small hours, dry apocalyptic thunder shook the building, and sheet lightning flared over the river below. I lay and shivered in the tumult, and thought of the horror of another hot June, in 1863, when Vicksburg suffered siege by Union forces. Confederate President Jefferson Davis said 'Mississippians do not know how to surrender'; after forty-seven days when the people sheltered in caves and 'ate horses, mules, cats and rats', Vicksburg learned that lesson, and the guns fell quiet. A satisfied Lincoln announced that 'the Father of the Waters flows once more unvexed to the sea'; the Confederacy was split in half, and the war almost won. They dig up bullets still, in the hills above the town, and sell them for fifty cents each to the tourists.

I woke to a still, hot little town, pretty with balconies and porches. An unpretending tripperboat takes parties out in summer, without folksy sternwheel or scalloped funnels: 'Because I wouldn't suit that,' says the skipper. James Neeld I found contented in his tiny pilot house, blond and grizzled, spinning a spoked wooden wheel. He was a musician, until eleven years ago he took to the river; and delivers a gentle blend of classical cassettes and mild historical commentary. On deck, Mrs Neeld sells peanut candy. 'Good way t'live, the river.'

We spun past the industrial dock on the canal, past timber barges and grain elevators, sawmills and scrap and the sad rotting sternwheel of the great steamboat *Sprague*, which set a record in 1907 by pushing 63,307 tons of coal downriver. Barges lay tethered to trees in a haphazard blend of industry and nature; Vicksburg has settled some twenty-five waterfront industries, and offers eleven hundred acres more. 'But Vicksburg,' said one leading citizen reflectively and unattributably, 'has turned away more chances than a lot of *states* have.'

Later that morning, coming back from the pitted battleground above the town, I threw a newspaper on my bed with the last days of the Falklands war in banner headlines across it. The black maid paused in arranging towels to glance at it contemptuously. 'They's always young men dyin' innocent for thuh greed an' lust for power of Princ'palities an' kings,' she said, and passed on down, smoothing her skirts for church. No point in wars. Vicksburg knows.

But I had not chosen to wait in Vicksburg for the steamboat merely in order to dissolve in melancholy peace. I had chosen it for the more bracing reason that the Corps of Engineers lives here. In a stately 1860s redbrick above the river, the Mississippi River Commission, nine strong, has its being. Every year it travels the river running public meetings on its works and duties; but the works themselves, mastered from the commission, fall to the lot of the US Army Corps of Engineers. They have done since 1824; West Point being then the only home of engineering in the growing nation. The corps got the job of shifting sandbars and easing the channels; later its brief was sharpened up to include flood-control levees and the maintenance of a navigable channel nine feet deep and three hundred wide. Under the suitably willing and cautious motto *Essayons*, they have been doing it ever since. Vicksburg masterminds St Louis downwards; the lock-and-dam upper river is dealt with from Chicago. On the Monday morning I presented myself to the Chief of Public Affairs, Herb Kassner, for an account of the task in hand.

'This river,' he said 'drains forty-one states. In five thousand years it has had seven deltas. The Gulf of Mexico used to be up at Cairo.' I remembered Mark Twain's cynical comment of the 1880s; that 'the military engineers have taken upon their shoulders the job of making the Mississippi over again'; for the twentieth century still more than the nineteenth has presumed to keep the river in its place. Settlements, towns, factories have become too valuable to wash away. In the 1930s, the corps created some cut offs of their own; but the price, says Kassner, was instability still now felt. So the keyword is stabilisation: even the most illogical and time-consuming loops may – indeed must – stay put.

Jimmie Graham, Chief of Engineering, does a lot of stabilising, 'as the budget allows'. The great trick is to force the channel to use its own power to your ends. Hence the wing-dams, or dikes – protruding at right angles to the bank in sets, they encourage the river to drop silt, form banks, and make the true channel narrower and swifter scouring. Hence the vast articulated concrete mats for revetment of the banks, and hence the points where reinforcement deliberately stops, to encourage a widening bend. The whole master-plan for the river's course was set down in the 1950s; it is nearly three-quarters finished, and 'holding up pretty good'. The ghost of Mark Twain spoke, distinct and contemptuous, at my shoulder: 'One who knows the Mississippi will promptly aver that ten thousand River Commissions . . . cannot tame that lawless stream, cannot curb it or confine it, cannot say to it, Go here, or Go there, and make it obey; cannot save a shore which it has sentenced; cannot bar its path with an obstruction which it will not tear down, dance over, and laugh at.'

I asked Jimmie if he felt a sense of mastery over the lawless stream, and he laughed. 'Yeah . . . we're awful cautious about the words – what is it we say, Max? – we have reasonable control. We don't believe you'll ever get the river whipped.' He beamed with approval of his wayward charge.

What he does is unique in the world; foreign powers arrive to confer on the management of alluvial Niger, Brahmaputra, Ganges or Orinoco; the Chinese come to see.

' 'Cos without what we do, there couldn't be life in the valley. Not without movin' on every few years.'

A reinforced bank here, a dredger there, a sand-bank cleared; all can be grasped. It is the bigger things that throw you off balance. Such as the fact that after creating seven deltas in five thousand years, the Mississippi is currently making a bid for an eighth. Some fifty miles north-west of Baton Rouge, the river is linked by an old loop to the Atchafalaya. And for half a century the latter river has been trying to usurp the main waters. Permitted thirty per cent of the flow to the main channel's seventy, it consistently took more; until it became dangerously apparent that the Mississippi itself intended a new short cut to the sea. 'The social and economic consequences of which,' says Kassner drily, 'are not acceptable.' For one thing, the massive industrial ports of Baton Rouge and New Orleans could barely drink, let alone navigate. For another, Morgan City in the Atchafalaya basin might well drown. Three hundred miles of carefully fostered waterway would vanish; a hundred and fifty rogue and dangerous miles appear. The old River Control Structures hold now, and have held well since a scare in the 1973 floods; they are, perhaps, above all other works, the symbol of this extraordinary job, and evidence of the river's determination.

So, *Essayons*. But our age is one of doubt and resurgent Rousseauism. Before I left, Bob Louque, a mathematical mind in the hydraulics section, dropped the most memorable aside of all. 'Maybe we shouldn't. Some people say we shouldn't have done any of it, ever. Left the river be. And maybe we should've left the Indians alone, and not had a country.' He shrugged for a moment, only a moment, in genuine doubt; then laughed, and showed me how the automatic rain gauges report in by satellite link.

Now I was impatient for the steamboat. Puritanical diffidence about taking such a Hollywood route southwards evaporated; the *Mississippi Queen*, however monstrous McGrew might think her, was at least a way to travel the last leg of this chained giant of a river. Besides, steamboat fever was stirring drowsy Vicksburg into some kind of life; every bartender, every shopkeeper and antebellum hostess, was talking about Tuesday and the influx of three hundred and sixty well-to-do passengers. A poster appeared, tacked crookedly in an office window on steep Clay Street:

WELCOME STEAMBOATERS! YOU'RE HALFWAY UP THE HILL!

A general tugging of collars and checking of buttons was in evidence.

I whiled the last evening away with Cecil, a kind, elderly antique dealer. 'I go inna a town, take a motel room, spot onna radio, say bring your antiques, and they come.'

He sticks to early American because 'don't know too much on foreign stuff'.

Cecil once trod on an alligator in the bayou country. 'Jus' like a log. I said, Merciful Lord, Protect thy servant!' As I stirred my last frozen daiquiri, a tousled girl shot in with news.

'*Queen*'s due in at nine! My husband's playin' trumpet in the Dixie band. Nine o'clock!' So I drifted to the levee alone, and sat with the mosquitoes, hoping for the lights, the whistle, the thrashing paddlewheel of the ship. The silence racketed with crickets; the air was thick and damp as soup. Small wonder, said Mark Twain a century ago, that small towns had made a legend of the steamboat. When it arrived, it was 'the grandest building in the town'. Three days in Vicksburg had taught me much about Twain's truthfulness. I longed authentically for a blaze of glory on the scummy canal. Instead, a boy dropped out of the darkness to the stones I sat on. 'Steamboat dock here?'

'Yes. About nine.'

'Wrong. About midnight. Becauzza me. I just got off her. My name's Dean Jaeger, OK?' He was young, and bedraggled in the soiled white jacket of a kitchen boy. Four days upriver from New Orleans, leaving St Francisville, the kitchen job had finished his New York constitution, and he collapsed with heatstroke. The ship turned back for Natchez and hospital; a few iced towels later, the boy had discharged himself and taken the bus upriver to Vicksburg. In the strange, cricket-sounding, pitch-black and shuttered town, he had groped down to the levee to look for his boat. 'Ah God, Southern mosquitoes.' He drank beer from a can wrapped in a brown paper bag ('Which law is it here? no drink, no drink in public, or drink in public 'f it's in a brown bag? States down South got so many different laws'). He was proud of his part in a sensation, and embarrassed at his weakness. 'Gotta get back tonight.' We wandered together up Clay Street, a little lost without a steamboat to hope for, and had a legal indoor drink.

In the morning cool, the *Mississippi Queen* was there at last, as white and stately as a wedding cake. There are two overnight steamboats left: *Delta Queen* is a restored original from the twenties, her larger sister a new confection. The cost, and clientele, are of luxury cruise-ship standard. I was whirled aboard in a fluster of hospitality by the purser. 'I'm Tom Murphy – have coffee – meet great couple from Liverpool, England – Bob Hope sposeta be joining us next week – come see pilot house, come see gazebo – origin of *stateroom* is decks named after states, like Texas Deck here, see?' We paused by the stern; the paddlewheel is real, and power thumps out to it from two thousand-horsepower steam engines drinking a hundred and forty barrels of heavy oil a day. She may look a fantasy, but she is real enough. The great red wheel is a remarkably neat means of propulsion; no propeller torque but a straight bash on the water from each long shabby bucket-board. Undocking, I watched the wheel swing to and fro, churning and reversing; behind me the gigantic gold-and-white calliope struck up its steamy festive wheeze: *Sailin' Down the River*. The sternwheel wash rose, a series of symmetrical following waves. Triumphally we swept towards the main river, gang-plank slung forward like a lance. I thought of Dan and his sweating palms, and the last time I had passed beneath Vicksburg Bridge with the barges; and wished that someone could be there to play Dan's triumphs too on the calliope.

Steamboatin' Times, laid in my immaculate veranda cabin, promised such diversions as a Grandmother's Tea and bragging party, bingo, *Showboat*, and gym. But she is a mercifully big ship, and if your tastes lie more towards gazing entrancedly into the pouring sternwheel, you can do so in solitude. The cheerful Mr Murphy had his work cut out to find my corner of the deck before evening, and escort me ceremonially to the pilot house. Pilot Harold de Marrero even looks like Mark Twain. 'Doesn't he?' said the captain critically. 'The mustash?' A steamboat is more grandly guided than a tow of seven times its area: two pilots with first-class licences (which entail drawing the river in detail, from memory, and which are no longer mandatory for tow operators) – plus a captain, in this case himself a first-class pilot, Arthur J. MacArthur. The captain and duty pilot were in merry mood, lords of creation; Cap'n Mac demonstrated the telescoping smokestacks, handy for low bridges and confusing passengers on the top cocktail deck; Cap'n Harold mischievously offered me a turn at steering. Such offers do not come twice. Besides, a man who has drawn the river from memory knows pretty well when a beginner has room to flunk. I took him up.

A steering-bar is not a tiller. Push it right, and the boat goes right. After a few false casts, I found the five rudders disposed around the sternwheel give a remarkably unsluggish response. Without too much difficulty I held the king-post steady on the far point, and edged the big steamboat towards Newtown Bend. Vastly entertained, the pilots called into the radio.

'Anybody northbound, Newtown?'

'Hey' – a flippant crackle. 'Dat sounds like me, man!'

Cap'n Harold is a fifth-generation river pilot, his son a sixth; he knows all the voices. He announced,

'Say, I got a lady steerin' fr'm London, England.'

'Reall-yee? Yay. Lady, say t'mater an' tater.'

I obliged, eye nervously on the rudder indicator. 'Tomato and potato.'

The master of *City of New Orleans* broke up laughing, and sobered briefly. 'Ya want room?' Harold demurred, we had plenty.

'Want t' wipe th' sweat off y' hands?' asked Captain MacArthur sweetly. I did.

'Say lady,' said our downstream friend, now visibly clearing us in the generous high-river channel. 'Howdya get a nigger down a tree in Louisiana?'

'Dunno.'

'Cut th' rope!'

De Marrero and MacArthur were concerned.

'Say, we have to kid a lot. Those guys, no life if they can't kid on the radio. We all got real close black friends. It's like, say, your Irish jokes.' I accepted the spirit, and waved to *City of New Orleans* in the correct two-arm gesture.

'I don't like Irish jokes,' said MacArthur reprovingly. His family come from County Cork. A final yell broke from the passing tow.

'I'm in favour of welfare, race equality, and the Equal Rights Amendment! A free black woman for every man over twenty-one!'

We swung round the next beautiful bend with a flaming tree-edged sunset to starboard. The steam pilot took the bars back, powerful and assured. He steered the biggest and best steamboat left on the river. We talked of ships; I briefly fell into an old enthusiasm, a past trip on HMS *Invincible*.

'That's a heck of a ship, you know,' I said. In the growing dusk, Captain Harold smiled over his greying Twain moustache.

'Ah now. All ships are a heck of a ship. You know that.'

I learned to love the lumbering white wedding cake with the big red sternwheel. Even if to a sea-accustomed eye she is absurd – fifty-five feet high, drawing only eight and a half, squared off each end – such strictures are irrelevant on the flat river. In her element she manoeuvres fast and neatly, barely needing the boost of her new bow-thrust propellers even to dock. She is a creation fit for Twain's description:

'Sharp and trim and pretty . . . clean white rails, decks black with passengers . . .'

The captain took me down to dinner, and talked steamboats. It is a shock to realise how lately and prosaically steam was plying the Mississippi; the *Sprague*, whose great sternwheel I saw on the bank at Vicksburg, was working till 1948.

'My daddy was on the building of her. Biggest thing on th' river. Big Momma, we called her.' He looked across at me suddenly, a man with forty-eight years of river life to haunt him. 'She had a signal. She'd raise her two searchlights right up – and cross them.' He crossed his forearms either side of his plate. 'And you knew it was *Sprague* coming, by the crossed lights on the bend. I never see no other boat do that since.'

'Nobody does it? For a joke?'

'Well, if some smart-aleck kid . . . if I saw it . . . no, nobody would.' It is a matter of respect. 'You knew it was *Sprague*. Big Momma.'

In the Thirties, the channel was so bad that men still went ahead in boats to sound it with leads. 'I've leaded every foot of this river from St Louis to New Orleans, don't you think I haven't.'

Outside the Grand Saloon, passengers bound for the Mardi-Gras dance scuttled along the corridors dressed as sailors and cats and witches. The bold spirit from Liverpool, England, had rouged his cheeks and come as the Mississippi Queen. Outside, the quiet woods slipped by; in kitchen and in laundry, projection room and purser's lair, the crew rejoiced privately at the prospect of Natchez that night. 'The bar under the hill stays open. Big night,' said the pilot. 'Only, cap'n doesn't like to git in before midnight. Spoils the Mardi Gras.' Once, steamboats raced with cargoes and impatient passengers; now cruise values prevail. De Marrero eased the ship under the bridge, turned, and made in the dark for Natchez. 'I've got a piece of land, 120 acres. One day I'm gonna build a model of the river. Be my hobby, sort of.' It will be a good model. Cap'n Harold has thirty years and more on the river, as pilot and public man, campaigning for higher licence standards, stirring it, sailing it, loving it. He docked by searchlight under the green bank, and went ashore to play the bar piano until three o'clock.

Natchez was wicked, once. Above the steep banks, the upper town was, and is, studded with graceful antebellum mansions; below the hill lay the gambling hells and brothels, and the murderers whose surfacing victims gave a name to Dead Man's Bend twenty-five miles downstream. But wicked old Natchez fell into the river; great fifty-foot caved banks now loom below Silver Street, and the balconied palaces above are free from vulgar neighbours. Coaches departed to tour them in the morning, amid sheets of rain and crashes of thunder. The blustery steam blowing over the dripping undergrowth brought on a terrible nostalgia for western Ireland; so after the briefest walk around the crumbling stucco town, I settled happily in the bar under the hill.

A fine-featured blonde in her forties strolled from the bar to the piano, and played with melancholy strength; then, the spirit suddenly fading, returned to her drink. Her name is Dorothy; she works in the ship's laundry, six weeks on and two off, 'so I can hardly hold it all together – I got two hours maybe in New Orleans, sort out my teenage kids, then off again.' Dorothy does not play the piano like a laundry maid. 'I studied at the Guildhall and the Royal

Academy, used to play harp, dulcimer, in concerts. Not for two years.' A man in New Orleans, problems, kids, a steady job. She laughed.

A dark, handsome boy from the crew came up. 'Dorothy, you'll come on the raft?'

There is a dream: a few crew intend to leave at Cincinnati, hitch up to Minnesota, build a huge log raft and float down to Baton Rouge in the footsteps of Huck Finn. 'So long as I don't haveta do the laundry,' said Dorothy, sucking at her straw. 'OK.'

We discussed financing; the boy considered sponsorship. 'Call it the peace raft, huh? The CND raft? Really though,' he added with a burst of honesty, 'it's just the wanna-go-down the-Mississippi-on-a-raft-raft.'

Dorothy smiled with her beautiful, worn eyes and strolled back to the piano. 'Half an hour, I go back. Oh God. Not more towels, sheets, not napkins . . . aaah.' She played sadly on.

Then the evening sun came out, the whistle blew, and we proceeded downstream in our dotty magnificence, calliope wheezing. In the pilot house Cap'n Mac raised hell about the lack of Saltine crackers, and the bouncing maître d'hôtel appeared with a basketful. 'Git a perm, JJ,' said the master ungratefully. 'Wanna be lashed to th' paddlewheel?' The boy laughed and bounced downstairs to make three hundred and sixty people feel loved. The captain cached his Saltines. 'You pilots bin eating my cheese, too.'

High on the bow gazebo roof, you cannot hear the blare of Dixie in the Grand Saloon, nor the babbling pilot radio; only the crickets on the bank and the flapping of the state flag in a light headwind. All evening the tows grew more frequent, the banks fuller; finally in the small hours, the port of Baton Rouge opened in a blaze of industrial light. This is the head of the deepwater channel, 150 miles from New Orleans. Deep-sea shapes began to appear; container ships, sharp-bowed ocean runners, oil rigs at rest. 'Intruders,' said de Marrero. 'Not river craft. We belong, they don't.' The two idioms run together all the way down to Orleans. I began to grasp why the Atchafalaya is not going to be allowed to sneak the water away from this vast industrial empire.

A smart excursion boat swept through the dockyard grime and the state-capital pomp of Baton Rouge next morning; and the master of the *Samuel Clemens* came briefly aboard to greet the pilots: Joy Manthey, aged twenty-five; a thick-set, cheerful, brown-haired girl. Joy has a first-class pilot licence; she sees no reason to consider another career. 'I did get a degree in social welfare, from Louisiana State University. But I was on the river selling popcorn when I was ten, and I know you won't find any better people anywhere. So I'm goin' towin' soon's I get a job fixed.'

'Yeah,' said de Marrero later. 'But I don't feel women belong on the river, somehow.' I still knew too little of it to argue, but looked wonderingly at the crowded anchorage as we moved down the narrow, deep, unfamiliar river between Baton Rouge and New Orleans. Tugs, tows, lighters, rigs, oilers, containers abounded even though the traffic is thirty per cent down on normal. 'Which makes it easier t'run the river. Only, it's jobs. Men's and women's. I know other people are hurtin'. So I don't feel too good about it.' We overtook a slow tow, with courtesy:

'Guess I'm slippin' up behind you, Cap'n.'

'Guess y'are. Which side ya goin' Cap'n?'

'Guess I'll make it easy for you, Cap'n . . .'

Later, the tug *Genesis* stood by to ease us into our berth by searchlight; music roared from Vieux Carré bars, and we lay still against the Poydras Street Wharf. We had arrived.

In the morning, I left the whirl of passenger-changing and rode a tug around the harbour limits. The *John G. Amato*, property of Crescent Towing, started life as an icebreaker, and now growls from New Orleans to the Head of the Passes: Mile Zero. At Pilottown, a lonely settlement ringed by water, the bar pilots come in from the sea with ships, and hand over to the rivermen. On *Amato*, Captain Walter Davidson whirled me round his harbour, pointing out the way downstream, the unpopular short canal to the sea, and the Intracoastal Water-way – 'Alla way t' Texas'.

He is young, and fair, and cheerful, and loves New Orleans as only a newcomer perhaps can. Here the world opens. 'People pay helluva lot for yachts t'do nothin' in. I git paid, I git somethin' t'do. Useful ships need us bad, in the river current, in th' fog in winter.'

The upriver world, from St Louis to Baton Rouge, had suddenly receded, a tree-lined, rippling dream of odd square boats and muddy banks. Below us, the sea and river slowly mixed in the brackish bayou country. I left *Amato* and walked the levee road from Algiers point; then took the Canal Street ferry back across the water to the most bewildering of cosmopolitan cities. New Orleans: the seaman's last fling, the riverman's Big Bad City; where highways are named for Jefferson and de Gaulle, districts for Gretna and Algiers, bars for Pat O'Brien and Louis XIV. Among Grecian pillars and Parisian balconies, voodoo shops and crucifixes, Holiday Inns and silent cobbled courtyards, I walked in the damp sunlight past Bourbon and Ursuline and Jackson; and caught a streamlined white-and-gold city motorbus, named Desire.

THE LOIRE

GEOFFREY GRIGSON

*T*here is a pretty grove and a statue of its goddess where the Seine begins; a Victorian Father Thames reclines (though not exactly in the right place) over the birth of the Thames; the first trickles of the Danube are balustraded and protected in a round basin. And the Loire, all French, one of the longest rivers of Western Europe?

The Loire comes to light, drip-drap (in a dry summer) from the end of an old, much-photographed pipe over a stone trough in a rough cow-shed. This cow-shed is 4,700 feet or so above sea-level, on the Cévennes, some 320 atlas-miles south of Paris, and so more than three-quarters of the way down France, not so very far from the Mediterranean. More exactly, it is thirty-four miles uphill from the pinnacled fantasia of Le Puy, under a road and below the small once volcanic peak called Gerbier-de-Jonc. This peaklet and this cow-shed of the Ferme de la Loire keep company on a broken plateau of sheep walks and occasional villages and farm sheds and more peaks, and uplifts of basalt also.

In spring the road up from Le Puy, wriggling and narrow but difficult only in snow, crosses slopes crowded with daffodils. In summer, late summer, the *sucs*, or sugar loaves, are shapes of blue bedded beyond magenta colonies of rosebay willow-herb. By that time bilberries will be ripening and you can sit on terraces of the small chalet hotel (closed till June), purpling your mouth with bilberry tart and bilberry ice-cream.

The Loire begins with good food. In the season stalls along this road below the chalet and Gerbier-de-Jonc will be selling bilberry sweets, bottled bilberries, Cévennes hams and sausages and goat cheeses.

The cow-shed is divided in two now, and fitted up for the sale of postcards and sweets. There is no statue of a river-goddess, but at least you will see one worshipful inscription, one sign of celebration and thanksgiving, which has recently been nailed to the stone wall above the trickle and the pipe. Unexpectedly, this inscription has to do with wine. Wine, really good wine, famous wine, begins some 320 miles downstream, and lower by 4,500 feet, where the no longer infantile Loire will be almost washing the vineyard slopes of Pouilly and then those of the great hill of Sancerre. So convivialists from Sancerre have fixed their inscription to the

70

cow-shed wall proclaiming the homage of the Sancerrois, the Sancerre district, 'to the Loire, Queen and Mother of its vineyards'.

Very French. But that is all – except the parked cars and the motor coaches – to signalise the coming to light of France's longest, most beautiful and variable, if not most useful or most constantly amiable river. I have come out of the cow-shed, after a glass of Loire water, wondering if some drops from the pipe will escape the hazards all the way from Gerbier-de-Jonc, and at last make the Atlantic, beyond the suspension bridge at St-Nazaire. If they manage it, such drops will have travelled 627 miles, no less; through gorges, over barrages, along meadows with Charollais cattle, under cathedrals and Romanesque churches, past Nevers, Orléans, Blois, Tours, Saumur and Nantes, past tarted-up and often tiresome châteaux, past nuclear power stations, deserted quays and shifting islands, until the water turns salt.

At first the Loire below Gerbier-de-Jonc is a small trout stream through upland flowers, very orange marsh marigolds, and orchids. It soon collects more and more contributions from its huge lonely catchment area, dives into secretive valleys, and wriggles to the suburban edge of Le Puy. The Loire is soon hidden so frequently, the roads above it and more or less along its course are so small and up about and down about and roundabout, that I have found these first miles towards Le Puy only intimidating. As it runs, so far, the Loire does not differ enough from 100 other rivers cutting down from upland Europe.

For my riverine taste the Loire still does not improve much after it skirts Le Puy and begins forcing itself northwards through the last main barrier of the mountains – through gorge after gorge, starting with the gorges of Peyredeyre. They are fairly deep, these gorges, and claustrophobic, though not very narrow. Three-quarters of the way – of some thirty, rather stifling uneasy miles – the Loire again takes to hiding itself below declivities, around bluffs, and under trees.

Its valley is an old route through the mountains; there are ruined castles on heights and Romanesque churches to visit, especially the strange strong church at Chamalières with its carving of the prophets, before you reach Retournec and its bridge. Yet judging by the scarcity of hotels and the shabbiness of the few villages all along the river road from Le Puy until the river breaks into lower country en route for the plains, the French themselves do not care greatly for these gorges. Where France is beautiful – or accessibly beautiful – every year it becomes more and more suburbanised for weekends behind prim garden fences, or defences, and geometric placing of conifers. But it is not really so along these gorges. The river line, though it does open here and there, is too twisty, the departmental roads are too narrow and often too steep to allow much commuting, I suppose, from Lyons or from the sulphurous iron and coal complex of St-Étienne, the 'French Birmingham', which is only a few miles east. However unexploited the gorges are, however unspoilt, the river here does contradict what the French come – lower down – to consider the special nature of the Loire: its wide dignity, its slow historical procession and, most of the time, its serenity. From this second mountainous run I value only a place or two where the eye is surprised and comes to rest on the delights of space and the shape and tint.

One such place is the little village of St-Paul-en-Cornillon (no hotel), where the Loire is slowed down by a barrage, and curves round a headland. Beech forests on the far bank make the river here a lake of green amber (green amber does exist – from Egypt); and then the

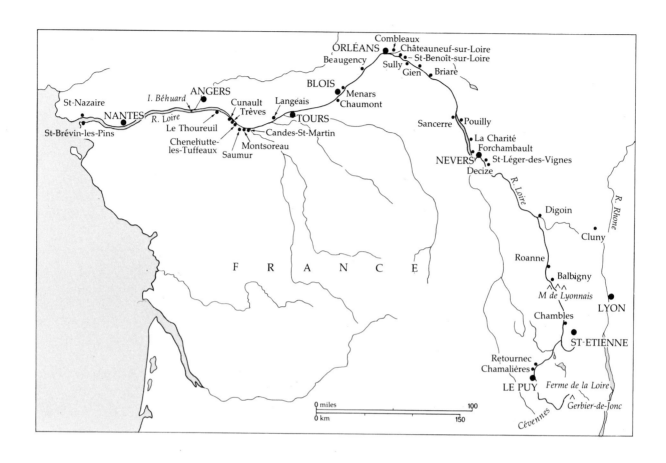

Captions for the following photographs:

1. A sumptuous château at Sully, surrounded by a moat flowing in from the Loire and back out again.
2. At Orléans the town and the river seem specially intimate, the Loire slipping under bridges, past quays and worn stone walls.
3. Complex fishing nets worked by ropes and pulleys at St-Brévin-les-Pins, opposite St-Nazaire.
4. At La Baule, in the estuary, neglected salt-pans turn crimson in the autumn with a growth of samphire.

3

4

beeches and the river as well change to an autumn amber, under a more or less southern intensity of blue. Delectable. Then further north, along this artificial Lac de Grangent, the road lifts to a view, hundreds of feet above the water, which justifies all the anxious driving from Le Puy. Rocky ground falls away from the skied red-roofed village of Chambles and a broken tower, down, down and down to the still water. On the far side of this great valley peak after peak of the Monts du Lyonnais, separating the Loire from the Rhône, form a long horizon of indented azure.

The Loire has now more or less freed itself of severe restriction, of considerable heights on either flank. Just north of Chambles, a turning off the river road (which is now D 108, at the bottom of fold eight on Michelin map seventy-three) leads to Notre-Dame-de-Grâce, a viewpoint; not so very high, but it shows the Loire 1,000 feet below, wriggling through its first long flats, still to the north. The view is a little deceptive, because after thirty miles the Loire does pick up its skirts and slope again through narrows. These additional narrows begin near Balbigny, and continue almost to Roanne, the first sizeable manufacturing town on the Loire. The Loire tears around rocks, it leaps something of a barrier (Digue de Pinay, Saut du Perron), thoroughly bad-tempered when full. It was a cause here once upon a time of many wrecks and drownings, and of wild ringings of the church bell of St-Maurice, up above the rocks, to summon rescuers for bargemen shooting the rapids with coal from the mines round St-Étienne – all this before the joining by railway of St-Étienne to Roanne. This is a twenty-four-mile section of the Loire not to miss. It can be reached easily by a small road running for some way alongside the river; and scenically it is much to be preferred to those big gorges or semi-gorges up from Le Puy. It gives more sense of the mighty muscle of the Loire before its final break into the plains.

When the railway came Roanne could go ahead and grow into the crowded, not very pleasant, town it is today. All the same it does have one grand distinction, the restaurant of the brothers Troisgros, one of the temples of the *nouvelle cuisine*, and one of the few restaurants outside Paris honoured by the *Michelin Guide* with three stars. I suppose such a restaurant here does have historical warrant. Roanne is on one of the historic routes to Paris from Lyons and the south as well as from St-Étienne–Roanne northwards to Orléans by the Loire and its boats, then from Orléans the rest of the way overland. It was famous for its unprovincial comfort. John Evelyn stayed there twice in Civil War times, in 1644 and again in 1646, on his way from Geneva to Paris via Lyons, in happy company with Edmund Waller, the poet. At Roanne they indulged themselves 'with the best that all France affords'. They slept there in damask beds, after a supper that 'might have satisfied a Prince' – much as the Troisgros brothers would now satisfy the lunch or dinner tastes of a Rothschild or an Elizabeth David. The celebrated mariners of the Loire, or the master mariners, monopolists, with their small fleets for cargo and passengers, were also well-to-do men who could afford the best in food and wine at the larger river ports between Roanne and the Atlantic.

Leaving Roanne – ugly Roanne, the Troisgros brothers or no – the Loire comes close to one building worth looking for, a charming little eighteenth-century chapel which those well-to-do mariners dedicated to their patron St Nicholas. But it is now locked, neglected and forgotten in the incessant clatter of lorries one side and the other. A river loneliness does reassert itself quickly enough – but with monotony. Meandering along to its westward turn below Orléans, the Loire is now a meadow river, taking shape, not yet very wide, but emptying often to shallows (so the now little-used canals were built alongside) and showing yellow sand-banks, edged with the silver-green of endless willows. And it is prone to floods, all the more so after the downstream junction of the Loire and the Allier, below Nevers. What makes for a really vicious and destructive flood for miles and miles is the coincidence of heavy rainfall in the catchment areas of both the Loire and the Allier.

For a long way now only a few riverine towns break the monotony. Digoin has a one-star and a two-star restaurant, and a noble nineteenth-century aqueduct, in stone, taking the Canal latéral à la Loire to a junction across the river; Decize is islanded in the river, and outside Decize, not to be overlooked, on N79, at St-Léger-des-Vignes, is the workmen's Café du Barrage – river rumble, tumbling foam, clouds of spray, red tables shaded by vines. Then comes Nevers itself – cool, nicely empty cathedral, edging dignified tree spaces and gardens above the Loire; and grubby Forchambault with its long, long river frontage, under trees, pretty and squalid and unloved, with angler's cafés serving *fritures de la Loire,* fry-ups of small river fish.

Soon after La Charité, with its pale Romanesque fragment of a once-great abbey church, second only to Cluny, its floor sloping down towards the Loire, there shows up the chalky hill of Sancerre, and the Loire widens and improves. It begins its westward bend, passing Briare under another huge canal aqueduct, designed and built by Eiffel, iron this time, and a pomp of sea-horses at either end; Gien; Sully – first major château, white, gaunt, not over-restored and fake-looking, surrounded by a moat flowing from the Loire and back again; and then St-Benoît-sur-Loire, where incense wreathes the cold pillars of the great Romanesque church built above the relics of St Benedict.

Orléans isn't far ahead, where the river begins its curve south-west, along – for all Frenchmen – the veritable, absolute Val de Loire, to Blois, Tours, Langeais, Saumur. But here I rest first of all a bit short of Orléans, at Châteauneuf-sur-Loire – and for several reasons. This little town, nothing much in itself, helps to explain the Loire in the geography of its nature and its history. Châteauneuf had its château – now destroyed, most of it. The town, though, maintains – and very pleasantly – the château gardens, lawns, trees, bedding-out, and a long low orangery, disgorging in summer its fruited orange trees in tubs. Beyond the orangery, steps descending towards the Loire arrive at the door of a little museum of sentiment about the once famous navigation from the sea to Orléans and Roanne – all about the mariners, their boats, their equipment, their cargoes, their passenger service either way; all about the floods, the terrible floods, which may always occur again since the river has been jacketed only here and there, and never – it becomes so strong – with entire success.

The mariners, in their blue blouses and pantaloons, red neckcloths and belts, with gold rings in their ears, wearing wide-brimmed black hats against sun or rain, were professionals. They knew the winds, the anchorages, the channels, the shifting sands and shifting islands. All along the river you can tell where the town or the village ports were by sloping or flat quays, grass-grown between the stones, still with their old iron rings for mooring. Wine, vinegar, grain, timber, stone, coal, iron, salt (salt especially, from the ancient saltings near the river mouth), sugar, cattle – for all such goods the Loire was a highway once essential to the economy of France. Goods for Paris went ashore at Orléans to go on by road, or (after the mid-seventeenth century) left the river at Briare for a canal going north to join up with the Seine. There were passengers too. Before the railways a favourite way from Paris to Nantes, and out into the Atlantic world, was by coach or carriage to Orléans, there entrusting oneself and one's trunks to the mariners.

Travellers might be unlucky. Madame de Sévigné took to the river at Orléans in September 1675, journeying to her château in Brittany. So low was the water that year that her boat kept going aground. Instead of making a quick passage to Nantes she found herself stranded at night, 100 yards out in mid-river. She floated down to Nantes again in 1680, in May, when the nightingales (there are still a million nightingales along the Loire) were in song, by moonlight. Most passengers were squashed in anyhow, but Madame de Sévigné sat all the time in her carriage, so fixed in the boat that she would be sheltered from the sun.

Now and then you find an old mariner's placard on a quay inscribed with the river distances. There is one here at Châteauneuf near the museum – Blois 89 kilometres, Saumur 213, Nantes 345, St-Nazaire 403, and so on.

This Châteauneuf museum documents the repeated and often vast flooding of the Loire country. Prints, photos, newspaper cuttings, faded old proclamations tell the horror. Children cling to chimneys. Houses, corpses, dead cows and pigs, uprooted trees, are swept along, boats toss in rescue. The floods can be very sudden and, luckily, very short. High up above Le Puy, last September, a storm over the Cévennes raised the river thirty feet in an hour, swept away houses, cars, holiday camps, drowned a person or two, over-threw a suspension bridge – and was gone. Tours, in this Val de Loire, has had much to endure. It suffered 153 considerable floods in 148 years, from 1820 to 1968. In the worst floods (1846, 1856 and 1866), the river rose more than twenty-three feet, invading suburbs and threatening to break the levees. Keep an eye, along the quays of the Loire, on walls, on gateposts, and you see lines cut to mark flood levels of this or that year. Opposite Gien, some miles up from Châteauneuf, I have noticed flood levels cut on the eighteenth-century gateposts of a villa. The highest of them shows that up here that flood of 1846 rose twenty-one feet. That would have filled the front rooms almost to the ceiling, nearly covering the gilt mirrors.

I am not going to personalise this dangerous Loire, or assign it a gender, or make cracks about the nature of rivers and women. But I am going to mention that this Châteauneuf was also the home in childhood of Maurice Genevoix, the French novelist, born upstream at Decize, who recognised part of his long life's reality in the mixed nature of the Loire. For Genevoix (who died recently, aged ninety-two) the only reality we can know is made up of the symbol and that which corresponds to it; which can be the more easily understood or appreciated if you take the river Genevoix knew most of his life, along the quays, and past the little Auberge du Port and along the Promenade de Chastaing. Here the Loire is a slow strong mirror moving forwards, a mirror of clouds and sky colours. And here as elsewhere one certainly needs to experience this great river by night as well as by day, in quiet, in half-darkness, reflecting stars. Genevoix presented such a summer night on his river in *Trente Mille Jours*, the autobiography he published just before his death. It was 1918, in July. He had left his writing, and walked out to a sand-bank which was cooling after the heat of the day. He sat there in the half-dark, watching circles from rising fish which broke the star images on the flow and turned them for a moment into elongated pearls. He heard silence, he felt happy in the quietude and serenity the Loire induces, then was made uneasy by faint pulsing sounds coming across the water. They weren't easily explicable. Then he realised he was hearing faraway guns, a monstrous bombardment 'shaking the night and the world'. From the papers next morning Genevoix learnt he had been hearing Foch's counter-offensive on the Aisne, away to the north-east, the beginning of the end of the war.

In an early novel of the 1930s, *Rémi des Rauches*, Genevoix is tender about the slow voluptuousness of the Loire, about the way it glides between sinuous banks, about its rosy mists and its reflections, and then gives what I suppose is an unsurpassed description of a major flood, from the first symptoms to its full chaos and horror. He dedicated that novel *à la Loire*.

Orléans next; and Orléans and the Loire seem specially intimate, the river slipping under quays and flood-marked walls, restaurants in which they serve wild duck from meres in the not so far off Sologne, and sloping streets. French people, English people too, say they dislike Orléans. But why? Because guidebooks and tourist leaflets go on too much about Orléans and Jeanne d'Arc? Because there is so much talk about associations, that very sure method of avoiding what is for what isn't? To me Orléans *is* – the best of the Loire cities, with the best shops, the best market (near the river), the most intriguing pedestrian alleys up to the best of main streets, an architectural unity end-stopped by just such a dominating cathedral as this street and this city need. And of all this much is owed geographically and historically to the river.

It is after Orléans that my scepticism sharpens – not at all about the Loire, but about the label VAL DE LOIRE, applied so with emotional capitals château by château; that cliché of tourism, that expression of *la gloire*, the blinding light which keeps so many French eyes from recognising so much of French actuality. In these 'châteaux of the Loire' – luckily not all of them perch on the river – kings and mistresses lived, noblemen were glorified, imprisoned, cheated, degraded, tortured, murdered. Very well. But these châteaux, occasioned as they were by the Loire and its slopes and vineyards and sunshine, have so often been restored by *gloire*-infected architects for *gloire*-infected owners; who have mostly sold out to the state. Guides drone on about the glorious grandees – and about the antique dealers' furniture and the few, but always fifth-rate, pictures with which the French state furnishes the châteaux so mingily and cynically. Three of the châteaux I would pick as adjuncts – two of them thrillingly so – to the splendours of the river. My first, in order of flow, is Ménars, on the north bank, my second Chaumont, my third Saumur, away and away downstream, in the prime country of the Loire wines.

At Ménars, which doesn't figure much in guidebooks, I must quickly correct myself and explain that the real wonder is less the château itself than its extraordinary park, parallel with the Loire, its main terraced walk seeming to reach a headland beyond and below which the Loire arrives out of infinite distance, as if to go on for ever and ever, amen. Then I must admit that Chaumont as well isn't so much in itself. What counts again is the position. Henry James long ago saw the truth about the château when he arrived one day to find it closed to visitors. He clambered up for a look, and found that the château resembled nothing so much as 'an enormously magnified villa'. That is true. Chaumont is a white, portly mixture of Renaissance and medievalism, looking faked externally into a bad illustration for a novel by Scott. But then the position, the wonderful position on the high lip of the river. As James says, Chaumont 'sweeps the river up and down, and seems to look over half the province.' Saumur, though, is the real thing. White towers of a real castle shoot up to blue sky. You feel genuine medieval power, you feel the height above a town which had to do what it was told, above the shining hugeness of the river. You feel the fact – to be deplored or no – of grandees having lived here in style. The oddity is that you can take the riverside road through Saumur along the quays without receiving a hint of that grandeur overhead.

Most towns along the Loire make a better impression outside than in. French towns-people do not care for the past, and like their towns to look modern, more or less, in a cheap way. So old façades are smoothed over. Of exceptions along the river, the best I know is Beaugency, between Orléans and Blois. It is as if small Beaugency lacked money enough to suburbanise itself along a delicious river-front, to spoil its Quai de l'Abbaye, to cut down its riverside plane trees, or somehow manage to hide the river and the twenty-six arches of its ancient bridge. Villages do better, as a rule; little port villages as they used to be, where clumps of tansy grow alongside the quays, and black punts are drawn up on levees and banks, or shoot off ahead of a curving wake. Often the best place for a picnic along the Loire is the river-front of a village or a small town, the perfect spot combining view and detail, distance and intimacy. Along what is more strictly the Val de Loire some picnic places I would choose include that Promenade de Chastaing at Genevoix's Châteauneuf, and nearer Orléans the flower-painted junction of the river and the Canal d'Orléans at Combleux. Then, again, Beaugency, along the Quai de l'Abbaye; and by Cour-sur-Loire a river lane of quays and rusty mooring-rings almost under that marvellous park of Ménars. Time and again I have had this river lane to myself, no litter, no other cars, only half a dozen miles as it is from the industrial zone of Blois.

Downstream, beyond Blois and Amboise and Tours (that spreading city which seems to reject its river), there is one corner I recommend for a picnic, a corner concealed and delightful – at Candes-St-Martin. It is one thing to stop at Candes – a necessary thing – for its white church, one of the most satisfying of the river churches between the Cévennes and the sea. But it can seem hopeless to find a parking space, unless there is room below the porch (which resembles Salisbury chapter-house in miniature). The main street, hiding the river, is narrow and hellish. Lorries squeeze through. But turn down a not too obvious or inviting alley, and there you are, at a green nook of the Rue Basse, in front of you the confluence of the Loire and the Vienne at a yellow sand-bank, and upstream the rounded willow-green of islands dividing, according to light, the blue or grey of the major river. St Martin died at Candes – '*Ici est mort Saint Martin le 8 Novembre 397*' says a floor tablet in the church. It was from here that greedy monks of Tours stole his corpse and sailed away with it upstream to Tours, where a basilica was built over him.

Candes introduces miles of exceptional riverside, before and after Saumur, a glittering succession of white villages between the water and a quarry cliff of chalk which was hard enough for building, a succession of the prettiest small seventeenth- and eighteenth-century houses among flowers, of early churches, occasional cafés, and wine caves saying come in and taste. Montsoreau is the first, then Chénehutte-les-Tuffeaux, where priory ruins topping the cliff have been made into a hotel, Trèves, and Cunault, with an extra-solemn Romanesque church which rivals St Martin's Church at Candes. Last of all, and I think most elegant of all, is Le Thoureuil. This length of cliff and river and wine recalls an oddity of the old traffic of the Loire. Coconuts from the French West Indies were shipped from Nantes to Saumur. Oil crushed from the coconut 'meat' was used to light the underground quarries along the river, and the broken shells were carved virtuously and profitably into rosary beads, sent all over France.

Nearing the sea, I still have to speak of Nantes, first and last of the Loire cities; and of one feature which diversifies the river – the islands. The islands, the willow-covered islands, create channels; and add mystery, so many being uninhabited and inaccessible. The painter Ben Nicholson, who lived for a while at Tours when he was young, has told me how he was intrigued by a sculptural quality he saw in river and island – here were three planes, a plane of river, then a plane of sand, then a plane of the rounding willows. It was these planes he remembered in the cutting and colouring of his celebrated reliefs.

Overnight floods have often washed islands away, altering the channels. So to be habitable an island in the Loire needs a core of rock. It is just that which explains the Île Béhuard, below the marriage of the Loire and the Maine. Don't fail to visit Béhuard. There is a bridge to it, then a road over sandy fields to a village, then among the houses a rock, then on the rock a church. Every house has steps to its first floor, since not every so often, but every year, Béhuard is flooded. The postman does his round by boat or on stilts. In summer you can picnic on sandy verges, alongside clumps of thorn apple or wilting sulphur patches of evening primrose, two characteristic plants of the river. There is no hotel on Béhuard, but there is a restaurant and a pleasant one. On the church rock a cross guided the mariners of the Loire; and from the rock you can see the vineyard village of Savennières, and La Roche-aux-Moines, where King John, that lackland idiot, lost us most of our French dominion in 1204. Sitting down to lunch on Béhuard, with a bottle of Savennières, you can savour our loss.

And Nantes, where you can buy books of Breton patriotism in the shops? Where cranes raise more and more tower blocks along the river? Nantes, which was France's chief gate to the world, especially the New World, before the rise of Le Havre on the deeper, more amenable Seine? All I am going to say is briefly gastronomic. You are near the sea. At 5 a.m. there is fresh turbot in the fish market; at 12.30, outside Nantes, on the levee protecting the market-gardens from the Loire, you can eat *turbot au beurre blanc* in that Restaurant Clémence in which Madame Clémence invented *beurre blanc* seventy years ago. Don't, by the way, believe menus up and down river when they offer *saumon de la Loire* or *alose* – i.e. shad – *de la Loire*. The Loire is polluted, and the salmon and shad are more likely to have come from Norway, frozen.

The Loire after Nantes broadens so prodigiously that refineries on the now un-charming north side cannot be seen from the now as uncharming south side. I sign off opposite St-Nazaire, at St-Brévin-les-Pins, by the first and last hotel of the Loire, the Debarcadière, standing on a German bunker, looking west to New York, east into the vast river, under the new suspension bridge which must be the most expensive in Europe – thirty francs a crossing. The Loire itself, though, signs off with a certain irony. You think it has finished? Not quite. Through the millennia, they say, it is the push of the Loire which has not only created, here at the mouth, the once important, still fascinating saltings, where neglected salt-pans turn crimson in autumn with a growth of samphire, but has also piled up – at a louis d'or the grain – the sands of that Blackpool of French millionaires, La Baule.

THE ZAIRE

NICHOLAS WOLLASTON

'A mighty big river,' Joseph Conrad called the Congo in his story *Heart of Darkness*, 'resembling an immense snake uncoiled, with its head in the sea, its body at rest curving afar over a vast country, and its tail lost in the depths of the land.' From head to tail is 2,900 miles, which makes it the sixth longest in the world, but in volume it is second only to the Amazon. Conrad's snake is immense indeed, and very fat.

It was the head of the snake that white men first discovered. In 1482 a Portuguese caravel sailed into a bay on the African coast, and by the colour and sweetness of the water and the islands of weed floating on a current far out to sea the captain knew he was in the estuary of a huge river. On a second visit in 1485 he sailed upstream towards the Crystal Mountains till he reached a gorge of boiling, impassable water – the Cauldron of Hell – into which the river came thundering down, hurled by cataracts from the unknown uplands beyond. It was the end of the voyage, but before turning back the captain asked the natives what they called the river, and was given a word that meant simply 'river' and sounded to a Portuguese like 'Zaire'. This hybrid is now its name – and that of the biggest state it flows through – but for a long time it was called after the tribe that lived down by the estuary, the people of the kingdom of Kongo.

Those cataracts – thirty-two of them, falling nearly a thousand feet in 150 miles and creating the biggest reserve of water power in the world – blocked any further exploration, and for four centuries the heart of Africa, the source of slaves and ivory, was a place of mystery. Guessing in the dark, and sometimes confusing the Congo with the Niger or the Nile, geographers believed that in the middle of the continent lay a *cuvette*, a vast basin in the equatorial plateau where the waterways were navigable and the riches unimaginable. But the Europeans on the coast and the Africans inland, though remotely in touch by trade, remained ignorant of each other. To the Portuguese, the country up beyond the cataracts was where the rays of the moon could make a man's head swell to twice its normal size. And to the Africans, the white men were the returning spirits of the dead, who lived at the bottom of the ocean. How else explain the rumour that when one of their ships approached the land, its masts rose out of the sea before the hull?

The tail of Conrad's snake wasn't discovered till the heyday of Victorian adventure, and still it was years before a firm connection with the head was made. Dr Livingstone died in Central Africa in 1873, believing that the great river he had found and explored was part of the upper waters of the Nile. It was left to H. M. Stanley in 1877 to follow it downstream to the mouth: to penetrate the *cuvette* and prove the truth.

The Upper Congo is the fusion of several rivers that spring from the swamps and savannas of the African watershed. The longest of them starts in the highlands between Zambia and Tanzania and flows through the lakes of Bangweulu and Mweru; another rises near the Zaire–Zambia frontier not many miles from the source of the Zambezi; a third drains out of Lake Tanganyika. They join to form the Lualaba, which heads northwards for almost a thousand miles up the spine of Africa, collecting the water of other streams along its course. It passes Kabalo, Kongolo, Kasongo and the old Arab market town of Nyangwe where Livingstone, still thinking he was on the Nile, was turned back because nobody would let him have canoes. It passes Kibombo and Kindu, flows through another two hundred miles of forest, crosses the equator and tumbles down sixty miles of rapids, the Stanley Falls, dropping the name Lualaba and becoming the full-grown Congo as it reaches the town of Kisangani.

On his famous journey of discovery, recounted in *Through the Dark Continent*, Stanley left Lake Tanganyika and plunged downriver, not knowing where it would lead him – north to the Sudan or west to the Atlantic. An Arab trader in Nyangwe told him that further downstream, where no white man had ever explored, there was 'nothing but woods, and woods, and woods, for days and weeks and months'. It was a country of cannibals, leopards and gorillas that 'run up to you and seize your hands, and bite the fingers off one by one, and as fast as they bite one off, they spit it out'.

Gorillas couldn't stop this man, though he didn't miss the chance for some timely rhetoric. 'What a forbidding aspect had the Dark Unknown which confronted us!' he wrote as his caravan set off, 150-strong with an escort of 400 provided by the Arabs. 'The object of the desperate journey is to flash a torch of light across the western half of the Dark Continent . . . A thousand things may transpire to prevent the accomplishment of our purpose: hunger, disease and savage hostility may crush us . . .'

Many things transpired in the next few months; none of them crushed Stanley. The first villages he came to were deserted, the natives vanishing at the sight of a white man with a small army, but the abandoned skulls and human bones told a grisly tale; and from the forest came the throb of drums, war cries and the eerie sound of horns. Though the first attack by yelling cannibals was beaten off, it left the party jittery. 'Better turn back in time,' the Arabs advised, but Stanley pressed on. Weeks of peril and uncertainty passed as the expedition paddled downstream, with spears and screams and poisoned arrows flying from the river banks, and a daily toll of corpses to be tossed into the water. Smallpox and dysentery broke out among people already dispirited by ulcers, pneumonia, typhoid; and then they came to rapids and whirlpools. And then the rains began. The Arabs had had enough and went back to Nyangwe, leaving Stanley to exhort the rest, though he was weakened without an escort and still not sure whether they were on the Congo, the Nile or even the Niger: 'Into whichever sea this great river empties, there shall we follow it . . . Many of our party have already died, but death is the end of all; and if they died earlier than we, it was the will of God . . . My children, make up your minds as I have made up mine . . . We shall toil on, and on, by this river and no other, to the salt sea.'

He got his people into the canoes for the journey on into the unknown, but many of them were sobbing with grief or fear. 'Lift up your heads and be men!' he shouted. 'What is there to fear?' But to Africans with no cares for geography, who had been through some nasty moments higher up the river, the terrors ahead were too real. 'Poor fellows – with what wan smiles they responded to my words! How feebly they paddled! But the strong flood was itself bearing us along . . .' It bore them along past villages from which fleets of canoes came skimming out to attack, full of warriors crying, 'Meat! Meat! Ah-ha, we shall have plenty of meat!' It carried them down through virgin forests where immense trees were hung with vines and orchids, where the only paths were made by elephants, and where millions of insects filled the air with incessant song. It churned itself into waves where boats were capsized and men were drowned. It took them among tribes who merely laughed at them, or exchanged chickens and bananas for beads and calico, or sent their prettiest women to gladden the white man and his friends. It swept them to the brink of the Stanley Falls, where they had to carry the boats overland, cutting through the jungle and fighting a running war with ferocious, hungry savages. And all the while, Stanley made notes of local customs, drew his map and took solar observations. At the bottom of the Falls, where Kisangani stands, he achieved his triumph. He boiled a thermometer and found that the altitude was lower than the upper reaches of the Nile. So this must be the Congo. And to convince him, it was already bending westwards in a wide untroubled stream, deep and full of promise, that could flow nowhere but to the Atlantic.

The middle stretch of the Congo is a huge arc across Africa, looping through the *cuvette* and draining an area one-tenth the size of the whole continent. Here Conrad's 'mighty big river' is deep, wide, swift – the great inland waterway of the early explorers' dreams, the embodiment of itself, the sum of one's own ideas about the Congo. Here, down the 1,000 miles from Kisangani to Kinshasa – taking one week for a journey that took Conrad nearly three and Stanley more than six – we went by boat. We were told by a man in Kisangani, who occupied an impressive office in the transport company, that the boat to Kinshasa would leave on Thursday. It is the sort of thing one is often told in Africa, and foolishly one believes it. The man wasn't being deliberately untruthful, though of course the boat didn't leave on Thursday, or on Friday, or that week at all, but on the following Tuesday. He was trying to be helpful, and hoping to make life a little brighter for us. He had no idea when the boat would leave, nor had anyone else, but to say so would be admitting ignorance, which is a kind of failure. He saw we were impatient to get going, and he could make us happy for a time.

The old name for Kisangani was Stanleyville, in honour of the man who literally put it on the map, but to modern Africa the word reeked of colonialism and it was rubbed out. Much of its prosperity went the same way. 'The place had had its troubles,' the novelist V. S. Naipaul wrote, for this is his town in *A Bend in the River*. 'What had been the European suburb near the rapids had been burnt down, and bush had grown over the ruins; it was hard to distinguish what had been gardens from what had been streets.' Patrice Lumumba, the fiery Marxist who became Congolese prime minister after Independence in 1960 – who first appointed Sergeant Mobutu as commander of the army, only to be toppled by Mobutu and sent by him to his death – came from Kisangani. And in 1964 it was the centre of a fierce rebellion among the same tribes from the Congo forest who had annoyed Stanley so much. Inspired by magic and drugs, they slaughtered thousands of people before being scattered by an army of white mercenaries and Belgian paratroops, leaving the streets and river full of blood. Downstream from the town, in a little cemetery above the derelict yacht club, thirty-four missionaries who died in the massacre lie together among the trees, and *les événements* are remembered with a shudder.

One of the tribes that troubled Stanley as he descended the Falls was the Wagenya, but he was a forgiving man and after escaping from their butchery he wrote of his admiration for their fishermen. His account of their fish traps in the lowest of the cataracts, and the engraving in his book, would do well to illustrate them today. Huge tree trunks are jammed into the rocks, anchored with liana ropes cut in the forest and twisted to great tension against the rapids. Tied to the trunks is a scaffolding of poles from which big baskets are hung, to catch the fish coming down in the roaring force of water. Wagenya men work like acrobats along the poles, balancing and tying and adjusting, while below them in the water canoes slip and sidle through the current, the paddles dipping in the foam. Sometimes there is a shout and a man holds up a big fish. It is a beautiful, exciting sight.

Capitaine, a delicious Congo fish, was usually on the menu at the Zaire Palace Hotel in Kisangani, and probably more authentic than the meat. From my room I watched two goats being dragged on their knees across the backyard into the kitchen, and next day there was *côte de veau* for dinner, rather dark in colour. One night we tried the casino restaurant, and had it to ourselves – frogs' legs in garlic and the reflection of the roulette wheel spinning idly on the ceiling, but no gamblers. They would come later, towards midnight, the waiter said, and stay till morning.

The rich men of Zaire, the neo-*colons*, can be seen at airports and hotels, swaggering in dacron suits, cravats and enamelled shoes. Their laughter rattles like tropical rain on banana leaves, and their tantalising chestnut women, with hair teased and twisted into electrifying puzzles, are wonderful to look at. At an airport the baggage carousel may be broken and the departures indicator stuck, showing flights that left ten years ago on defunct airlines; and the hotel water supply may be cut off, the lifts out of order, and the air conditioner rattling intolerably or merely leaking water. But a traveller can take heart from the cheerful Africans around him, for whom these gadgets are not worth fussing about – just Western inventions, rather funny and slightly contemptible; though imported beer at £8 a bottle is preferred to the local brew by anyone with discernment and the money.

Most people live less stylishly. A worker, if he earns the price of ten bottles of local beer in a month, is doing well. When a petrol station has some petrol, drivers line up the previous day and sleep in their cars all night, hoping for five litres in the morning; and the pump man, softened by a bribe, might stretch the ration. Even the government machine sometimes begins to wobble. An official who was scrutinising our papers – *'vous êtes en danger,'* he said angrily because I hadn't got my passport on me – suddenly broke down. His stern face crumpled, he hid it in his hands and sobbed over his desk about the difficulties of life. He was hungry, his wife was ill, he couldn't afford medicines for her . . . He only recovered when we pushed across a handful of *zaires*. The currency, called by the same hybrid name as the river and the state, is an expensive joke, almost worthless at official rates. A copy of Naipaul's novel in the land that inspired it costs £52. Luckily the black market isn't hard to find, and on our first day in Kisangani an officer of the dreaded CNRI, the national centre for research and investigation, offered to buy our dollars at three times the proper price. It seemed safer to look for another bid, and a missionary had some suggestions: there was a Pakistani who might be useful, in an office above an empty motor showroom, or failing him there was a Greek in the bazaar, at the back of a department store behind shelves of tomato paste and tuna fish. It was straight out of Naipaul. We came away with blocks of notes the size of *Who's Who*, and felt rich until we started peeling off a few packets for another meal.

It is easy to poke a finger at the corruption, the decay, the collapse. Anybody can see the peeling plywood, the falling concrete, the potholes that spread over the roads and join up; or the cars lurching along, their bodywork flapping, their gaskets blown; or the abandoned boutiques, the boarded-up patisseries and beauty salons, the deserted temples of an empire that lasted barely one man's lifetime. What is harder to define is the continuity, the essential stream of Africa. The white men implanted a fragile order more real to themselves than to most Africans, and fostered institutions, erected monuments and invented frontiers hardly more substantial than the bush paths that are washed away in a heavy rainy season. A good deluge – political, economic, tribal – and the whole lot might go. Meanwhile quaint Europeanisms linger in the newspapers: in a solemn article on the use of the word *citoyen* or in a long correspondence about the meaning and morality of *Dallas*, currently being shown on TV. But the papers on sale in the street are a week old, which suggests a degree of fatigue, or more likely of indifference. It isn't a matter of lagging behind and not trying to catch up: Africa has its own speed, like the Congo but not so fast.

On Sunday in Kisangani there was a cycle race through the town, an echo of Belgian days. A band thumped out some brassy imperial rhythms and a man with a microphone whipped some enthusiasm into the crowd. The riders came round the corner like thorough-breds, their thigh muscles glistening and pumping as they sped along the pitted streets. They raced all morning; and in the cathedral down by the river where Pope John Paul II once celebrated mass the congregation raised its voice in Greek – *Kyrie eleison* – and a Belgian priest in golden robes, the cuffs and collar of his sports shirt showing, swung incense up and down the aisle. Afterwards we sat in the garden of a Greek restaurant and watched a cool Nilotic houri, delicate as a forest antelope, toy with a pork chop while her Belgian lover absorbed several beers. A party of Africans nearby, tricked out in sunglasses and crocodile belts and big gold rings, got through quantities of chicken curry and wine, then called for *crêpes suzettes* and sat back to admire the sparkle of their jewellery in the flames. Outside in the street a leper rose in front of us, holding up his finger stubs.

Eventually the boat departed for Kinshasa. Joseph Conrad, who was once captain of a Congo river steamer, would smile at the modern version. His was a wood-burning stern-wheeler that stopped at night to cut fuel along the shore. Ours was a big diesel ship with a doubledecker barge tied alongside and four more of them in front, two by two, all bigger than the ship that pushed them. The whole cumbersome juggernaut was immense: a travelling town with perhaps two thousand people on board and all their animals; a floating market slipping down the river with its own shops and store rooms, laundries, barbers, butchers, several kitchens, a beer hall and, if not quite a brothel, a number of busy market girls. Unwieldy as a ship, as a town it was crowded, noisy, full of discomfort and squalor, but prosperous and generally good-tempered.

We occupied a first-class cabin, among traces of another era. Wash basin, wardrobe, coat hooks, reading lamps, mosquito shutters – nothing was left but the marks where they had been. In the bathroom, without window or light, we shared the darkness – the broken toilet, the missing taps, the suspicious floods, the cockroaches – with an endless African family from next door. The *maître d'hôtel*, in a sprightly yachting cap, asked for complaints, but with worse things elsewhere on the barges it was hard to grumble. He warned us of thieves, and for a wad of *zaires* he lent us a padlock for our cabin. The only other white passenger was a young American from the Peace Corps, with long renaissance hair and alienation problems. For three years, while teaching mathematics, he had been trying to merge into the culture of his students, to identify with Africa. Perhaps he should have got married, he thought, for total empathy. But even that might not have been enough. 'In Zaire,' he announced before the voyage began, 'if you're not having metaphysical experiences, you're being superficial.' It was a challenge, to stimulate one's vision of the river ahead.

Past the first bend when Kisangani disappeared, and past the last mission – a church and cool buildings on a lawn among the trees – the picture opened. On each side of the river, smooth and grey as steel under the metal sky, lay an infinite band of green. Sometimes the density of green was broken by a tree with copper leaves, or a crimson vine creeping into the light, or a fringe of water hyacinth along the shore, with purple flowers. Sometimes a dead tree, bleached white like a prehistoric signpost, pointed across the forest to nowhere. But to left and right in different shades for a thousand miles, the rule was green.

'Going up that river,' Conrad wrote in *Heart of Darkness*, 'was like travelling back to the earliest beginnings of the world, when vegetation rioted on the earth and the big trees were kings. An empty stream, a great silence, an impenetrable forest. The air was warm, thick, heavy, sluggish. There was no joy in the brilliance of the sunshine. The long stretches of the waterway ran on, deserted, into the gloom of overshadowed distances.'

Going down it, we were travelling into that old yet ageless world, primitive but still valid. The broken taps and empty light sockets of the boat were meaningless in that tremendous, daunting scenery. There were channels and branches and islands of all sizes, though it was the end of the rainy season and the mud-banks were submerged. There were occasional arrows nailed to the trees to mark the route, rather unconvincingly. There were reaches of unimaginable beauty, and of incredible tedium. There were nights when our searchlights, playing on the passing scene, cast a theatrical fantasy over it and turned the trees into castles and cathedrals. There were morning mists that wrapped the river and lifted with the sun on another patchy day of grey and green. There were swamps clogged with greenery and mosquitoes, and creeks winding secretly into the forest. There were beds of water hyacinth that had broken away, emerald and purple, like watery funerals floating down the river. There were rainstorms that stirred the trees into a boiling stew of leaf and branch and water.

And there were the villages: every few miles another one, thatched, clustered, trapped between the forest and the river. Before we reached it, the dug-out canoes were already launched and waiting, like the fleets that had attacked Stanley. The men – or women and children – paddled furiously as we came close, snatched at the ship, hung on and jumped aboard. We didn't stop for them; it was a chancy business. Sometimes a canoe lost its grip or missed us completely and was left astern, to wait for the next boat in a couple of weeks or so. Once or twice a canoe was swamped and overturned, spilling people and goods into the river.

Usually they caught us and often, by day or night, we had twenty canoes tied alongside, being towed downriver.

For the villagers it was market day. They brought their produce to be sold, and stayed for hours on board to talk and drink and laugh with the bright-eyed girls and spend their money in the stalls on soap, razor blades, fish hooks, nails, batteries, aspirin. Then they dropped into their canoes, cast off and turned upstream to begin the long paddle home. Many passengers took the chance to do business on the way, and we carried traders too who were working up and down the river. Leaning from the ship when the canoes came out, a man would throw a piece of rag on to something he wanted – a pig, a load of manioc roots, a bundle of monkeys – to claim it for himself. But nothing was sold without a dispute, and the bargaining could get very rough.

Somehow space was found in the overloaded barges for more cargo: baskets of fish, fresh or smoked, or even live fish in tanks, and bags of meal, and chickens, ducks, goats, monkeys – delicate grey ones, fox-coloured ones, black and white ones, their tails slit and looped over their heads to make a handle – and smoked ones, black and sticky and done up in parcels with a rich dark smell, and antelopes tossed aboard and haggled over, and crocodiles muzzled with a stick tied between their jaws, trampled on and poked with paddles, thrown upside down among the monkeys – it was possible to feel sorry for a crocodile; and tortoises, tubs of palm oil, jars of palm wine, peanut butter, edible slugs, pieces of handicraft, native chairs and carvings, more monkeys – all brought out of the canoes and packed away into the corners of our floating town. 'Sometimes in this environment,' the American from the Peace Corps sadly confessed, 'you feel kind of superfluous.'

Soon the decks were awash with blood and excrement and feathers; and every day, as the barge roofs were spread with more bits of fish and flesh to dry, the smell rose higher. The noise rose too, from pigs, goats, cockerels, babies, though mercifully the monkeys were beyond speech. Once, above the din and diesel roar, I heard the shriek of exotic birds and felt a modest thrill at journeying through the forest, until I traced it to the two lifeboats that were supposed to save us all from shipwreck; one of them was full of fish and ducks, but the other contained a cage of exquisite grey and scarlet parrots.

In midstream, even with the engines stopped, we could never have heard the drums and war cries that pursued Stanley from the shore. All we got was a pair of vultures winging purposefully across Africa and once or twice a gaudy, silent butterfly flying round the ship like a spy.

On the second day one of the barges was found to be leaking; already the water was breaking over the deck. The captain steered his monstrous vessel into the bank where we lay for hours, nudging the greenery, while the barge was pumped out. It had to be done again, every day for the rest of the voyage. But pressed against the trees we could at last catch the small sounds – the rattle of a falling leaf, the throb of cicadas and bullfrogs at night – that came out of the otherwise silent forest. 'This stillness of life did not in the least resemble a peace,' Conrad wrote. 'It was the stillness of an implacable force brooding over an inscrutable intention.' It worried him that men were living and hunting in there, and somehow threatening his own precarious confidence: 'The consciousness of there being people in that bush, so silent, so quiet . . . made me uneasy.'

Our own captain, Conrad's successor, was less bothered. He had left his principal wife at home but had brought along another, and with friends and relations they took up several cabins and much of the upper deck. It was a small village of its own, with children crawling among the ducks and chickens and a cassette-player blasting everyone with a mix of Euro–African music. At any moment there might be a woman hanging a fresh goatskin over the rail with the washing, and others stewing the goat, chopping spinach, mashing boiled plantains or grinding tapioca; a man teasing a pet monkey, boxing with a chimpanzee, drilling a hole through a turtle's shell to stop it diving overboard; a girl, with her hair tied into a mass of prickles, twisting her sister's into two sharp horns; a boy pulling the wings off a moth; a pair of lovers slipping into a cabin; a baby sitting in a bucket of water under the fire hydrant.

The captain himself could leave much of the navigation to his quartermaster and was free for business, for he was a trader too, buying cheap along the river and sure of a profit in Kinshasa. Every day his stock of meat and fish and vegetables grew bigger while his ship, a teeming urban island, crept across the map. 'It's wonderful,' the American said, 'how they take this great object of modern technology and convert it to their own culture.' His desire for empathy was being partly satisfied in the cabin he shared with an African; it was now a dormitory crowded with his companion's friends from elsewhere on the barges and their casual women. 'They're not like whores in America,' he said. 'There's no vice in them at all – they're *happy!*'

At Bumba, our first stop, near the Congo's most northerly point before it turns south-west towards the sea, the American had his wallet stolen when he went ashore. It was the seventh time since he came to Zaire. 'I don't even get angry any more,' he said, feeling a welcome identity with the thief. Next day at Lisala a fish merchant fell into the river and was drowned. His widow wept terribly and wanted at least to have his body, but it would be twelve hours before it floated up and we couldn't wait.

Among the passengers was a colonel, a gentle, quite un-military man who, like the captain, had left his first wife behind and was travelling with his second one, much younger, and their child. Years ago he had been on an army course in America and would like to have settled there, but he felt friendly to the English, too, having once spent a holiday on the Isle of Wight – a remote but happy memory for him on this equatorial river. When we got to know him we raised the risky topic of the president, whose familiar portrait in cravat and leopardskin hat hung in the dining room. For nearly twenty years ex-Sergeant Mobutu has run the country rather in the way that King Leopold II of the Belgians ran it at the end of the last century, with spectacular advantages to himself. Was he popular, we asked?

'Very popular with his friends,' the colonel said, speaking as one soldier of another. Recently he had been arrested and kept for four months in the underground barracks of the BSP, the president's special brigade, in a room that was dark even by day and had no light at all at night. Nobody told him the reason, and after thirty years in the army he knew better than to ask. Men with no training, often with no education, were promoted over him because they were Mobutu's men, picked from his family or his tribe. The president's latest wife's uncle or his childhood friend from the same village could be made a general, the colonel's boss, and might sometimes want to demonstrate his rank.

There are favours for the few, fear for the rest; huge fortunes for some people, the secret fate of the *disparus* for others. While the elite rise higher, the mass get left behind; or worse – they slip back into Conrad's silent bush, a modern variant of his darkness. 'As the

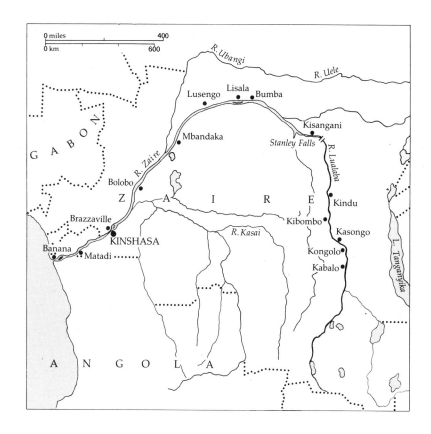

Captions for the following photographs:

1.   Intending passengers paddle furiously to bring their canoe alongside the Kinshasa-bound river boat – which neither stops nor slows for them.
2.   Wagenya fishermen at the Stanley Falls cataracts, near Kisingani. They work like acrobats along the poles – from which baskets are suspended to catch the fish – while below them canoes slip and sidle through the current.
3.   Everyday life on the Zaire. The passing of the boat is a major event, and villagers living along the river paddle out to buy and sell their produce, exchange news and gossip. The boat is their floating marketplace.
4.   Many passengers take the chance to do business on the way. The ship also carries traders who work up and down the river.
5.   The decks are littered with baskets of fish, bundles of smoked monkeys, goats, antelopes, even tied and muzzled crocodiles.
6.   The villagers bring their produce to be sold and stay for hours on board to drink and haggle.
7.   On the Zaire a canoe provides the only access to the other bank.
8.   A thatched shanty on stilts, backed by impenetrable jungle.

poor man reaches upwards,' another colonel said in another novel, John Updike's *The Coup*, 'the ground is sinking beneath his feet, he is sinking in the spreading poverty, the muchness of humanity divided into the same weary constant, the overused, overpopulated world.'

There must also be fear at the top. A minister is paid thirty times a doctor's salary, or a colonel's, but the court cards are often shuffled and some are thrown away in case anyone gets ideas of his importance. Even Mobutu is frightened. He sends an army ahead of him when he travels, and the only place where he walks freely – where he lavishes his favours – is his own village.

'What you need is a madman,' the American said, 'a fanatic like we get in America, who'll shoot him.'

'We have no fanatics,' the colonel said, apologising. And he wasn't sure that assassination was the answer. The people wouldn't stop at Mobutu's portraits; they would destroy the whole notion of him, starting in his village. A palace coup could become a tribal war which the colonel, who knew something of Africa before the days of Stanley and King Leopold and had fought in *les événements*, didn't look forward to. For himself, he would like to leave the army. He knew he was in danger, he wouldn't survive a second arrest, he could begin a small business. Already he was trying his hand, buying fish along the river to sell in Kinshasa, though it was tough to compete with the traders; and the jar of palm wine he bought, beery and slightly sour, didn't last long among his friends on board. But it's easy to make money, he said, if you have something to start with – an outboard motor, a truck, a building to turn into a little factory. Of course it helps to be one of Mobutu's men, but the colonel had his modest dream of riches and one day, perhaps, of another holiday on the Isle of Wight.

We steamed on down the Congo: another bend, another sultry reach, an endless downhill passage. The market was busy round the clock, the hours passing like the villages. Some villages were a mere grass hut or two on the bank, with a child in a canoe and a wisp of smoke. Others were large settlements dominated by a mission church, with dozens of canoes coming out to meet us. A big dugout makes an impressive picture, driven by a crew of men standing up and bending to the rhythm. Stanley admired their paddles and they haven't changed: slender and pointed, carved from a red wood like mahogany. One day they will be replaced by the Suzuki and the Yamaha, and one day perhaps the Congo will be trivialised by tourism, but not yet.

At Lusengo a canoe brought out a load of smoked meat, masses of unpleasant burnt stuff. The American said it was hippo, but the colonel said it was elephant – tastier and more valuable, since killing elephants is forbidden. A soldier, a giant in US combat kit, jumped down into the canoe and a fight began. The villagers thought he was arresting them for selling illicit meat. A man picked up a machete, another speared the soldier with his paddle, someone slipped, someone grabbed, and the soldier punched out. It was one man against six, and from the boat we cheered. At last the soldier made his point: he was arresting nobody, he only wanted to buy the meat.

We had a squad of police on board to keep order and see that no one was travelling without a ticket. Every day they caught a few stowaways, missing hundreds more, and at Mbandaka half a dozen cheerful youths were taken ashore under guard, roped together. A body on a stretcher was also carried off, followed by its relatives. Who had died, we asked? Nobody yet, the colonel said. But there had been a fight, a man was felled with a piece of wood, his skull was cracked, his mouth and nose were bleeding, he wasn't conscious and probably would die. It would be the second death on the voyage, which is about normal.

Mbandaka is where the Congo crosses the equator for the second time, and where two more of our barges were found to be leaking. The town looked abandoned: a concrete hotel smashed like an old teapot and a street of shops, once busy department stores but now repositories for the world's jetsam – talcum powder, electric toasters, stereo recorders. We were puzzled by the number of photocopy shops, but they were deserted and probably didn't work. Only the big brick church was holding out against the dereliction. Even the bollards along the quay were broken; it takes a lot to knock a bollard off. Close by lay the hulks of old river boats, rusty sternwheelers with deck boilers and tall funnels like Conrad's, now occupied by squatters. On the warehouse doors were painted some of Mobutu's sayings: 'The people must understand that if each of us does what pleases him and pursues his own ambition we shall have anarchy.' And another: 'We shall see who is best among us at cultivating his field.' Every dictator must have his joke.

Graham Greene came to Mbandaka in the Belgian days when it was called Coquilhat-ville – 'coq' to him – on his way to the leper hospital of *A Burnt-Out Case*. In his notebook he wrote of 'the huge Congo flowing with the massive speed of a rush hour out over the great New York bridges'. He recorded the motto of a local tribe – 'the mosquito has no pity for the thin man,' which he put into his novel – and noted the thin fine hands of Africans, their laughter and their deep sense of despair. He appreciated the excellent cheap wine and the creamy, mature Camembert cheeses flown from Europe. They aren't available now. But his experience when he tried to go up one of the Congo tributaries is familiar. The boat had a hole in the bottom and was said to be dangerous: 'Perhaps the boat could go next week – or next month . . . If they say it is safe it will sail. Otherwise no. I distrust the whole affair.' He got away in the end, having stocked up with mosquito bombs and whisky and taking with him, as we all do, a copy of *Heart of Darkness*.

After the barges had been pumped out, after the grubbiness of Mbandaka, it was good to get back into the river – the great cleansing, ultimately benign stream flowing through Africa. 'One searches the forest for a sign of life,' Graham Greene wrote, but perhaps it was the emptiness that began to be attractive. The younger novelist, John Updike, was more sympathetic to 'this continent whose most majestic feature is the relative absence of Man'.

Below Mbandaka the Congo is joined by the Ubangi river from the north and becomes the frontier between the Republic of Zaire and the People's Republic of the Congo. The grey pall of warmth above us began to melt, and bright savannas rose behind the swamps; we were reaching the rim of the *cuvette*. At Bolobo the canoes brought out oranges, bananas and pineapples. The stretch between Bolobo and another tributary, the Kasai, was once the scene of some rough colonialism. Africans along the river had been trading for centuries before Stanley's discovery, but the tales he told in Europe of the riches to be had and his own return to the Congo as agent for King Leopold brought a type of commercial white man, often in official uniform, who thought little of the black man's cares. 'There is no question of granting the slightest political power to the Negroes,' Stanley was told. 'That would be absurd. The white men, heads of the stations, retain all power. They are the absolute commanders.' One of them, the Belgian officer who gave his name to Coquilhatville, found that by shipping Congo ivory to

Liverpool he could make a profit of over 1,500 per cent. No wonder that most of the Africans were driven out of business, though some defended themselves to the end. In 1891, fourteen years after Stanley came down the river in canoes and one year after Conrad went up it in his steamer, a military expedition was sent to punish the natives for being so reluctant to lose their trade. Every village between the Kasai and Bolobo had to be destroyed and a great number of people killed.

'The horror! The horror!' were the dying words of Conrad's sinister, shadowy trader in *Heart of Darkness*. The horror was in the massacres, the decapitations, the severed hands, the agonising souls that balanced the profits and filled the darkness of King Leopold's monopoly. One of the men who brought news of the scandals, who had already spent several years on the Congo before Conrad met him there, was Roger Casement. In this handsome Irishman there was a touch of conquistador, according to Conrad, who watched him disappear into the wilderness with a servant and a pair of bulldogs and come back a few months later, leaner and browner but quietly serene, as though he had been for a stroll in the park. 'He could tell you things!' Conrad wrote. 'Things I have tried to forget, things I never did know.' Some of those things, and something of Casement, too, perhaps, found their way into *Heart of Darkness*. Casement told them again in a report on the atrocities of Belgian rule, when he was serving as British consul at Boma down on the Congo estuary. He travelled up the river collecting evidence of killings, floggings, mutilations and mass deportations, with details he couldn't bring himself to describe. Privately Casement, who many years later and far from Africa was to be hanged for treason, called the Congo a 'horrid hole'.

Towards the end of our voyage everyone got listless; we were thankful not to be going upstream, which takes twice as long. Graham Greene also had had enough after a week on the river, and hankered for a bath in the Ritz and a dry martini; for him, in *A Burnt-Out Case*, the Congo was a region of the mind. Some of our noisiest animals – pigs, goats, chickens – had been eaten, but the babies were screaming louder. More palm wine and tapioca brandy was drunk, and the market girls ran out of customers. The beer ran out too, and the *maître d'hôtel*, his yachting cap less sprightly, announced that the drinking water was finished. But we should reach Kinshasa tomorrow, he said; and then it was the next day, because we had to stop so often to pump out the barges; and in the end it was the day after.

We steamed on, the savannas lifting slowly into sunlit hills, and suddenly on the river ahead we saw another boat coming up towards us, faster and with no barges tied to it. From the fresh paintwork and the buzzing helicopter and the electronics on it we should have known whose it was; and hadn't Stanley, coming down the Congo in 1877, noticed that the aristocratic leopard headdress was worn only by the tribal chief? There, on a platform of his yacht, was the old sergeant himself – President Mobutu Sese Seko Kuku Ngbendu Wa Za Banga in his leopardskin hat. We were supposed to hate and fear him, but as he passed everyone raised a terrific cheer; and the Father of the Nation, Guide of the Revolution, a black King Leopold for our times, waved back.

We came through the hills into the Stanley Pool – now called Malebo – a wide lake with islands dealt over it like cards and always the drifting lumps of water hyacinth; some had white egrets pecking in the foliage as they rode across the Pool. On the far side, where the banks close in again and the water begins to dip towards the cataracts, the cities of Kinshasa and Brazzaville face each other across the Congo: the ex-Belgian and the ex-French, the capitalist and the Marxist, one with Americans and Israelis to give advice and the other with Russians and Cubans.

Our captain wheedled his juggernaut into the dockside at Kinshasa and put ashore the reeking, laughing load he had brought a thousand miles downstream from Kisangani: the traders with their purchases; the colonel with his dreams of peace and wealth; the young American with his rucksack and ambiguous identity; the market girls, quick to vanish in the city streets; the children with pink bubblegum bursting from their lips; the bundled women, loud-mouthed or battered, sinewy or plump; and washerboys, butchers, fishmongers, peanut sellers, soldiers, stowaways, issuing endlessly from the barges: the hundreds of faces we hadn't seen before, though we had been passengers together for a week.

Kinshasa, formerly Leopoldville, hasn't been flattered by its visiting writers. In 1890 Conrad, who was struggling with his first novel and had taken nineteen days sweating on foot up the path from the coast, wrote in his diary: 'Mosquitoes – frogs – beastly! Glad to see the end of this stupid tramp. Feel rather seedy.' But Kinshasa, the trading station on Stanley Pool described in *Heart of Darkness*, was a dump: 'It was on a backwater surrounded by scrub and forest, with a pretty border of smelly mud on one side, and on the other three enclosed by a crazy fence of rushes. A neglected gap was all the gate it had, and the first glance at the place was enough to let you see the flabby devil was running that show.'

In 1959, in the last days of the Belgian empire, Graham Greene found 'a brand new city with miniature skyscrapers' and streets patrolled by tanks and black troops that reminded him of the Indo–China war. He escaped over the river to Brazzaville, 'a far prettier, more sympathetic place than Leo. Europe in Leo weighs down on the African soil in the form of skyscrapers; here Europe sinks into the greenery and trees of Africa. Even the shops have more chic than Leo. The inhabitants of Leo call this a village, but at least it is a charming provincial village and not a dull city.'

In 1975, like the others before him, V. S. Naipaul was touched by the feeling of despair. He watched the acquisitive black bourgeoisie copying the white *colons* and grabbing what they could in an unreal world of imitation. He sensed the danger of an African nihilism, 'the rage of primitive men coming to themselves and finding that they have been fooled'. He called it 'a city detached from the rest of the country, existing only because the Belgians built it and today almost without a point. It doesn't have to work; it can be allowed to look after itself. Already at night a more enduring kind of bush life seems to return to central Kinshasa, when the watchmen bar off their territory, using whatever industrial junk there is to hand, light fires on the broken pavements, cook their little messes and go to sleep. When it is hot the gutters smell; in the rain the streets are flooded. And the unregulated city spreads: meandering black rivulets of filth in unpaved alleys, middens beside the highways, children, discarded motorcar tyres, a multitude of little stalls, and everywhere, in free spaces, plantings of sugarcane and maize: subsistence agriculture in the town, a remnant of bush life.'

We didn't linger in Kinshasa. There were suits for £400 and shoes for £200 and champagne for £100 – the meretricious trappings of a different Congo world – and Belgian tennis girls parading their pale limbs in the Boulevard du 30 Juin like pretty bits of froth left on the banks of an alien stream that once passed this way. A black man in a suffocating city suit complained that it was '*terriblement chaud*'. A white man in an embassy had another word, 'vandalised', and we saw what he meant: the junkyard of river boats along the waterfront, some of them quite new, and the acres of broken-down buses in the suburbs, rotting for lack of spares. The forest was coming back, and since Naipaul was here it has advanced a little further: not quite Conrad's primeval forest, but he might recognise it.

From Kinshasa, following the Congo downstream, there is a railway and a road and, fitfully, an Air Zaire flight – *Air Peut-Etre*, they call it. We could have gone to Inga to see the hydroelectric works, and to Matadi where the biggest suspension bridge in Africa is being built across the Congo, a link in a plan that is still a dream, so the bridge will be useless for many years; and on to Boma and Banana where the Congo, now the frontier between Angola and Zaire, runs into the Atlantic. But we came away.

Stanley went on down. He had taken six months from Lake Tanganyika to Stanley Pool, which he named himself, and had fought thirty-two battles on the way. Ahead were the cataracts, also thirty-two, which lower the Congo from the upland *cuvette* to the coast: the cataracts through the forest and the Crystal Mountains which for so long had stopped explorers coming upstream. It took Stanley nearly five months to bring his bedraggled party down them, with the loss of many men and canoes.

'We have a horror of the river now,' he wrote, when his only surviving white companion was drowned. His men were riddled with dysentery, ulcers, worms and fever, and some of them believed there was no end to the river, but he got them to the estuary at last: 'Ah! the hateful, murderous river, now so broad and proud and majestically calm, as though it had not bereft me of a friend, and of many faithful souls, and as though we had never heard it rage and whiten with fury, and mock the thunder. What a hypocritical river!'

Two days later he took his incredulous men aboard a 'big iron canoe driven by fire' and sailed out into the salt sea where, four hundred years earlier, the captain of a Portuguese caravel had found evidence of a river mouth. Forgetting that the Nile is longer than the Congo, but perhaps remembering that he had lost at least forty people on the river, Stanley allowed himself a last emotion: 'I felt my heart suffused with purest gratitude to Him whose hand had protected us, and who had enabled us to pierce the Dark Continent from east to west, and to trace its mightiest River to its Ocean bourne.'

THE DANUBE

PIERS PAUL READ

B etween the Fürstenberg Palace and the parish church in Donaueschingen, a small town on the fringes of the Black Forest, there is a large pool where clear water comes quivering out of the ground. This is the official source of the Danube, and in the nineteenth century a circle of paving stones with ornate balustrades was built around it. The reigning prince commissioned a marble monument from a Professor Adolf Heer representing the local district Baar as a mother with her arm around her barely clad young daughter, the Danube, showing her the path she must follow to the sea. This symbolic sculpture is somehow appropriate, for as I travelled along the Danube from its source in the Black Forest to its delta on the shores of the Black Sea I came increasingly to see her as a woman who in her youth has no notion of either the glory or the sadness of the life ahead – a woman with a charmed childhood who marries well but is suddenly widowed, and thereafter leads a long, dignified but uneventful life.

Her actual birth is not beneath this ornate monument in Donaueschingen, but twenty or thirty miles further west by the watershed of the Black Forest. Here, beneath a copse of spruce trees, water flows up from beneath a rock into the thin, cool, pine-scented air. Only 100 yards distant the land falls away towards the Rhine and the North Sea. From this spring a little stream called the Brege runs down the mountainside past dark green pine forests with banks of dirty snow still lying in their shade, then alongside great bald patches of yellowed grass and massive peasant dwellings with their stables, barns and human living quarters all cosily contained beneath one huge shingled roof. In only ten miles the beck becomes a small river, but it is not until Donaueschingen that the Brege is joined by another stream, the Brigach, and is christened *die Donau* – the Danube. Through the royal park, the shallow, graceful river moves, with the sunlight dappling the stones beneath the surface, and adolescent girls – who might well have been models for Professor Heer's statue – catching minnows in the clear water.

For the 400 miles that it flows through Germany the Danube is not a grand river – hardly larger than the adjoining rivers like the Lech or the Inn – and it avoids the great Bavarian cities of Nürnberg, Augsburg and Munich. It is not a rational river like the Rhine, and from the very start presents this paradox – though it is more than 1,700 miles long, the longest river in Europe after the Volga, and although it touches on the territory of eight different nations, the Danube never plays the role in the European consciousness that its size and centrality would suggest. Several cities have grown up on the banks but only one – Budapest – makes the river part of the city, and Budapest, as we shall see, is herself forlorn.

In Germany, however, there is no intimation of this disappointing future. After Donaueschingen, the river falters for a moment as the water seeps away through the porous chalk into the Bodensee, but after the town of Tuttlingen (where I spent my first night) it cuts a path through the Swabian Alb, making curling wooded valleys of exceptional beauty which reminded me of the River Rye in my native North Yorkshire. There was in particular a moment when the road, having left the Danube to cross a spur of hills, suddenly looked down through the trees at the huge, silent monastery of Beuron clasped by a curve of the river; and I thought myself back in Ryedale overlooking the ruins of Rievaulx Abbey. If the Rhine is a river of castles, then the Upper Danube is a river of monasteries, of which Beuron is the first. Not only are there monasteries built on the banks, but in each Swabian village of tall timbered houses with pretty blue shutters there are large crucifixes adorned with life-sized statues of the suffering Christ.

There are also secular fortresses – castles like Wildenstein, which stands on a crag above the Danube soon after Beuron, and the fairy-tale castle of the Catholic Hohenzollerns at Sigmaringen, which sheltered Pétain and the Vichy Government at the end of the last war. But these secular citadels are cottages when compared to the great churches and monasteries of Zwiefalten, Obermachtal, Ulm, Ingolstadt, Regensburg, Weltenburg, Niederaltreich, Passau and Melk. They are all, with the exception of Ulm and Regensburg, vast masterpieces of baroque art – and there are those who find baroque (and more particularly rococo) too rich for their taste. Certainly the onion towers of Zwiefalten appear squat and complacent beside the soaring lace-work spires of Ulm Cathedral; and the faces of the gilded putti in the baroque churches are bland and empty compared with the fifteenth-century figures carved on the choir-stalls of Ulm: but with baroque the whole is greater than the sum of its parts, and these great churches – like wedding cakes turned inside out – demonstrate a cheerful, celestial exuberance which is quite as true to my idea of God as the geometric austerity of the earlier Gothic cathedral.

Ulm, dominated by its cathedral, is the first town of any size on the banks of the Danube. Although it was here that I saw the first boat on the river – a pleasure craft covered by an elegant awning – the combined waters of the Iller and the Danube flow outside the city walls and are too fast and shallow for any significant river traffic. Small streams are diverted beneath the walls and run down between the tall houses of the fishermen's quarter to sluices built for trapping trout. When peering over a bridge I saw some fat fish swimming motionlessly against the oncoming current. I regretted the roast pork I had eaten for lunch and wished instead that I had chosen trout.

Thirty miles or so beyond Ulm the Danube flows by the village of Blindheim – anglicised to Blenheim – where in 1704 the Duke of Marlborough and Prince Eugene of Savoy defeated the armies of Louis XIV and the Bavarians in the War of the Spanish Succession. I could find nothing in my Michelin guide to commemorate this historic event – which was perhaps only to be expected – but it reminded me that the Danube, which here flows over flat countryside, is also a river of battles – not just the battle of Blenheim but also of Ulm itself where Napoleon defeated the Austrians; of Wagram, outside Vienna; and further down the river in Hungary, Mohács, where in 1526 the Turks under Suleiman the Magnificent defeated the Hungarians under their King Louis II, and then were themselves defeated in 1683 by the Austrians under Charles of Lorraine and Louis of Baden.

Battles, however, leave little behind. The monuments here in Bavaria are not to blood and steel, but witnesses to the intangible faith of the Catholic religion – triumphant churches dominating the historic cities and monasteries of Donauwörth, Ingolstadt and Weltenberg. After Donauwörth, Ingolstadt, though still pious and cultured, possesses an oil-pipeline terminal from Marseilles, Genoa and Trieste. Now the onion-domed towers of the churches are dwarfed by the chimneys of power stations and petrochemical works.

At Regensburg, politics intervene. Deep and wide enough to accommodate steamers and barges, the Danube becomes a thoroughfare of some strategic significance. It also changes direction. Having flowed north towards Prague, Warsaw and the Baltic, it is blocked by the Bohemian Alps and turns to the south-east and a quite different destiny. For the Romans the Danube was the northern frontier of their empire (the line between barbarism and civilisation) and here at Regensburg they built a garrison town which centuries later became the seat of the parliament of the Holy Roman Empire – a prototype capital city for an all-German state. In the event, history passed it by and the imperial mantle fell first on Vienna and then Berlin. As a result Regensburg remains much as it must have been in the days of its glory – a charming, unspoilt, unmistakably German city with a fine stone bridge which crosses the river to the old city gates. The long, steep roofs of tall houses with striped shutters flank the clock-tower; behind them rise the turrets of the merchants' houses, and soaring above them all are the twin spires of the cathedral.

Despite the devastation visited on most German cities by air raids during the war, Regensburg retains not just its fine old Kornmarkt and Rathaus but also a maze of crooked streets and narrow alleys which, in a most un-German way, are rather scruffy. As I wandered through these streets in the evening I came across a Weinstube advertising *Forelle* and, remembering the trout I had seen in Ulm that afternoon, I went down and ate one – long, plump and adorned with onions and fennel – beneath the blackened barrel-vaulting of some medieval merchant's house.

I would like to have stayed longer in Regensburg. I had a large, light room overlooking a courtyard in a hotel which had once been a Carmelite monastery; and when I left this monk's cell with bathroom en suite it was to walk through a pleasant and cheerful town. Young Germans with open, idealistic faces much like those on the choirstalls at Ulm were collecting money for Solidarity. Outside the station a band in black and gold uniforms with black and red plumes in their black caps was playing to celebrate the centenary of the Regensburg Station. I felt that Regensburg symbolised the best moment in Germany's unfortunate history – an attempt by the converted Barbarians to embody the values of Rome and Christianity.

Seven miles down the Danube the Walhalla, a huge doric temple built as a monument to the greater German nation by King Ludwig of Bavaria, brings to mind the other, darker side of the German character. After the innocence and exuberance of the baroque churches and romantic castles of the Upper Danube, this is the first intimation of the ugly side of what is to come. On a clear day, from the Walhalla, you can see the Alps and that small village of Branau am Inn on the Austro-Bavarian border where Hitler was born. As I drove on from the Walhalla through pretty riverside villages, it seemed inconceivable that this rural paradise could have been the homeland of the demented dictator. In the balmy spring weather it seemed impossibly paradoxical that the waters of the Inn, which join the Danube in the magnificent city of Passau, should flow not just from Hitler's birthplace but also from Salzburg, where Mozart was born.

Passau is built on a tongue of land between the two fast-flowing rivers, the Danube and the Inn, and it is here that the Danube becomes the national river of Austria. Before engines were built to push barges as far west as Regensburg, Passau was the terminus of all river traffic from the east – particularly the cargoes of grain from the Hungarian plains. The Danube was the principal thoroughfare of the old empire and remains the route by which Russian coal and iron ore are imported into the modern Austrian republic. It is also at Passau that the river, after flowing across the flat Bavarian plateau, enters a defile between the Bohemian Forest and the Alps, plunging between steep wooded banks to provide a river landscape of exceptional loveliness. The road I followed from Passau to Linz went in and out of wooded hills; where the land became flat again there were apple trees in blossom scenting the evening air. Then another castle, another monastery: I was at Wilherring where the road rejoins the river and follows it into Linz.

There is something wretched about Linz. It is a large city, the third largest in Austria, and it has a fine main square which slopes down towards the Danube, yet despite this the place seemed dour and dead. This may have been because I was beginning to tire of travelling alone. The restaurants in the city were all empty, and the one I went to for supper took an hour to produce the dish I had chosen. But I was also reminded by the unmistakably Third Reich style of the arcade at the foot of the main square that this was the city of Hitler's schooldays – its cathedral the church where the future Führer was confirmed. I spent the night in a small hotel on the promenade, and the next morning continued my journey by train, rattling along the river bank until I was rewarded with the sudden sight of the two green-domed towers of the largest and grandest of all the monasteries on the Danube, that of Melk. Since I was educated by Benedictine monks in England, my feelings when I saw this paragon of all Benedictine monasteries – comparable only to Monte Cassino itself – were mixed. I could only marvel at this Versailles perched on a rock above the Danube like a beached, baroque Noah's ark with an ochre-and-white striped prow and three angels standing on the bridge; but I could not but wonder whether such a palace was a proper architectural expression of St Benedict's ideal. It seemed less a memorial to the greater glory of God than a monument to the vanity of man.

I spent the night in Melk and, at half-past eight the next morning, caught a steamer from the pier beneath the monastery which took me downstream to Krems. This part of the Danube, called the Wachau, descends fifty feet in twenty miles as it passes through a narrow valley studded with castles and churches – first the Schloss Schönbuhel, an eighteenth-century building with an onion tower, then, almost immediately after it, an older Servite monastery with *Gloria in Excelsis Deo* painted on its white walls. It was such a beautiful morning that I was certainly in a mood to glorify God. There was a faint blue tinge in the air, but no clouds in the sky: the ruined keep of Agstein was high above the river on a wood-covered hill. Black rocks stuck up like sharks' fins through the soft green fleece of the trees. At Weisenkirchen the valley widened out to allow vines to grow on the hillside. As a climax to this, my first passage on a Danube steamer, we came in sight of Durnstein, the castle where the Austrian Duke Leopold captured and imprisoned Richard the Lionheart on his way back from the Crusades. The boat stopped at Krems, where I took a train to Vienna. By midday I was in another tall, old-fashioned room in a hotel on the Grashofgasse.

Vienna is where the Danube becomes wholly identified with Austria, heir to an empire which once stretched from Bavaria to the Carpathians, from Silesia to the Po valley. But though it was a Viennese, Strauss, who named his most celebrated waltz after the Danube, the river stays outside the city walls. Twice besieged by the Turks, Vienna looks in upon itself behind its ramparts. Even when these were demolished in 1857 to provide handsome boulevards to circle the city, it only further removed the river from the town; and in 1868 the Viennese diverted the fast-flowing water from the front of the city to a drab suburb. On the one bank were warehouses and a railway; on the other a wasteland of shingle.

In 1914 the Austro-Hungarian Empire, which was never based on a people but on a dynasty and an idea (the idea of a Christian empire which first saw expression in Aix and Regensburg), overreached itself; four years later, after tens of millions of dead, it came to an end. Vienna, once the nominal capital city for fifty million people, now caters for only seven.

Forty miles from Vienna, the grim fortress of Bratislava looks down on the Danube. Bratislava, once Pressburg, is the capital city of Communist Slovakia. Neon-lit red stars shine from the top of the factory chimneys: armed guards in turrets placed on stilts peer through binoculars at the passing boats. This political reality – the Iron Curtain – helps explain why a cabin had been booked for me on the Soviet MV *Moldavia*, which I found tied to the Präterkai in Vienna. To step into the foyer on the main deck was like walking into a grand hotel. A smartly dressed Soviet sailor took my suitcases; a young Ukrainian 'passenger director' took my passport and, after checking my reservation, asked if I was the author of *The Professor's Daughter*, which he had studied at university in Kiev. Made to feel welcome in this way I went down to my light, spacious, air-conditioned cabin and then, before my fellow passengers returned from their sightseeing in Vienna, I explored the boat.

The MV *Moldavia* was long, wide and flat – more like a royal barge than a steamer. It had been built by the Austrians in their shipyards on the Danube but was owned and operated by the Russians, who kept it impressively clean. On the top of the boat, behind the bridge, there was a large flat deck with a small swimming pool and numerous deckchairs. Beneath this there was a dining room, bar, lounge, television room, sports room, sauna and eighty-five cabins for the passengers. Somewhere on the boat there must have been accommodation for the crew of ninety – clean, youthful Russians who seemed to have been employed as much for their pleasant appearance as their abilities. My fellow passengers, when they returned, turned out to be mainly Germans – 150 of them – with a small party of elderly Americans, mostly from California. They were in the charge of two young and able German girls, Brigitte and Elvira, who like nurses or air stewardesses, shepherded their guests with a steely sweetness. At dinner I shared a table with two enchanting ladies from San Francisco – a widow and her sister – who were to be my companions for the rest of the voyage. As the boat backed slowly out into the mainstream of the Danube, and then turned towards Bratislava, a pretty, smiling Moldavian stewardess wearing a white blouse, black skirt and high-heeled shoes traipsed back and forth from the kitchen to serve us with a good supper of smoked sturgeon, pork cutlets and fruit.

With Czechoslovakia on the left bank and Hungary on the right, I saw for the first time, the kind of landscape that was to be typical of the remaining 900 miles of my journey towards the sea – marshy lowland screened from the passing boats by willows and poplars planted on the river bank. Then, as the river pushes through the Pilis and Neograd mountains, the land rises again and there – high on the right bank – is the huge cathedral of Estergom. At this point, after having flowed from west to east for 750 miles, the Danube suddenly turns towards warmer climates and flows due south.

Twenty-five miles further downstream we arrived at Budapest, at once the most beautiful and the most tragic of all the cities on the Danube. Only Budapest embraces the river – the double city strung together by five long and lovely bridges. On the right bank the old city of Buda towers behind dignified ramparts; on the left bank the more cheerful and commercial Pest sprawls with more modern boulevards. Built along the banks on the Pest side are new, modern hotels but the most outstanding building is the huge neo-Gothic Parliament building designed by Emmerich Steindl in the late nineteenth century. Its design is a hodge-podge of styles – a cross between the Houses of Parliament at Westminster and the Doge's Palace in Venice, topped with a cupola similar to the celebrated St Stephen's crown. Looking out over the wide, fast-flowing river at the Disneyesque Fisher Bastion on the opposite bank, one gets an overall impression of a glittering city, a ferment of culture and vivacity.

What then goes wrong? Why does the city suddenly seem so melancholy – all dressed up with nowhere to go? I turned to my guidebook (Baedeker's *Austria*, 1929), which suggested that what was once the Franz Joseph Quay was now called the Belgrade Quay. 'This superb street,' writes Baedeker, 'to which carriages are not admitted, contains large hotels with frequented cafés, and is the favourite promenade of Pest. It is planted with trees and on fine sunny evenings is thronged with a gay crowd, threading its way between hundreds of benches and chairs.' Alas, not today. Now creaky Balkan buses belch black fumes as they trundle along a busy thoroughfare. The hotels have been rebuilt – nondescript, air-conditioned piles with names like Hilton, Hyatt and Intercontinental – for government functionaries and Western businessmen. Certainly you can sit in their 'coffee shops' if you can pay the price of a cup of coffee in Deutschmarks or dollars.

The life of the city was obviously not to be found on the Belgrade Quay, so I walked around in search of its new location. I walked for hour upon hour but saw only melancholy Magyars with doleful expressions on their faces. Was it poverty that made them depressed? The shops, though well stocked with food, showed none of the glittering display of consumer goods behind glossy, plate-glass windows that characterised Vienna only fifty miles away. Or was it that lack of political liberty which made the streets drab and the mien mournful in the passersby? Certainly liberty was something which the Hungarians had always sought and which had somehow always eluded them. First the Turks, then the Austrians and now the Russians had put their foot on the neck of this old, isolated race. The very magnificence of Steindl's parliament house made it a poignant monument to Hungary's hopeless democratic dreams. In the afternoon I walked over to the Gellert Hotel – an *art nouveau* building on the right bank of the river. Inside was not the foyer I expected, but a huge hall filled with the smell of hot damp air. A few old ladies sat at various kiosks, some wearing white coats; old men sat on benches as if waiting in a hospital out-patients' department. I walked further into the hall and realised that this was one of Budapest's famous hydropathic centres. There was a covered swimming pool filled with plump, unsmiling Hungarians waiting for individual treatment in booths off the main hall. Whatever relief they expected for their bodies, they did not look as if they thought that the waters would do much to make them more cheerful.

Despairing of ever finding any sign of vitality in the city of Budapest, I went back towards the *Moldavia* over the Szabadsag Bridge, but noticed on the Belgrade Quay an amiable crowd moving in and out of a large building like bees from a hive. I followed them in and found myself in a huge covered market crammed with people buying chickens, salami, smoked pigs' trotters, bread, mushrooms, peppers, strawberries and live carp. Each stall advertised the price of its produce, and the only queue I saw was for small tomatoes. This was undoubtedly a free market at work, and at the same time the only manifestation of animation and vitality that I had come across in Budapest. It seemed to confirm Adam Smith's adage that political and economic freedom are indivisible.

We left Budapest during the night and the whole of the next day – a Saturday – was spent sailing due south down the river. On the left bank was the now familiar line of willow trees with swampy land beyond the dyke; on the right a raised bank with the occasional settlement – a huge modern city at Dunaujvros and later the town of Mohács. At 4 p.m. we reached the Yugoslav border. Here the *Moldavia* was tethered to the shore for several hours while Valery, the passenger director, went ashore with our passports. He returned with two tough-looking uniformed Yugoslav officials and we were all summoned to the dining room to face them. One by one they took each passport and called the name of its owner to check that the face matched the photograph. One or two Germans looked uneasy – they were of an age, after all, to have served in Yugoslavia in less happy times – but the only one who seemed to me to have the undoubted face of a war criminal turned out later to be one of the nicest Americans. Eventually we set sail again and I went up on deck to enjoy one of the most beautiful stretches of the river which followed the Yugoslav border. The Danube divided into different channels and wandered in and out of islands covered with forests of willows and poplars. Solitary fishermen sat with rods; one of them had lit a fire on the river bank, and so still was the air that the smoke lay in a long, low line beside the trees. The river, too, was calm. The only sound came from the lapping of the water at the bows. I saw a large bird on top of a tree which an agreeable German with binoculars identified as a heron. He told me that the Yugoslavs had gone through the pantomime with the passports just to annoy the Russians.

By seven the next morning the *Moldavia* had already docked in Belgrade. I went up on deck to look at the ramparts of the fortress but saw only some run-down waterside buildings and a church tower. We had tied up, properly speaking, on the banks of the Sava: Belgrade is yet another Danubian city where the Danube is hard to find. After breakfast I set out with my fellow passengers in a coach to tour the city. Our first stop was the fortress, where I discovered that its ramparts are barely visible because they have been razed so many times by so many different conquerors. The internal fortifications were more impressive, although the gateways smelt of urine and the park, laid out on the ruins of the Turkish city, was strewn with litter – not just odd sweet papers or cigarette packets, but piles of rubbish as if litter bins had been overturned by hooligans. Without doubt Belgrade is a dump. When Brigitte had wrinkled up her nose and told me it was dirty, I had assumed this was just the prejudice of a fastidious German: but because there is so little to see (our guide was hard pressed to stretch the tour over two and a half hours), either in terms of public monuments or old buildings, one notices the dirty streets, the unwiped tables and unemptied ashtrays in the cafés. Of course Belgrade has had a hard time. The city, as our guide told us, has seen forty foreign occupations – each change of rule being accompanied by a partial destruction of the place. All the same, while the Poles and Hungarians have painstakingly rebuilt their capitals as they were before, the Yugoslavs seem to have devoted their resources to the tawdry Bauhaus megalopolis of New Belgrade on the other side of the Sava.

I slept through our departure from Belgrade and awoke early in the morning as the boat approached the defile between the Balkan mountains and the Transylvanian Alps. I went up on deck. The river was calm and so wide that it seemed that we were sailing on a lake. A slight mist made the air opaque, yet the blue sky and distant mountains were quite clearly visible behind the watch-towers on stilts along the Romanian side of the river. Then suddenly, after Moldova Veche, between the Turkish fortress of Golubac and the romantic rock, projecting from the water, called Babakai Felsen, the river is squeezed between the steep sides of the mountains. The lake narrows to a swift stream only 150 yards wide. The rock formation on the river bank was like squashed Battenburg cake. A Dutch-American geologist who was among the passengers told me how 'geologically interesting' this area was, demonstrating with his hands the impact of shelf upon shelf of rock. On the bank we could see marks of its strategic significance from prehistory to the present day – the prehistoric settlement of Lepinski Vir, then Trajan's memorial carved into the rock and the road he built along the precipitous gorge during his campaigns against the Dacians, and finally the Iron Gates and the enormous dam at Djerdap.

We knew that we were approaching the dam some time ahead. Several villages had been rebuilt higher on the river bank. There were also the towers of a submerged castle sticking out of the water, and a lovely but forlorn church standing with its feet in the river like a confused poodle. The dam itself is a considerable monument to Energy, the Baal of modern man. Built in partnership by the Romanians and Yugoslavs, it provides almost half the electricity for both countries. It also facilitates the passage of boats and barges along this hitherto treacherous part of the river. The *Moldavia* glided easily into a massive lock. An enormous 'iron gate' rose out of the water behind us and as the water was released beneath the boat we sank into a pit of glistening concrete. Then another gate opened, we sailed into a second lock, and the process was repeated – this time with a view of the whole dam – until we were free in the river once again, sixty-five metres nearer sea-level.

After travelling for a week on my own, I was grateful for the company of my fellow passengers on the *Moldavia*. Fortuitously my two table companions were both fellow Catholics, which added to, or perhaps explained, the spontaneous sympathy we felt for one another; but the other American passengers were also amusing – and daunting in their drive and curiosity. The tour company which had brought them all from California to the wilds of Central Europe was called Lifelong Learning Inc. Their motto was 'New Horizons Through Travel', to which I would have added, 'Never Say Die.' Old age and arthritis did not deter them from moving around the world. One couple told me that they only spent the summer months at home: the rest of the year they spent travelling. Indeed the only complaint among these senior sightseers was that there was nowhere else to go. China, India, Indonesia – they had done them all.

The German passengers were different – the majority being bucolic Bavarians who made the most of the dance floor, cavorting late at night to the sounds of the deadpan Russian pop group. There was a minority, however, of sedate and dignified north Germans, one of whom – a harbour-board official from Bremerhaven – told me that he took these river cruises whenever he could because they reminded him of his childhood on the Oder. His father had been a shipowner whose boats had traded up and down the river from Frankfurt to Stettin, and he had often sailed on them as a boy. It made me wonder if my own preference for the first fifty miles of the Danube – the wooded valleys around Beuron – sprang from happy child-hood memories of picnics on the Rye, and if the vivid impressions of childhood affect our appreciation of everything in later life.

The company of Germans from Bremerhaven and Americans from San Francisco, however agreeable in itself, cannot be said to have contributed much to my understanding of life on the Danube, and were it not for the fresh scents of river water or hawthorn blossom which wafted on to the deck, my view of the bank might as well have been on a television screen. The fishermen on their boats, or the villagers whom I occasionally glimpsed through binoculars, remained quite unknown to me.

In the evening sunlight we passed first Calafat on the Romanian shore – a charming town of bright yellow stuccoed houses and a triple-domed church; and two miles further down, on the right bank, the Bulgarian town of Vidin. The Baba Vida fortress which faced the river was dotted with people sitting out in the warm sun. At the foot of the walls, by the water gate, boys bathed in the muddy water. Further along the ramparts the entire population seemed to be taking their evening stroll. I longed to mix with them – to sit at a café and study their faces – and could only console myself with the beauty of the sun setting through faint cloud, creating mother-of-pearl ripples behind the ambling boat. Early the next morning the *Moldavia* docked at Giurgiu, the Danubian port nearest to Bucharest. After breakfast most of my fellow passengers set out in a bus for a quick tour of the Romanian capital. Since I had spent some time there on a cultural exchange, I remained on board; and at nine set out on my own to look around Giurgiu itself.

It is not a town to tempt the tourist – indeed to use the language of the Michelin guide, it is probably worth a detour to avoid it. My impressions, certainly, were prejudiced by having to walk a couple of miles through an area of dockyards and industry to reach it. Giurgiu is connected by pipeline to the oil fields of Ploeisti, and its chimneys gave off a cocktail of fumes into the air which made my eyes smart and my throat ache. The town was mostly under repair: it had suffered, I was later told, from an earthquake. The streets were nonetheless crowded with people, some of whom seemed to be working in a desultory way – digging holes or replacing kerbstones – at a pace to suggest that they knew they were unemployment in disguise. Young men queued for a 10 a.m. performance of a Charles Bronson film. Schoolchildren sat around a small park beneath the busts of famous Romanians. I went into two Orthodox churches. Both were empty – not just of people but of pews. Their floors were covered with rugs like those of mosques. I was half in the Orient already – women as well as men were doing heavy manual labour – but somehow I felt less helpless here than I had in

Budapest, perhaps because so many words seemed to come from the French – Farmacia, Librarie, Braserie, Alimentara, Port and even, in a quiet cul-de-sac, the Hotel Victoria.

We set off again in the middle of the afternoon beneath the huge Friendship Bridge which links Bulgaria and Romania ('Not much traffic,' as one American passenger said). Quickly we escaped from the cloud of polluted air which covers Giurgiu and Ruse on the opposite bank and, once again, found ourselves in the kind of wild, marshy wilderness which typifies most of the Lower Danube. By the next morning we were already in the Danube delta. The river, which had started out so fast and straight, was now old, sluggish and distracted – meandering into twirling cul-de-sacs, its actual flow hard to distinguish from marsh and lake. On both banks there was a vast expanse of flat, grassy land with small settlements of low thatched cottages, some painted a bright blue and with carved and decorated gables. There were barns with mud walls beneath their thatched roofs, and peasants driving horses and carts – scenes from a hundred or a thousand years ago.

Egrets, storks and terns skimmed and glided over the water near the river bank. High above, a grey crane flew on a fixed course at right angles to the river. It was a wilderness until suddenly I caught sight of towering derricks – perhaps the Romanian town of Tulcea. We left it on our right-hand side. The *Moldavia* seemed to sense that she was near home, and kept to the Soviet side of the river. In time she was rewarded. The land rose a little and once again cranes like pylons rose above the willow trees, then the masts of ships and finally blocks of flats with the odd mosque and a church set incongruously among them appeared in view.

The *Moldavia* docked in her home port of Izmail. Alongside was the larger MV *Ajwasowskij* which was to take us out into the Black Sea and on to Yalta and Istanbul. I packed my suitcases, and when my cabin number was called collected my passport, took leave of Valery and walked along the quay to the new ship. The *Ajwasowskij* sailed at midday – moving slowly up the northernmost arm of the Danube delta through the mottled brown water. Sheep and horses grazed on the spits of land. Domestic birds like ducks and geese swam side by side with egrets and cormorants. Slowly the grassland turned to reeds, and a green sea seemed to stretch to the horizon.

I became impatient to reach the sea but it was impossible to tell from the deck of the *Ajwasowskij* where the land ended and the sea began. Then, at four in the afternoon, I caught sight of two or three large ships and realised that the sea was not ahead but beside us. Very slowly the enormous liner passed down this last narrow channel of the delta. With the silt washed down from the mountain ranges a thousand miles away the Danube fought off the sea, clinging to life, fighting against dissolution in the massive void of salt water. The spits of land grew narrower and narrower until finally, with a last clump of rushes, each came to an end. The brown water was lost in the blue. The *Ajwasowskij* sailed out into the Black Sea.

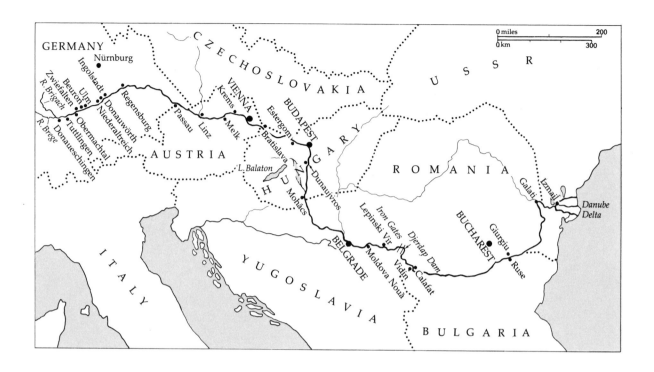

Captions for the following photographs:

1.   At Durnstein in Austria, where vines grow almost to the Danube's edge, Richard the Lionheart was imprisoned on his way back from the Crusades.
2.   Budapest on a misty morning. It is the most beautiful and tragic of all the cities on the Danube. Here, on the Pest side of the river, stands the huge neo-Gothic Parliament building, a cross between the Houses of Parliament at Westminster and the Doge's Palace in Venice.
3.   Secular and spiritual symbols side-by-side in the delta. A Russian Orthodox church towers over a ship flying the Soviet flag.

THE AMAZON

RONALD FRASER

A short hour before, flying out of the Peruvian desert, we were bouncing over the scalped flanks of the Andes. A long canyon and a winding dirt road, which led in a last desperate ascent to snow-capped peaks and glaciers, appeared with familiar, lung-aching intensity below. A turquoise lake, then another lined with the green tin roofs of a mining encampment, came into view. Rapidly I asked the steward for the captain's confirmation. As rapidly he returned with the captain's regrets. His charts did not mark this place. It was hardly surprising. Military survey maps had been of little more help. The source of the Amazon – or of the Marañon as it is known for its first one thousand miles or so – was nowhere definitively located. A couple of days earlier, as we drove to the summit of the last pass, we knew only that we were searching, amidst glaciers and peaks, for Lake Santa Ana, reputed to be the great river's source.

Gasping for breath in the rarefied air, half asphyxiated by fumes from a leaking petrol can, we had arrived at the Raura mining camp. An engineer came out of an office. 'Lake Santa Ana? Well, there it is. . .' I looked down in dismay at a crater-like chasm half filled with water. The company had drained the lake. 'But that's not the source. Come, I'll show you.' Again heading upwards, we soon crossed a small mountain torrent. 'That's the Marañon.' He laughed. 'We use it for drinking water for the camp. Over there is the source . . .'

A glacier, curled like a grey peruke round a massive head of magenta and ochre rock, rose at the end of a small lake. From separate mouths between scree and ice flowed two streams of clear white and blood-red water which mingled before being lost in the turquoise depths of Lake Niñococha. The silence was mineral, the air at over fifteen thousand seven hundred feet like an edge of steel at the throat. We stumbled along the lake for a closer look. The engineer pointed to other glacier-fed lakes hanging in the distance below. They, too, added their waters to the torrent that rushed down to Lake Lauricocha and on, ever larger and faster, through the Andes for 700 miles before breaking out to meander through the rain-forest delta. Roadless, there was no way of following it. We turned back. Quechua miners turned gravely to look at the jeep. The roar of an avalanche fractured the air. Beside the track llamas grazed on parched grass. The clouds were again closing in as the plane passed overhead and no doubt snow would be falling soon. When the cloud next broke, the barren Andean vastness had given way to a solitude even vaster, the trackless, shimmering forest and the great waterway winding through it.

Signs of human presence were barely perceptible in the wilderness below. An occasional small, irregular clearing cut out of the trees, the trunks lying like blanched spilikins on the reddish-brown earth, revealed that someone was trying to win a living in the midst of the tropical exuberance. The forest, I knew, had evolved over millennia to complex and delicate laws of its own, and still hides people, animals and vegetation unknown to science. But I was unprepared for the perfection of this vast *trompe l'oeil* which nature has painted in protective abundance over some of the earth's most barren soils; a perfection which, perhaps not surprisingly, has hypnotised Western civilisation with its illusion of limitless wealth for over 400 years.

C hugging through the creamy mud water, the palm-thatched river boat headed downstream. Iquitos's tin roofs and cracked concrete streets, its vultures and scrap-heap taxis vanished temporarily in the green distance. An outpost, a random contingency in the wilderness, the Peruvian Amazon's capital has the open amiability of a frontier town. Men call 'Brother!' to each other in the streets, and strangers are made to feel welcome. Accessible only by water and air, steaming in ninety per cent humidity for most of the year, languorous and quick-moving, Iquitos with 200,000 inhabitants is the Amazon's third largest town. A thousand miles of water separate it from Manaus, the next major town downstream.

Under an arching blue sky and towering cumulus, the forested banks ahead of the boat receded to the horizon where river and sky joined indistinguishably in the early morning light. Behind, a maze of channels and vivid green islands obscured the tributary's mouth. For a moment I looked back to one of those rare dates when, at this confluence, the line that divides history from prehistory was precisely drawn.

On Sunday, 12 February 1542, a small party of Spaniards, led by Francisco de Orellana, a one-eyed conquistador, rowed out of these waters of the Napo river and chanced on the Amazon. Their awe and amazement at the river in flood registers on heart and eye to this day. 'It came on with such fury and with so great an onrush that it was enough to fill one with the greatest fear to look at it, let alone to go through it . . . and it was so wide from bank to bank from here on that it seemed as though we were navigating launched out upon a vast sea.' Part of an expedition which had come in search of cinnamon and Eldorado, the mythical kingdom of gold, the fifty-odd Spaniards had set off to find food for their stranded comrades. After more than a week in their roughly made boat, they found food all right, but lost the will to row back up the Napo. Following the current, fighting warrior tribes, plundering villages for food, they became the first whites to voyage the Amazon's length. After seven months they sailed out of the river's mouth and up the Venezuelan coast to safety. With them they brought reports of real and imagined riches, of temperate and fertile lands, of settlements that extended for many leagues along the banks, of 'large cities that glistened in white'. And, of course, an account, related by an Indian captive more cunning than they, of the warrior women who held sway in the interior.

With the inevitability of an equinoctial sunset, Orellana's discovery ensured that Europeans would descend on the river of the Amazons. And so they did. Up and down the waterway Jesuit missionaries brought God and the discipline of hard, settled work to the semi-nomadic pagans they corralled in their missions. In the estuary, English, French, Dutch and Portuguese settlers introduced European warfare and virulent diseases. When, less than a century after the Spaniards' discovery, the Portuguese assumed mastery of the greater part of the river, only a handful of the original million or more Amerindians – no one knows their exact number – were left to exploit.

In the first of many Amazonian ironies, Western colonisation fell to a nation far advanced in its decline. Too few colonists and too few exploitable natives left this vast region undeveloped and semi-deserted. The size of Europe, Amazonia remains today as sparsely settled as the Sahara.

*T*he river boat's outboard puttered and stopped. We hung in the water for a moment, then the current spun the bow round and we drifted downstream. Impassively, the owner examined the engine and decided that the breakdown was irreparable. He took off his shirt. We had covered a good number of miles back from the Napo, but Iquitos was still out of sight. The current, which otherwise seemed not too fast, pushed the boat along rapidly the way we had come. No other craft was in sight. From between banks of high rainclouds the sun shone heavily, seeming to deaden all sound. The café-au-lait river was warm to the touch, impenetrable to the eye, calm as though coated with a layer of palm oil. And then, suddenly, inexplicably, whirlpools eddied and broke on the surface.

We drifted peacefully. When the rain came, torrentially, pearls sprang up on the river's ochre water. The sun returned and the air was a steam bath. In the distance the sound of an outboard chattered through the silence. The owner waved his shirt but the craft continued steadily downriver. It was half an hour or more before a tin-roofed boat turned from the opposite bank to take us in tow. Four hours later, hugging the bank to avoid the full force of the stream, we passed the point where the outboard had broken down.

The slow passage upstream afforded time for reflection. Who lived and how in the solitary desolation of the riverside huts we were passing? Palm-thatched and raised on stilts, their weathered and roughly sawn boards were symbols of poverty. And so, also, were the small stands of plantains, sugarcane, manioc, palms and papaya which grew in the clearings around them. Women looked up calmly from washing in the river, men glanced indifferently, a child now and again waved. They were small, dark, delicately boned, these people, with a coppery sheen to their skin and hair. They could, I thought, be mistaken for the original Amerindians, but a Peruvian sociologist had told me that most were the multiracial and impoverished heirs of the Eldorado of a century ago.

There was time enough, too, to recall the moment of history when the West exploited and then destroyed an Amazonian wealth more fabulous than any conquistador had dreamt of; time enough to search on the bank, among the branchless grey forest trunks rearing their delicately leaved umbrellas high in the sky, for the *seringa* which brought fortune and misery to these banks. To my untrained eye it was not easy to single out. Except for its height it's an undistinguished tree, as Henry Bates, the great nineteenth-century English naturalist, observed – rather like a European ash in bark and foliage. The Amerindians called it *cauchuc*, the wood that weeps; the colonists continued the native custom of making syringes from its sap and renamed the tree. La Condamine, the French polymath who travelled down the river in 1736, sent a specimen to Paris. But for a century the West had no serious need of rubber.

The industrial revolution, and in particular Charles Goodyear's vulcanisation process which ensured rubber's constant consistency, changed all that. Rubber-producing trees grew elsewhere, but nowhere with the yield and quality of the *seringa* (*Hevea Brasiliensis*) which was native only to the Amazon. The patenting in 1880 of the rubber tyre gave a new boost to the West's increasing demand. The Amazon became a second Klondike and rubber its black gold. Thousands of adventurers, financed by commercial houses which in turn were backed by London and New York syndicates, descended on the river to stake out an estate. They had one overriding need: labour. Amerindians fled the harsh and unhealthy tapper's life. Boatloads of immigrants from Brazil's drought-ridden north-east, and from the upper reaches of the Peruvian Amazon, were brought in. They arrived indebted to the owner and remained in debt at his riverside store, the only source of supply, where they were charged exorbitant prices for the staples of life. As a final indignity, they could be sold to a new owner for the price of their debt.

In the nature of free enterprise it was, of course, those with capital who reaped the largest spoils. In frenzied emulation of their European peers, the new rubber barons were soon raising works to the glory of God, culture and capitalist progress in their jungle towns. Stained glass and tiles from France, Italian marble, building stone from Scotland, iron and steel from England transformed Manaus from its 'most wretched plight' into a city of palatial private mansions and public opulence. Electricity and telephones, trams, the world's largest floating dock, champagne at $50 a bottle and brothels by the score added to the lustre of civilisation. The crowning and almost mythical glory was the opera house; the most ironic, perhaps, the splendid Palace of Justice built across the street.

The Eldorado of the few became the Green Hell of the rest. For the Amerindians it soon became even worse. Hunted down to meet the insatiable labour demand, they were carted off into forced labour. The chance discovery of a concentration camp on the Putumayo river, set up by a Peruvian rubber baron's company which was quoted on the London exchange, forced the British Government to investigate. Roger Casement, who had exposed the Congo atrocities, was sent out in 1910 at the head of a commission of enquiry. His findings echo through the barbarities of a more recent past. Amerindian men, women and children were flogged to death for failing to bring in sufficient rubber, burnt alive or used as live targets by overseers who, to prolong their agony, sometimes cut off their arms and legs and left them to die. Children's brains were dashed out, young girls forced to become concubines, women publicly raped. Casement's report caused a fervour of indignation in Britain, but the major torturers escaped unpunished despite his attempts to bring them to justice.

In the same year, 1910, Amazonian rubber production reached a record 62,000 tons. The price was also a record 12/9d per pound. The barons of Manaus, Belém and Iquitos (where, in manifestation of the economic reality underlying the boom, the pound sterling was common currency) had made their fortunes on prices much lower. Looking to a future of unparalleled wealth, they saw no need to improve production methods or to plant trees. In their splendour they counted without the long-term designs of a greater power: British imperialism.

Thirty years earlier, under the auspices of Kew Gardens, Henry Wickham had shipped – smuggled, local legend still has it – 70,000 Brazilian rubber tree seeds to London. Only 2,000 germinated, but they were enough. By 1914 plantation production in Malaya and Ceylon exceeded that of wild rubber for the first time. The price slumped to 2/7d per pound. The lights went out in the jungle towns, the Manaus opera house closed its doors and Eldorado vanished into the green vastness once more. But the boom left an indelible mark, for many of the immigrant tappers, stranded by the crash, remained to eke out a living on the river's banks.

I asked the boatmen to stop. Obligingly, they ran us on to the high red bank. Above, there was a small settlement of palm-thatched huts lining two sides of a luxuriant 'green' on which grey, humped cows were grazing. We walked past the huts where women were pounding manioc (or cassava) and dehusking rice. Our sudden intrusion was received with a friendliness that encouraged us to stop. A woman, no doubt much younger than she appeared, explained the long process of making manioc flour. The plant's root contained a poisonous juice and to make it edible it had to be peeled, soaked for a time in water, pounded, put in a press, sifted and finally heated. 'It's a world of work, mister,' she said. Her maternal grandfather had been a tapper, a mestizo from the Upper Amazon whose wife had been Amerindian. Her father, of Spanish and Negro descent, had come to the Amazon from the Peruvian coast to seek his fortune as a *regatón* – an ambulant river vendor – and had failed.

I asked where the manioc she was pounding grew and she indicated tracks through the forest to a clearing half a mile away where her husband was to be found. He was squatting on his haunches, weeding between the leafy plants with a machete. Neither spade nor plough could be used, for the rain-forest soil tolerates no turning, he explained. Large, charred tree trunks lay on the clearing, which was near the end of its life.

'The soil is exhausted after two or three years and then we have to open a new clearing.' Sweat ran down his reddish-brown face. 'With a couple of hectares a man and his family can live.' He described the age-old rain-forest technique of opening a clearing: undergrowth and lianas have to be hacked down, the trees felled and everything set fire to when it has dried. The ashes fertilise the soil. 'On my own it'll take a month or more to clear a hectare (2.5 acres) . . .'

To reach his new plot he would have to travel by canoe downstream; there was little land left to clear round the small settlement. On sand-banks, which usually appeared during the low water season, he grew a cash crop of rice. Sometimes he grew maize and, on an island upriver which flooded, he had in the past grown jute. Now he preferred to keep a couple of cows on the green and sell the milk. He had no clear title to any of the land he cultivated. To supplement his family's basic diet of manioc flour, rice, beans and plantains, he had to hunt and fish. The latter he could do – sometimes using a spear – only when the river was low. But game nearby was becoming scarce and he spent up to a week away at a time in the forest to shoot deer and peccary, a species of wild pig. Life was much the same for any riverside dweller, he said, a bit better or worse but always precarious, determined by a river which was both provider and destroyer. In flood it spread silt from the Andes over the banks, fertilising the soil. But it also tore away the same banks, flooded crops before time and left the land usable for little more than six months of the year. The great bulk of the land received no benefit from the annual flood waters. This could be cultivated the year round, but the soil was so poor that, as we had seen, it had to be left to revert to forest after two or three years.

We returned to the settlement with him. On the 'green', youths were shooing the cows away in preparation for a football match. Local inhabitants had been joined by spectators who had paddled from isolated huts up and downriver. A match, said the man, was an occasion for getting together, exchanging news, having a drink. The blare of pop music suddenly broke from a battered transistor in a hut behind the goalpost. Indicating that we might have a drink there, the man led the way up the steps. Watching the soccer game, the sound of John Travolta blaring out from behind, bottles of Coca-Cola on the table in front, it was apparent that Western modes had not spared even these distant banks.

The man accompanied us to the waiting boat. For a moment he stood looking out over the water and the forest stretching to the horizon under the afternoon sky. The river was his only connection with the world. 'Can you clear up a doubt for me, mister?' he asked at last. 'Is it true that in Europe there is no land left for a man to move on to freely and cultivate?'

*T*he water lapped gently at the boat's prow. Its flow induced a sense, at first contradictory, of stillness in motion. It flowed through the mind, leading the imagination along its vast course to the ocean and continents beyond. And so, too, it seemed to flow through the lives of its river-bank people. Their calmness – apathy, some said – was immediately apparent; and so, too, their mobility. Farming, hunting, fishing by turns, opening new clearings every few years, seeing banks crumble and vanish under the flood, seeing new islands thrown up and old disappear, movement became a constant expectation of life.

'It's a frontier land where people move on a whim or because the river forces them to,' said a sociologist in Iquitos. He had given up the task of mapping the smaller settlements on the Upper Amazon because each time he returned most had vanished or been re-established in other locations. 'But they move also to settlements that provide schooling for their children, medical facilities and work opportunities. Those are their three priorities now . . .'

Late at night, the boat pulled in to Belén, the waterfront slum of Iquitos. All the while, the man's question had tantalised my Eurocentric imagination. How to envisage scale in any other terms than one's own? It was difficult, and to simplify I placed the Amazon on a more familiar map. With its source at Gibraltar the river's mouth was north of the Crimea. Its course traversed Portugal, Spain, France, Switzerland, Austria, Hungary, Romania and a large part of the Ukraine. Its longest tributary, the Madeira, rose in the Sahara, bisected the Mediterranean and joined the Amazon in Austria. The Rio Negro's source was a couple of hundred miles south-west of Land's End and it cut through France, southern Germany and Austria to its confluence with the main river.

Not everything could be transposed on to the map. Of the Amazon's eleven hundred tributaries with a combined length of fifty thousand miles – twice the earth's circumference at the equator – seventeen are over one thousand miles long. (An uncharted tributary twice the length of the Thames was discovered by satellite only a few years ago.) Ocean steamers can penetrate two thousand miles up the main river. And yet the fall over that distance, from Iquitos to the Atlantic, is only 300 feet – half the height of London's Post Office tower. As much water pours out of the Amazon in twenty-four hours as passes under Westminster Bridge in a year. The river's flow is five times that of the Zaire and more than twenty-five times that of the Nile in flood. It contributes one-fifth of all the river waters received into the world's oceans in a year and pours into the Atlantic over 2,500,000 tons of silt every day.

It is this suspended matter which gives the Amazon and many of its tributaries their muddy brown colour. But then, too, there are black and clear water rivers which rise in the geologically ancient and eroded mountains to the north and south and carry no silt.

Were it not that the Amazon lies on the equator, the extreme flatness of this one-time seabed would ensure that it was permanently flooded and uninhabitable. As the northern and southern tributaries, however, rise in different hemispheres with different rainy seasons, and the ones are in flood as the others are falling, the Amazon itself rises on average only thirty feet every year. Any extension of the rainy season in either hemisphere can cause serious and sometimes disastrous flooding.

Extending over 2,700,000 square miles, Amazonia comprises one-third of the world's forest area. A couple of acres can contain up to three thousand different species of vegetation, half of which may not be found in a similar area half a mile away. Fauna repeats the pattern of flora. Eight times as many species of fish have been caught in an Amazonian pond the size of a tennis court as exist in all the rivers of Europe. More species of insect, more species of birds inhabit the basin than in any other single area of the world. This tremendous biological diversity is explained by the forest's shrinking, during geological periods when rainfall decreased, into large but separate 'reserves' in which speciation could occur, and its subsequent regrowth under more favourable climatic conditions.

'We are the victims of a rationality which must *measure* everything for it to appear real.' The European-born priest gazed reflectively on the river where small craft moved like water beetles. Overhead, above the jumble of palm-thatched and tin roofs, vultures circled endlessly in the sky. The array of shacks raised high on stilts or battened to large tree trunks which will float riveted the attention. Pools of liquid mud covered the concreted street, fetid swamps crossed by occasional logs formed a pavement. Strewn with detritus and crossed by open sewers, the waterfront slum of Belén appeared a threatening tropical miasma. The priest laughed. 'Amazonians like to live near the water, it's their natural habitat. They want to wash and fish in the river, be able to move with ease . . .'

Port of entry for riverside produce, the slum is where the peasants come when they give up the struggle on the banks and try to establish a foothold in Iquitos. Early each morning boats and canoes laden with produce arrive and are fallen on by the Belén inhabitants, who buy and resell the produce. Amidst the bustle of people trying to earn a penny, no one affected surprise at seeing strangers. But beneath all the movement there was an extraordinary calm, the calm even of death: under a shack, among chickens and pigs, a corpse covered by a blue plastic bag lay in an open coffin on trestles awaiting a final resting place.

Across the river several rafts with thatched roofs were being rowed slowly by men at long oars. Quechua Indians, explained the priest, who were bringing their rice crop to market. They were nearing the end of their seven-day voyage. The priest's eyes were watching the rafts. Across their course, a square-stemmed boat with a flat roof headed for shore. Lining its side, life-jacketed tourists stood peering out, as though doomed to sink in the muddy waters.

He turned away. 'The same "progress" is beginning here. The rain forest is being

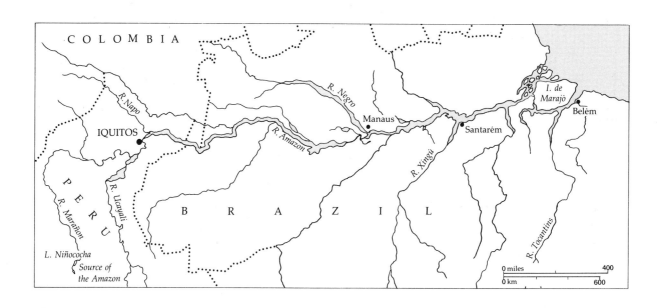

Captions for the following photographs:

1. This glacier, high in the Peruvian Andes, near Lake Niñococha, is the source of the world's mightiest river.
2. The confluence of the Marañon, which flows direct from Lake Niñococha, and the Ucayali, west of Iquitos. These are tributaries. The river hasn't even become the Amazon yet.
3. A pretty child at Belén, the waterfront slum of Iquitos.
4. Manaus in a tropical downpour. Here forty thousand workers make motor-bikes and TV sets in the midst of the rain forest.
5. The Manaus docks. The long-distance river boats sail at nightfall, after porters have loaded drinks, food and cargo.
6. The river is the region's main highway. With little else to do, boat passengers drowse through the heat of the day.
7. An assortment of the country boats that work passengers and freight up and down the river.
8. Fishermen at Santarém, a town of 100,000 with its own computer-processing company and satellite-tracking system.
9. A picture which reflects, sadly, the widespread burning of the rain forest to create space for cash crops.
10. One of the Amazon's countless tributaries; recently a tributary twice as long as the Thames was discovered by satellite.

6

7

opened to capitalist development. And still we have so much to learn from the Amerindians' long experience of living in harmony with the forest. They see beyond the frontiers of the immediately visible, have a direct and reciprocal relationship with nature, retain senses that have atrophied in the evolution of Western rationality . . .'

A nd now,' said the woman guide, pointing into the gloom, 'we go down into the Green Hell.' She slapped a fallen tree trunk with her machete in case of snakes. 'This is primary or virgin forest.'

A hush fell over the tourists, just a few of the thousands who visit the Amazon every year and whom we had joined on an excursion to 'the end of the world'. The sun vanished in an aquarium-like greenness. Tall, buttressed trunks reached up out of a green tangle of undergrowth to a tangle of green canopy overhead. Aerial roots hung in festoons and cords, lianas snaked up trunks in search of the sun. High up and almost invisible, bromiliads and orchids grew from the branches of trees. The silence was oppressive, broken only by tourists slapping at mosquitoes. 'D'you know which way we're heading?' asked an elderly American, sweating profusely. But there was no way of knowing in this sunless penumbra.

'There isn't much colour, it's just all green,' said an American woman. 'Uh-hu,' muttered another, 'it sure earned its name.' Their dejection was no more than a hangover from their frenzy a few hours before when, in barter for blowpipes, arrows and beads, they stripped themselves of watches and blouses at the tour's tame Indian village. Brandishing a blowpipe ten feet long at the guide, one of them cried: 'Look, I've got a real one!' 'Well, almost real,' came the answer.

Once upon a time, I reflected, Indians bartered their wealth for a few beads. But that was before the age of mass tourism. Now the beads hung from other necks.

Sensing despondency, the guide hastened to distract attention by pointing out mushrooms that cured diphtheria, earache and diarrhoea. The tourists reacted with indifference. Not so science, however, which is beginning to study the Amerindians' extensive natural pharmacopoeia, including fifteen different plants used as female oral contraceptives.

The expedition returned safe and thirsty from the Green Hell. Shortly their package tour would be returning them to the comfort of the Iquitos Holiday Inn. What brought them this far? 'Why, the Amazon – it's the unknown, the romantic. It's like you've crossed a frontier into . . .' he grappled for the right word, 'into, that's right, an alien world.'

I t was a world far less alien but even more strange which we descended upon a day or two later.

Light grey against the gathering storm cloud, the smoke curling up above the bluffs came not, as usual, from forest clearings but from factories turning out consumer goods. Like the phoenix, Manaus has risen from the ashes in an industrial and commercial blaze. Such an achievement is, of course, immediately quantifiable. Forty thousand workers in the midst of the rain forest assemble and produce colour TV sets, music centres, motor-bikes, watches and electric razors worth $2,000 million in 1979–80. Taking advantage of the thirty-year free port status the Brazilian military regime decreed in 1967, and of the minimum wage of $80 a month, Japanese and US multinationals have established plants here. In the past seven years, the city's population has more than doubled to 800,000. In this time it has become one of – if not the – largest South American centres of production for this type of consumer goods. Grand Swiss watches, a famous line of French lighters and pens, are assembled and exported to Europe.

Lying on hills overlooking the River Negro, a few miles from its confluence with the Amazon, the skyscraper city centre is a huge emporium of duty-free goods, some still stacked in packing cases, all promiscuously arrayed. Outboard motors nestle against sofas, vibrators are delicated poised on cameras, carpets hang on sale in hi-fi shops. Shelf-loads of decanters grotesquely shaped as knights' heads, outsize model cars and Pierre Cardin clothes – all awaiting the newly wealthy who jet in from southern Brazil to buy cheap in this jungle entrepôt.

No city of comparable size lies less than two hours' flying time away. 'It's an island in the jungle,' said a British bank manager resignedly. 'The edge of civilisation . . .' By road it is 3,000 miles to São Paulo in the south where all the major industrial decisions are taken. Metalled for only 500 miles out of Manaus, a large stretch of the highway beyond is impassable during the rainy season. 'Supermarkets and grocery stores have to lay in three months' supply to get through the winter.' It has become so large and sprawling that the very forest seems to have been concreted over. And yet, across the river's black waters, the low line of trees is clearly visible on the distant bank.

T he long-distance river boats left as night fell. An hour before, the low-water beach and the jetty, where a motley array of double-decked boats was moored, swarmed with people. Stripped to the waist, barefoot porters carried aboard crates of Coca-Cola, bags of cement, boxed TV sets and refrigerators, sacks of manioc flour. Passengers arrived and started to sling their hammocks of coloured cloth – segregated by sex – on either side of the two decks. Adding to the confusion, hawkers came round selling soft drinks, watches, fruit and even Indian beads. With a blast from its hooter a neighbouring boat set off. Under its lights the slung hammocks looked like brilliantly coloured bats hanging upside down.

It was a relief to feel the river's movement again. Flashes of rose-coloured lightning illuminated the black sky, and a soft breeze, which later turned fresh, rose from the water. Soon the deck lights were turned out and only the engine's throb and the sound of the water disturbed the silence.

Life began again with the dawn, with breakfast at a long table below the folded hammocks. The passengers patiently waited for the hard biscuits, yesterday's bread and plentiful coffee. With equal unhurriedness they waited to wash in the muddy Amazon water provided by a single tap in the men's and women's basin at the far end of the table. Close by, a large glass container produced a lighter coloured version of the same water for drinking.

In mid-morning, the passengers assembled quietly and good-naturedly at the table again for a game of bingo. The counters were corn kernels, the prize a chicken.

The creamy brown water flowed past the boat. Dolphins rose lazily now and again above the surface. The river was not so wide that the banks were invisible; or so it seemed until one of the banks was revealed as an island stretching for miles and the course we were following as no more than one of its channels. Mainland or island, the luxuriant monotony of the banks was broken only by isolated clearings, an occasional settlement and three or four towns. The unending sameness of the scenery underlined something I had found hard to believe in advance: the essential similarity, over so great an extent, of the riverine peasants' life. 'Along all the main rivers and many of the smaller tributaries, people eat the same food, wear similar clothing, live in the same kind of house and share the same beliefs and aspirations,' an American anthropologist, Betty J. Meggers, has written. It took the river itself to show how this could be so.

It was the end of summer, the beginning of winter, and soon the river would begin to flood. 'Often the water rises into the riverside huts,' said a local journalist who was travelling downstream with us. 'The floors are built to be raised, and inch by inch they are kept above water until, sometimes, only four or five feet are left between floor and roof.' He went on to describe a visit he had made to a hut nearly under water. The inhabitants had almost no headroom left. Tied to the iron legs of the charcoal-burning cooking stand he saw several lines running through the floor to the water beneath. He looked down. Securely hooked on the end of each line swam a fish which the occupiers pulled up to eat when the need arose.

'It's a life of misery and sacrifice,' put in a woman who was returning to a settlement downriver. Her peasant sons were on board and with them and I had been trying to calculate how much the family might earn from their cash crops of jute, water-melon and fishing. We had arrived at something like $700 a year. 'Well yes,' agreed the journalist when the woman had gone, 'they lead a very hard life.' But on the flood plain at least, which comprised only two per cent of the Amazonian basin, they could live better. All sorts of vegetables could be grown; but poverty, lack of education and ingrained habits prevented them from cultivating anything but traditional crops. 'And of course for a large part of the year their land is under water. Looking at the banks now you wouldn't believe it . . .'

The lights of Santarém came into view. The boat moored on a low-water beach next to a sewer, and a plank was thrown across. Porters came aboard and soon a bright red double-door refrigerator was being manhandled across, followed by a wardrobe many times larger and a stream of passengers carrying their luggage. The sand as we walked across was warm underfoot.

'A mazonia today is an internal colony of southern Brazil. São Paulo is our United States,' said the radio commentator privately in Santarém. 'The south takes our raw materials and sells us its finished goods, and Amazonia ends up the poorer.'

Timber, fish, Brazil nuts, jute, essence of rosewood – not so long ago exports were those that grew in river or rain forest. But now development has prospected new fields: huge cattle ranches, reserves of bauxite and iron ore which are among the world's largest, rich diamond and gold fields. Sixteen years ago, Amazonian per capita income was fifty-seven per cent of the Brazilian average; today it has dropped to thirty-seven per cent.

'Look at the contradictions of development. 17,000 kilometres of roads and only 15,000 kilometres of waterway in use. Here in Santarém, a town of 100,000, we have colour TV, a computer processing company, a telephone system which allows you to dial London direct, a satellite-tracking station, two cancer clinics *and* increasing poverty, illiteracy, unemployment and some of the worst shanty towns in Brazil.'

Such contradictions are not new. But what is particular to the Amazon is that capitalist development threatens to produce a large scale environmental disaster. Ten years ago, the military regime began to push roads, including the famous *Transamazônica*, through the forest. Their objective was to settle hundreds of thousands of land-hungry labourers from the north-east and to 'integrate' the Amazon into the national economy. The subsequent failure might have been foreseen if the ecology of the rain forest had been taken into account.

Flourishing on land that in a temperate climate would be barren, the rain forest lives more from the air, rain and itself than from the soil. The dense canopy captures and stores nutrients, while its heavy leaf fall provides humus for the shaded soil. When the vegetation is cut the impoverished soil is exposed to high temperatures, compaction and erosion. Very quickly every trace of fertility is removed and the land turns to desert. This the Amerindians and their peasant heirs have always known, and the hapless north-eastern immigrants were soon to discover. After a few years the soil was exhausted and most of them gave up the unequal struggle.

But the Brazilian economic 'miracle' was not to be denied. Eldorado might escape the labourer but not the large corporation or multinational. To the tune of $1,000 million over thirteen years, the government subsidised a new chimera: cattle ranching. In return for enormous tax concessions on their other operations, the corporations moved in. They made quick and large profits. But soon it became evident that the pastures on the huge ranches deteriorated after a few years, and that it was more profitable to convert new tracts of forests rather than rehabilitate the old pasture.

In the course of 'developing' the Brazilian Amazon, 30,000 square miles of forest – an area nearly two-thirds the size of England – had been burnt to the ground by 1978. Overall, this represents only 1.5 per cent of the Amazonian forest; but it has been concentrated in certain areas where up to twenty-five per cent of the forest has been destroyed. And each year the rate of destruction intensifies. Vast amounts of valuable timber, unknown numbers of species of flora and fauna are irretrievably lost. Scientists have made dire predictions about the effects on the earth's climate if the massive destruction continues. Some of these, like the drastic reduction in the world's oxygen supply, have been misinterpreted; others, like the increase in the atmosphere's carbon dioxide content and the attendant increase in the earth's temperature (with the accompanying threat of melting the polar caps and causing sea levels to rise), are still being debated. But one thing is certain: if the forest is burnt to the ground, a desert the length of Europe will take its place.

*T*he breeze from the Atlantic 500 miles away was fresh and the muddy river choppy. Over the wide reaches downstream from Santarém the vermilion sun was rising rapidly. To the west, pale in a lilac sky, the full moon was descending towards the horizon.

With equinoctial regularity Eldorado has been discovered and lost on these forested banks. Alone of all species, mankind records history, and has the capacity to learn from the past. Will it?

THE NILE

NORMAN LEWIS

*T*he people who should know differ strangely as to which is the longest river. The *Times Atlas* casts its vote in favour of the Amazon, the *Encyclopedia Britannica* says the Nile, while the *Guinness Book of Records* cannot make up its mind. Whichever the winner in this photo finish, one thing is certain: the importance of the Amazon in the human scheme is slight, that of the Nile huge. The one, majestic and aloof, has no history, enriches no land, supports only a handful of fishermen. The other is currently responsible for the existence of fifty million people, and even in the time of the pharaohs may have supported a population half that size, which, ruling out China, would probably have exceeded the number of inhabitants of the rest of the globe.

The Nile brought glittering civilisations into being, wholly dependent upon the annual bounty of its floods, and a single year's withholding of its waters from the parched lands awaiting them would have been enough to obliterate an empire. 'Egypt,' said Herodotus, 'is the gift of the Nile.' And not only Egypt but that 3,000-mile-long ribbon of fertility which uncoils through the deserts of the Sudan, where local wars of extermination have been fought when an occasional drop of a few inches in water levels meant that there was not enough food for all.

Khartoum, capital of the Sudan, seemed a likely starting-off place for explorations of the Upper Nile. It turned out to be a somewhat caved-in town with an embalmed colonial flavour, an occasional leper in sight, isolated grand hotels, and a Sudan Club where the many British expatriates that remain appeared to spend much of their lives. The Chinese had built a sumptuous Friendship Hall and glutted the town with Double Happiness matches – now serving as small change – while the Japanese kept the broken streets filled with yellow Toyota taxis. A thousand elephants had died to stock main-street shops with banal ornaments carved from their tusks, and the skins of such endangered animals as leopards, cheetahs and crocodiles were on offer at bargain prices.

I stayed at a new hotel in the centre where the novelty and the charm of the Orient fully compensated for faltering Western technology. A little Arabic, not well-learnt so many years ago, had been resuscitated for the occasion, and this permitted a proper exchange of courtesies with spotlessly robed fellow guests queuing for the lift. 'Peace on you.' 'And on you peace and the blessings of God.' 'They say today that if you wish to reach floor three you must press button six.' 'Let us do that. *Inshallah* we shall arrive.' '*Inshallah*.'

The doorman swept off his hat in the way Sudanese servants probably did thirty years ago. Fifty yards from where he stood smiling and bowing, a beggar advertised his plight by a strong-voiced cry, 'God is merciful,' repeated with unflagging conviction every ten seconds throughout the daylight hours. According to a printed warning it was as strictly forbidden to photograph him, or any other 'debasing sight', as it was a power station, a military establishment, or a bridge.

Down on the waterfront the scene was a lively one. Khartoum is built at the confluence of the Blue and White Niles, the first gathering its waters in the Ethiopian Plateau; the most distant source of the second being the Kagera river in Burundi, some 1,500 miles to the south. It came as a surprise to find that one river is actually blue, and the other, if not quite white, at least a palish green. It is regarded by many visitors as an emotional experience to discover a spot on one of the sand-banks where this separation of colours is clearly visible, enabling the pilgrim to stand with one foot in each river.

Hotels and government buildings impose a stolid conformity along the city waterfront – one could be anywhere – but at Abu Rof, just outside the town limits, the Nile comes into its own, and could almost be mistaken for the Ganges. Here people strip off to wash down, having pushed their way down to the water through the herds of cows and goats that are brought to drink. Here, taxi drivers back their shattered Toyotas into the shallows to sponge off the dust, and here – inevitably – the donkey-drawn municipal water-carts are brought to be filled. This is a playground to which men bred in deserts are attracted by the mere presence of water. They sit here in rows in barbers' chairs to have their heads shaved, and before the lathering begins the barber adjusts the mirror to enable his customer to enjoy the reflected scene of all that is happening down by the river at his back.

Abu Rof fosters the intense sociability of lives lived outside in what is for the most part of the year a good climate. Neighbours carry out their beds to sleep on the beach, which is furnished like a communal room with domestic objects, chairs, the occasional sofa, a kitchen stove, most of them softened in outline by pigeons' droppings. The villagers swap tall stories, pray a little, brew up tea, and polish each other's shoes, and turbanned and immensely dignified men gather in clear spots among the domestic litter for a game of marbles.

The backdrop to this amiable scene is the brown ramparts thrown up by the Khalifa and held with hopeless courage for an hour or two against the cannon fire of Kitchener's expedition sent to avenge the death of Gordon and to recover the Sudan. Kitchener's gun-boat, the *Melik*, with its paper-thin armour and single three-inch gun, is still tied up a mile or so upstream. Sheikh Hamid el Nil's cemetery, and the tomb of this holy man, whose name implies his mystic involvement with the river, is a short taxi-ride away. It has become the centre of a dervish cult, hardly more than tolerated by Islamic orthodoxy, which views gymnastic devotions with the same uneasiness a practising Anglican might feel in the presence of Holy Rollers at worship. I drove out on Friday evening, when all Khartoum relaxes, to see the dervishes whirl. About 100 of them had marched in under their flags and were engaged in a preliminary workout. The drums crashed, and the dervishes began to jerk and twitch.

There was nothing exclusive about the occasion. Any bystander could join in, and many did. A hard core of devotees whirled in professional style, but the onlooker caught up in the spirit of the thing was free to improvise. The drums imposed their own tremendous rhythmic discipline, but within this framework anything went. One pranced about, leapt, galloped, whirled until eliminated by vertigo, howled, shrieked, frothed at the mouth if possible, while the dervishes cracked their whips and lashed out with their canes. It was to be enjoyed by all; all good, therapeutic mania, like a *Come Dancing* session with ten marks out of ten for contestants who could throw a trance or work themselves up into a fit. My driver, who had been standing by his taxi, soon began to suffer minor convulsions and, after grabbing at the steering wheel through the window in an effort to hold himself back, suddenly tore loose, picked up a stick, and went bounding away. A few minutes later he appeared again, exhausted and reeling, but spiritually renewed. 'If you believe in God, sir,' he said, 'why do you not join us?' It was an experience he thought I ought not to miss.

I had no objection when he suggested a visit to the nearby tomb of the Mahdi, liberator of the Sudan from Gordon and the 'Turks'. It proved to be a garish edifice of recent construction, reminding one of a space-ship on its launching pad. Kitchener destroyed the original tomb. He had the Mahdi's body dug up and went off with the head with the intention of turning it into a drinking cup, deterred only from doing this by Queen Victoria's startled outcry. Winston Churchill refers with distaste to this incident in 'The River War'. He speaks of the Madhi's 'unruffled smile, pleasant manners, generosity, and equable temperament'. 'To many prisoners he showed kindness . . . to all he spoke with dignity and patience.' His limbs and trunk were flung into the Nile. 'Such,' says Churchill, 'was the chivalry of the conquerors.'

The driver obtained my admission into the enclosure from which non-Muslims are normally excluded, on the promise that I would join him in a prayer, and I duly stood with him and did my best to recite the words of the Arabic formula.

The Nile is rarely easy to approach. In the Sudan river steamers only operate for about a quarter of its length, and roads following the valley are usually out of sight of the water. I had arrived with an introduction to the owner of a motorised felucca, but he had gone out of business, and the only man prepared to offer long-distance transport was a Mexican white hunter who offered twenty-five days' hunting for £15,000. He mentioned as an inducement that on a recent expedition a client had had the good luck to shoot a bongo, an exceptionally rare species of antelope, only to be taken in the Sudan.

It would have been nice to go to Juba, capital of the deep south, to visit at least the fringe of the extraordinary papyrus swamp known as the Sudd, and stay in Juba's hotel where colonial nostalgia is so acutely felt that friends who had been there were prepared to guarantee that Brown Windsor soup was served with every meal. There were severe impediments to this project. In the Sudan communications are coming close to total breakdown, and this vast African country offers a foretaste of the likely predicament of the Third World when, in the end, petrol ceases to flow.

The beautiful lady in the tourist office broke the news to me that such were the fuel shortages that the plane to Juba could be held up there for as long as a week, or, at worst, a month. Shortages of this order might delay, once I got there, the proposed return by river boat,

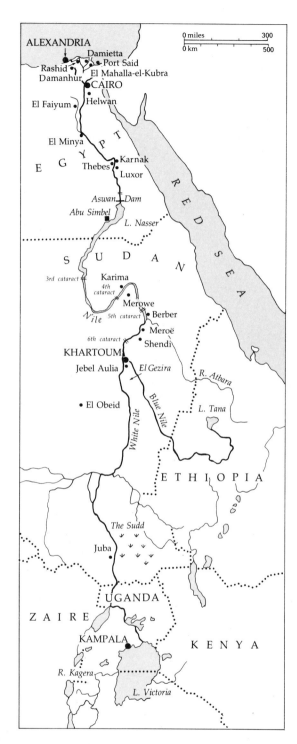

Captions for the following photographs:

1. Feluccas moored near Minya, accepted as the capital of Middle Egypt. Here on the Nile, the river of Victorian watercolour painters, nothing has changed for a century.
2. Feluccas, perhaps the world's most graceful river craft, under sail.
3. The desert begins only yards from the river's fertile banks.
4. A ferry completes its crossing in the Delta.
5. At El Faiyum the river is still tapped by a system of ancient water-wheels.
6. Delta fishermen set off through the reeds at dawn.
7. In the Delta child labour is commonplace. Work starts at 7 a.m. each morning; each receives 20p a day.
8. A felucca loading grain at Minya.
9. Sudanese tribesmen on the road to Khartoum. One appears to be transporting a small office safe.
10. A selection of the 200 ancient pyramids on the site of the ancient Nilotic kingdom of Meroë. The tops were dismantled by an early Egyptian military expedition seeking gold.

9

10

and it was hard to come by precise information as to what was happening in the south because the telephone lines were out of order.

Every world traveller will assure you that the Sudanese are the nicest people you are ever likely to meet, and I was beginning to agree. It was Saturday morning and there seemed to be a faint whiff about the place of the aphrodisiac smoke of acacia wood burnt in certain rituals on Friday nights. Young ladies in flowered chiffon saris came and went, smiling and giggling, shaking hands and touching their hearts, while the lady in charge of the office broke her depressing news. 'You could go by car,' she suggested, 'but you may have to queue eight hours for petrol.' She added that the car would cost £125 a day, mentioning that the journey to Juba occupied at least five days in each direction, and that 250 gallons of petrol would have to be carried. It was a moment, if ever there was one, to seek refuge in the art of the possible.

I ran to earth the only man in Khartoum with a Land-Rover for hire; he found enough petrol to fill his tank and for two spare cans, and we set off with the object of travelling as far south as this meagre ration would allow. An asphalt road took us to Jebel Aulia, where we crossed the dam built in 1934, which was covered as if by graffiti by the great names of British engineering of those far-off colonial times. Here fishermen, casting their nets under a screen of herons and fishing eagles, were taking Nile perch from the water. These they bartered with the villagers for such things as firewood and eggs. Beyond Aulia the road, marked as confidently as ever on the map, turned into a tangle of interlacing tyre tracks in a near-desert. Its surface was as flat and hard as a cricket pitch and once in a while we drove into a drab village, overtopped by a chocolate and green minaret, with the mirage lying like stagnant water, and creeping back as we charged up the streets. Such villages, just beyond reach of the Nile floods, were so poor that even the vultures had given them up. Nothing, absolutely nothing, was ever thrown away. The rains came in autumn, the villagers grew a single crop of sorghum, and after that their lives teetered on the edge of survival for the nine months to the next rains.

When we stopped for a midday snack a chance remark by the driver put the whole predicament of the underfed four-fifths of the world population in stunning perspective. Schooled in the proprieties of the well-nourished fifth, I made a move to gather up our litter. He was horrified. 'Leave everything,' he said. 'The goats will deal with the orange skins, even the paper, and the Arabs will turn the beer-cans into cups. Come back here in an hour, and you won't see a trace of anything.' Since the vultures had lost hope and gone away, animals that had died from natural causes lay scattered about these villages quite intact, but mummified by the sun.

We turned away to the east, passing without warning across the frontier between arid savannah and the brilliant fertility of the nearly two million acres of the Gezira, the great garden of the Sudan filling the triangle south of Khartoum between the Blue and White Niles. A glum prospect of mud huts afloat in the mirage still showed through the rear window, but ahead was a soft bedazzlement of green fields moated with running water, and sparked with the refulgence of brilliant birds; great wading storks in absurd postures, ten kinds of kingfisher, green cuckoos and crimson bee-eaters, insect hunting from the telegraph poles where they perched in their hundreds. The Nile valley, throughout the length of its passage through the arid lands, is the paradise of birds, drawn to its water and the teeming insect life of its marshes and its saturated earth.

It was intended back in the 1920s that the Gezira project should provide cheap cotton for the Lancashire mills, but each year less cotton is grown for export and more food for home consumption, although the Gezira still provides most of the national income. It is not quite the success story it was, and production in most sectors is in decline. The management of water on this scale is a complex affair and technological breakdowns are compounded by a brain-drain to the affluent Gulf States. Water levels are maintained by specialists at pumping stations and irrigation regulators, who are required to be in constant touch with one another through the telephone network. This has begun to break down, so that canals frequently overflow and land is damaged by excessive flooding.

It is said, too, the canals are no longer kept as free as they should be from weeds. This not only reduces the efficiency of irrigation, but has provoked a marked increase in the incidence of bilharzia. I was told that eighty per cent of Gezira children before the age of ten now suffer from the disease, and the anaemia and chronic diarrhoea it entails. The shells of the snail that acts as host to the parasite in an intermediate stage of its development were to be seen everywhere in the mud excavated from water-courses.

A quick forage round the market was to produce enough fuel, a gallon here, a gallon there, for a two days' trip to the north, and our first stop was at the sixth cataract of the Nile, where the river slips between burnished coppery hills and a miniature gorge. The description cataract over-dramatises a fall in the water, rippling over pink stones hardly more than a few feet high; but here the boats taking part in Kitchener's river war had to be dismantled once again to be reassembled only a few yards further on (nuts and bolts had sensibly replaced rivets in their construction), and there is a local legend that here they were bombarded by Mahdists who remained miraculously immune from the Maxim guns by reinforcing the chainmail they wore with pages from the Koran.

*T*here were wide, tranquil waters above the babble of the cataract, with palms, beanfields and birds and butterflies galore, and little girls were tugging goats by the ear, one by one, down to the water and actually persuading them to drink. Here I ran into the corruption spread by tourism even in this remote place. A year or more back, before petrol shortages had closed them down, an agency had been accustomed to send parties of trippers to this enchanted spot, and a local peasant, under the pretence that he owned the land, had levied a toll on access to the river. Watching from his lookout he spotted the Land-Rover's approach and hurried to lay branches across the path, charging £1 per head before he would remove them. It was the first and the last time that I heard the hateful word *baksheesh* in the Sudan.

The track leading to the north followed the railway line and in the space of an hour we passed the wreckage of two derailed trains. They had become a centre of local pilgrimage, and while we were examining the second train several goat-herds came into sight from behind the rocks to make a cautious, tiptoe approach as if for fear of disturbing a sleeping, but potentially dangerous animal. One of them picked up a stone and threw it at a mangled tanker-truck, and the sound of the stone striking metal was shrill and bleak in the dry air. They came up and shook hands with us repeatedly, delighted at the relief from the terrific monotony of their lives offered by the wrecked train and the sight of fresh faces.

In this vicinity, at the approach to the important river junction at Shendi, we found ourselves among 100-feet-high mounds of immense ironstone boulders, heaped together in such a way that it was hard at first to accept that they had not been built by human hands. Scattered over the sand the shapes resembled squat armless Venuses, 100 tons of sand-polished sculpture by Henry Moore, sand-logged dinosaurs, black iron shards, and meteorites.

Shendi, at one of the old crossroads of Africa, had always lived off the river traffic and the caravan routes crossing the Nile at this point. It had been an emporium of ivory and slaves, particularly the slave-girls brought down from Abyssinia, those highly valued harem items whose jet-black skin was – as an early writer put it – as cool to the touch as a toad, mentioning that a toad was sometimes kept on hand to enable the would-be purchaser to convince himself of the truth of the claim. Shendi had fallen into a decline highlighted by the loss of one of its ferries. It had been out of action for a year, although the spare parts necessary to get it going again had been delivered some months before, remaining in their crates by the river bank where they had been dumped from a lorry, and probably forgotten. Here a pull-in for market traffic offered the huge and expensive luxury of Pepsi-Cola, English cigarettes (high-tar content for the Third World), a packet of which cost an average Sudanese worker a day's wages, and hardboiled eggs by way of a snack. Children were waiting to seize upon and suck the discarded shells.

A hard day's drive brought us by evening to the site of the ancient Nilotic kingdom of Meroë where we camped for the night among the low pyramids – there are about two hundred in all, clustered in groups over the low hills. They remain so well preserved, so clean-cut in their outlines that a few of them could be mistaken for follies built here by some Sudanese Victorian eccentric. The obvious clue to their antiquity lies in the fact that so many have lost their tops, dismantled in search of treasure by an early Egyptian military expedition tricked by an impostor into coming here in search of gold.

Throughout most of its course through the Sudan the Nile is surprisingly difficult to reach behind the green mosaic of its gardens and its innumerable irrigation ditches. All this invaluable land has remained in the same families for many generations, producing a precisely calculable return and a sufficiency of food for all, based on a stable equation of birth and death. Antibiotics have destroyed this equilibrium. Until now epidemic sickness has carried off most of the children of the Third World in the first year of their lives. Now they survive to compete with each other for food supplies that have reached their limits. Up to four crops a year are raised at Meroë, but there is no way of coaxing more food from the soil, and even the volume of water supplied by the Nile has come close to its limits. Too many heirs divide the family plots into smaller and smaller segments, and too many peasants are already struggling to survive on the produce of a rectangle of land the size of a suburban front garden. Malaria, typhoid and hepatitis have been almost eliminated, but only at the expense of strengthening the hand of starvation.

There seems to be no remedy in sight for this situation, which is allied to another long-term threat in the Sudan – that of desertification. There are more mouths to be fed everywhere, not only in the Nile valley itself but in the vast arid areas of semi-desert that border it. A few years back the greatest drought of this century coincided with the quadrupling of world petrol prices. The annual grasses failed to come up because there were no rains, and the herdsmen, impoverished by the loss of their stock, and no longer able to buy kerosene, began to cut down the last of the trees. No one is more keenly aware of the function fulfilled by the trees than the desert nomad, but he was up against the wall. The acacias and the desert apples were turned into firewood, and the desert was on the move again.

The first symptoms of this creeping sickness of the earth were to be seen at Meroë, where sands were blowing into the green fields by the river, and one saw lorries stuck in sand-drifts where only two or three years back there had been a surface as hard as concrete. A few weeks before, my driver had made the trip up to the north, passing a spot between Karima and the Egyptian frontier. Last time he had been in the vicinity there had been a grove of date palms there, with a bit of a garden producing a few cucumbers, with a well and a donkey turning a water-wheel. Of this nothing remained but a few palm fronds sprouting like feather dusters from the top of the dunes.

I flew to Cairo, passing over the Aswan High Dam and the 300-mile-long lake it has created. Lake Nasser came as a surprise. The mind's eye had presented an immense version of a Highland reservoir, and I was unprepared for this great sprawl of water, for its headlands, capes, its inlets and creeks by the hundred – even its fiords – all of them alien and out of place in this dry and incandescent land. Egyptians will say of this much-advertised solution to all their problems that it has turned out to be a mixed blessing, and there is an undertone among them of murmurings and doubts. A typical Third World thirst for industrialisation, cost what it may, has been satisfied by the dam and the electricity it has generated, and it would be unfair to suggest that many of the factories brought into being have been as disappointing as the one that produced so many millions of headless pins. The question is whether in the long term Egypt's capability as the most lavishly endowed of all agricultural countries may have been placed at risk.

The natural rhythms based for thousands of years on the annual flooding of the river and the soil's renewal by the silt deposited by the floods have been disrupted by the dam. Artificial fertilisers, expensively produced, will be required as a substitute for the silt, but the perennial irrigation – which replaces the annual flooding, and drying off – has entailed problems of drainage which can only be solved by an expensive system of deep drains, which Egypt cannot afford. In the absence of drainage the build-up of salt carried in the river water will lead to a decline in the soil's fertility. It has recently been discovered that the loss of silt has accelerated the river's flow, eroding the banks and threatening to undermine the bridges.

The peasant shakes his head cannily, and the fisherman wrings his hands. This year the cauliflowers were smaller, and this year fewer fish are being taken. The fisherman blames his poor catches on a change in the water and claims, too, that many fish that once came down from the upper reaches of the river are now held back by the dam. He is probably right. What advanced technology provides with one hand, it may be taking back with the other.

It was remarkable to find the river at Cairo, rather more than 100 miles from the sea, not noticeably wider than it had been at Khartoum, 2,000 miles closer to its source. The dry season had laid bare a wide border of mud, and this had been invaded by colonists who had staked out gardens, while slime-covered figures down by the water's edge were filling buckets with precious mud, to be carried away.

*   *   *

I n Cairo one was trapped in the noise, the convulsive despairing crowds, the entangled traffic of an urban population of nearly eight million imprisoned in a city designed to house a third of that number. Virtually nothing but luxury flats has been built since Nasser's reforms drove the speculators out of land into property. High-rise blocks, Centre Point-style, have gone up by the hundred, many of them left empty, although frequently changing hands at ever-increasing prices. A million of the homeless of Cairo now squat in its great cemetery where they share the tombs with the dead. The traffic follows no rules other than those of total war, and as the Islamic faith fosters a belief that one's destiny cannot be avoided, crashes are frequent and spectacular. Because most garages, lacking the space to house them, decline to recover crashed vehicles, they are normally shoved off the road and abandoned.

Egyptians tackle all their problems with ingenuity and resource. I saw a Volkswagen crushed absolutely flat used to plug a hole in the wall of a department store. Larger wrecks had been expanded by the use of hardboard, and taken over by homeless families. When fatal crashes happened, the bodies were sometimes, if space allowed, pushed under the car, reverently covered with flowering branches, and left for the arrival of the police – which might be long delayed.

Those who wish to escape the bustle and the clamour of the capital are recommended by an official guidebook to make a move, as soon as they have seen all the sights, to Helwan, eighteen miles away on the banks of the Nile, described in *Tourist Information Egypt* as 'this city of sunshine, health and beauty . . . always noted for its marvellous dry climate, and for its mineral waters . . . one of the famous health resorts of the world.'

A leading article in the *Egyptian Gazette*, dated 11 February 1981, brought the record up to date:

'Unauthorised property development is continuing unabated in Helwan. The value of government land appropriated by private property speculators there is estimated at £500,000. With impunity they bring in the bulldozers, level down whatever lies in their way, and arrange their bricks and mortar with such panache that unless you know, you would never guess that the whole operation was a flagrant breach of the law. With alacrity the more brazen among them put up fences and signs warning trespassers, and then sell off further tracts of land to a second generation of speculators.

'One individual who seized the hill situated by the continuation of Riyadh Street built an attractive villa at the top and planted an attractive garden. Water and electricity were laid on, rubble and rubbish were discreetly dumped on the other side of the hill. He then started selling off the rest of this well-situated piece of land. He is now abroad, but assures everyone that he is now rich enough to buy and bribe his way through any legal proceedings that may be put in his path.'

The writer then went on to speak of the pall of smoke lying over the town, discharged by the string of factories that had been built along the river. I went there and was reminded of my experience of the eruption of Vesuvius back in the 1940s. People who had come to Helwan for the sake of their health were groping their way about with handkerchiefs held over their mouths, leaving their footprints in the grey fall-out that covered the promenade and extinguished the flowers in the celebrated gardens. The view of the Nile might have been through a dirty curtain. The remedy, said the *Gazette*, was to compel factories to pay their corporation tax 'and to fit chimneys on the equipment which is polluting a district once famous for its balmy perfumes of jasmine, date and guava trees'. It seemed to doubt that much would be done about it.

Upmarket package tour operators switch their attentions to Egypt in winter. The news was of all the hotels of Luxor and Aswan chock-a-block, of the Valley of the Kings glutted with multitudes, of fashion models being photographed on the knee of every god at Karnak, of *Son et Lumière* and of belly-dancing, barbecues and even sangria at Abu Simbel.

Minya, accepted as the capital of Middle Egypt, where there are antiquities enough to be visited, is no longer in fashion, and I went there, staying at the old Savoy. The hotel is full of sepia photographs and nostalgia, and possesses a new dining-room ceiling pierced with 830 illuminated holes, representing stars, which has so far not quite succeeded in drumming up new business. There was pigeon in saffron rice on the lunch menu, followed by a majestic sweet called 'eat it and thank God', but the peace of the surroundings was disturbed by an upper-class Egyptian woman who grumbled loudly at the absence of a buffet. A waiter quietened her with a mish-mash of the negatives pervading a language which insistently tempers deprivation with hope. *Ma'aindish* (I have none), *ma-fish* (It's off), *khallas* (finished), *bukra inshallah* (tomorrow, God willing).

No town by the water in the good old days was conceivable without its half-mile of promenade, and Minya had this to offer, although the parapet dividing it from the river was now used to dry washing, many of the garments on display being colourful in the extreme, some extraordinary. Across the water a vast cemetery extended for miles, with thousands of tombs, some dating back 4,000 years. I arrived at the moment when the males of a funeral party were about to embark for the further shore. Local custom excludes women from the final scene of the human drama, and they were left to screech and tear at their garments.

The Nile here, and in all the other towns forgotten by winter visitors, was the river of the Victorian painter in watercolours. There was nothing in the scene that would not have been witnessed 100 years ago; girls in garnet velvet robes carrying watercress on their heads, the low horizon of palms scythed by sharp, white felucca sails, a buffalo with a heron picking at its ear, fishing boats painted with holy tombs, trees of wisdom and crescent moons, a child playing on pan-pipes to advertise the huge eel he had for sale, curling like a python from his wrist. For those who crave peace it was here.

The pyramids start at El Faiyum. Few of these southern pyramids are visited by tourists, although they are remarkable enough, in particular the steep, white fortress shape of El Maidum. El Faiyum uses an ancient system to raise its water from the Nile and the town is full of the unearthly sound of water-wheels grinding on their wooden bearings, resembling only the underwater song of whales. The oasis contains a shallow lake, twenty-five miles in length, which entices wading birds to leave the safety of the river, and here they fall to cohorts of Italian sportsmen in ambush.

A party of thirty Romans – most of them fantastically uniformed for the sport – had just come in for their midday meal at the Panorama Hotel when I was there. The morning had been a good one. The Italians, having brought provisions including spaghetti, cheese and even spring onions from Rome, did not eat the birds they shot, but sold them to an Egyptian dealer, who killed any that were still alive before thrusting them into a sack. One of the sportsmen told me he had shot about 100 *anitre* that morning, but his ducks turned out to be sandpipers, avocets, phalaropes and ruffs – many of them of great rarity by our standards. He had bagged quite a few small birds such as wagtails, too, but these the dealer discarded contemptuously, flinging them into the water. The total bag for the morning weighed seventy kilos, totalling possibly 1,000 birds, and the group expected to shoot as many again when they went out in the early evening. It was the best place they knew of its kind anywhere in the world, but they thought it was too much to expect things to go on much longer like this. Three or four years, at most.

N orth of Cairo the Nile divides into two channels, one reaching the sea at Rashid, near Alexandria, and the other at Damietta, about forty miles from Port Said. From these two main courses spreads the vast fan of the Delta, the greatest vegetable garden on earth, which is in its way a secret place, hardly visited by anyone without business there, ignored by the tourist.

The Delta is beautiful in all its parts. A soft light, sharpened with a little sand, billows over the fields and haloes the peasants at work with their buffaloes. The canals breed their own mists, and there are naked boys everywhere stalking moorhens with their nets, and delving for catfish in the mud. Ninety per cent of these children suffer from bilharzia.

For much of the estimated forty million years of its life, the Nile has been depositing silt in the Delta. This jet-black, crumbling, crystalline, almost vivacious substance bears no resemblance whatever to the grudging soil tilled by the English gardener. It grows all the familiar vegetables in sizes that are so monstrous that a good Delta cabbage has to be picked up in both arms, and one can see a man bent under the burden of an enormous cauliflower carried on his shoulders. Methods of cultivation remain primitive in the extreme, but they are totally effective given a bottomless reservoir of cheap labour. I covered 500 miles of Delta roads without seeing a plough in action. The earth was being chopped and patterned everywhere, by peasants using the adze, which, say the landlords, is 'kinder on the soil'. Water is shifted daily, by the thousand million gallons, from river to canal and canal to ditch, but there are 100 water-wheels turned by a donkey for every pump. These are supplemented by gangs of freelances who scamper from property to property shouldering the device known as the Archimedean screw, used to move small quantities of water. The severe time and motion principles of antiquity prevail here. No one in the Delta falls asleep, Mexican-style, with his hat over his face.

Arrangements are feudal, even by comparison with, say, some of the less-developed rural areas of Latin America. Outside Damanhur, near Alexandria, a gang of men were waist-deep in stinking water, cleaning the sludge from a canal with their hands. They were working at great speed, urged on by two overseers on the bank above, and when one of the men began to show signs of fatigue, and began a blubbering protest, an overseer picked up a large stone, threw it, and hit him in the chest. The man began to scream, came charging up the bank, and grabbed up an adze in a threatening manner, but was soon overpowered. For his insubordination he was told that a quarter would be deducted from his day's wage, the equivalent of £1.60. 'If you want to eat, you must work,' the overseer said. He was quite happy to discuss this incident, and labour relations in general, with an utter stranger. Unemployment was very high, he said, and his firm were able to pick and choose when it came to employing labour. They would only use men prepared to drive themselves hard. When asked why dredging equipment was not used, he said the high cost of fuel made it uneconomic. For the price of a gallon of petrol a man would do more than the machine.

There was no shame, no concealment, about such transactions, no desire to avoid publicity. They were the facts of life in the Delta, recognised and accepted, likely to have drawn only a foreigner's attention and comment. The overseers were not psychopaths but ordinary men doing a regular, respectable, no less well thought-of job than, say, greasing cars. A half hour later I saw a gang of young children, guarded by a man with a switch, who were engaged in clearing stubble from a field. The man was delighted to stop for a chat. He was benign-looking and genial. We wished each other peace and the mercies of God, shaking hands and touching our hearts. He told me that the youngest of the children was about eight, and they were paid the equivalent of 20p a day, starting work at 7 a.m. 'I love them all,' he said, lashing out playfully at a nearby slacker. He prided himself on knowing how to get the best out of children. 'Encourage them,' he said. 'Kid them along, praise them when they do well.' He held up the switch and shook his head disapprovingly. 'I really hate to have to tickle their hides.'

The Delta population doubles every few years. Everyone has heard of the Pill, but despite the urgings of the government it is rejected by the very poor. Children here, just as in the slums of Naples, are a source of income, and as they undercut the price of adult labour they can find employment however short work may be. The driver lost his way in the labyrinth of mean streets of Mahalla el Kubra, and we were instantly adopted and taken into the confidence of an assortment of males sucking at their hookahs outside a café. One of our new friends provided facts and figures. He himself, he said, seemed to spend most of his life out of work, but his two daughters in their late teens had jobs in the brickyards of El Rashid, where they were paid £1 each a day. Three of the younger children, ranging from five to twelve, did odd jobs in the rope factory. Nothing too strenuous, he said, and it kept them out of mischief, and brought in another 80p. His wife's contribution raised the family income to a level which at least filled all their stomachs. She did the daily shopping for a rich woman, who was so fat, he said, that she could not stand up, only kneel, and even then she had to be supported.

Fat women in these small Nile-side towns were everywhere to be seen, and a man had just come into sight manoeuvring his enormous wife, like a piece of stately furniture, into a position where she could be propped against a wall across the road and left. He came over and introduced himself in English as a high-pressure welder, producing a sheaf of testimonials given him by companies he had worked for in Britain and West Germany. His wife had been joined by several elephantine friends, dressed like Madonnas of the Florentine school in black biblical robes. They wore patent-leather shoes with gold buckles, and small girls in attendance, squatting as necessary to wipe flecks of mud from their sparkling footwear, completed the feudal picture.

It was a scene without appeal for the welder, on a month's leave from Hamburg. The hookah, pulled from a neighbouring mouth, was thrust between my teeth, while he plied me with all the questions indispensable to the protocol of such meetings, and exposed the secrets of his own unsatisfactory life in Mahalla. 'What is your affliction [work], sir? Don't talk about daughters, but how many sons have you? How is King George? I love Miss England. The ignorant woman over there is my wife. She eats every day one kilo of nuts, and on Friday four pigeons.'

A t El Rashid – once Rosetta, where they dug up the famous stone by which ancient Egyptian hieroglyphics were deciphered – the mouth of the river was finally reached. Cold Mediterranean rain was spattering on the yellow water and in the muddy streets, but it did nothing to damp down the animation of an intensely oriental setting. Perhaps there is something in the story that the gypsies passed through Egypt on their way to Europe, for the streets were full of objects, carts, barrows, market-stalls, even the occasional wraith of an American car, painted in exuberant gypsy style, largely with rambling roses. El Rashid gathered the harvests both of the sea and the land, a bustling, prosperous place where business and pleasure had reached a civilised agreement. A fleet of taxis (half-fare travelling on the luggage rack, a quarter in the boot) brought buyers and sellers from all the villages, and they went about embracing each other and roaring with laughter.

The deals done, a man could seat himself in one of a row of golden thrones for his shoes to be polished, while dictating a letter to a scribe, nibbling at a calf's foot from a charcoal brazier, or perhaps having his blood pressure taken by a doctor who operated from a 1938 Studebaker, with a blow-up of an electrocardiograph plastered by way of advertisement over his back window. Camels were debarred from the town's centre, but while I was there, one had managed to sneak through and pass down the main street, and was cropping geraniums.

In the background the Nile moved in its last sluggish curve to the sea. Its great rival, the Amazon, is 150 miles across at its mouth, containing the Island of Marajó, roughly the size of Belgium. One could sit in a golden, plush-bottomed throne in the muddy square of El Rashid and look across the waters to the Nile's further bank, which might have been 200 yards away. There were five months to go to the end of the dry season, by which time not a drop of the waters gathered in Ethiopia or the mountains of Equatorial Africa would reach the sea. A little would have been wasted, but the rest would have been taken up by a million gardens, their boundaries touching each other for nearly 4,000 miles. A river of life indeed.

THE ZAMBEZI

NICHOLAS WOLLASTON

More than any of the others, the Zambezi is one man's river. He was a pious, brave, ruthless Scot – missionary, explorer, liberator, prophet – who first saw the Zambezi in 1851 and became inspired with its promise as a waterway into Central Africa. Up it, from the coast to the high plateau of the interior, would travel the agents of trade, civilisation and Christianity. The failure of his idea, the fallacy of God's Highway, was the tragedy of that extraordinary man. He was Dr David Livingstone.

But though he spent years camped beside it, though he mapped nearly its entire length, though he buried several of his companions and his wife along its banks, though he was the first white man to gasp at its most stupendous feature – the biggest waterfall in the world which he named after his sovereign queen – and though he spent thirteen years exploring it in the belief that it could bring enlightenment to the black man and an end to 'that curse of Africa', the slave trade, Livingstone never went to the Zambezi's source.

I flew there from Lusaka, 400 miles away, and landed on the grass beside a lonely mission school run by Plymouth Brethren. I was just in time for morning coffee with the teachers. We said a prayer, thanking God for the biscuits and the lovely day and asking Him for the success of my trip, and then the headmaster took me in his pick-up to the famous spot. He would cut his lessons, he would devote the day to me. Fifteen miles away, over a track through bush and elephant grass, we left the car and dropped down a path into a corner of the tropical rain forest. Twilight flickered between immense trees that rose from the damp underbrush. From among the roots, gurgling and cool, came the new-born stream. I scooped up a few handfuls to drink, and a one-eyed man came with his small boy to fill a plastic can. There was a sense of genesis, of a life beginning. I dropped some sticks and dead leaves into the water and watched them float away, downhill towards the Indian Ocean. This is the watershed at the heart of Africa, where a corner of Zambia pushes up between Angola and Zaire. Not far beyond the frontier another river rises, which joins the Congo and flows into the Atlantic. The two springs are forty miles apart; a continent separates their mouths.

After lunch at the mission the headmaster took me to a favourite place downstream where the young Zambezi, like a Highland salmon river, comes tearing over slabs of rock, twisting under trees, slipping joyfully into pools. The mission children, for a treat, ride down the rapids on inner tubes. There should be heather on the hills, but the butterflies make up the loss. An old woodcutter with an axe launched himself knee-deep from the other bank to greet us, clapping his chest in the local way. I waded to an island and was attacked by red ants which injected me with formic acid in 100 places.

Perversely, the Zambezi heads north, then turns west into Angola for a couple of hundred miles before swinging south and east on its great loop towards the sea – 2,200 miles from start to finish. I caught up with it again in the village of Balovale, now renamed for the river itself – Zambezi. Huge trees give shade to the government offices. People sit idly on the verandas, as always in Africa, waiting for something to happen. Soft voices come through the windows of the courtroom, pleading or persuasive. After dark, the cicadas tingle against the throb of drums on someone's radio. At the foot of the hill the bountiful, stately Zambezi flows past at four miles an hour: 'This magnificent stream,' Livingstone called it. In the rainy season it can rise forty feet above low water.

I went across in a dug-out canoe with dried fish, firewood, maize meal and two bicycles. The ferryman edged up the bank before turning slantwise to the current, while I baled out with an old cow horn. The midday heat was flavoured with the whiff of river water and African sweat. From the other side a herd of cattle was driven into the water by three boys who pulled their pants off, tied them over their heads to keep dry, grabbed the cows' tails and were towed across the river – a flotilla of shouts and whacks and glinting horns. A fat grey snout broke the surface, turned over and was gone: a hippo had come up to breathe.

The Zambezi is fed by tributaries that drain into it from huge swamps clotted with weeds and singing with mosquitoes. I flew downstream, a few hundred feet above it: a king of rivers winding through a park, down an avenue of trees. Then it enters the Barotse Plain, a sort of vast bladder to absorb and store the flood water in the rains and release it under decent control. There is a harbour on the marshes at Mongu, though it is ten miles from the river, where people from the villages across the plain wait for a boat to take them home.

In a canoe with an outboard motor, I went speeding through the marshes: like the Norfolk Broads on an African scale, with tropical exotica. On the banks, crouching fishermen watch their lines and nets. Canoeists, poling along channels in the reeds, ply from island to island in the brilliant sun. Many of them wear denim jackets, even city suits, which would have pleased Livingstone: he didn't care for nudity. Not much else has changed. It is a paradise of birds – herons, cormorants, geese, hornbills, ibis. The nests of weaverbirds, like precious purses, are tied delicately to the reeds. A fish hawk sits in a dead tree. Dragonflies dart among the waterlilies. May it be long before the tourists reach these enchanted Barotse marshlands.

Each small mound of dry land has a hut, perhaps a village, with a few trees and a patch of cultivation or grazing. One of them, Lealui, is the island capital of the Litunga, paramount chief of the Barotse tribes. I tied up my canoe and walked through the village to his palace, a big thatched house defended by a spiked stockade. In Livingstone's day, there would have been enemy heads on those spikes. At the gate a sentry challenged me. We sat under a tree and talked for a long time, and at last he agreed to take in a letter to His Highness. Half an hour later a message came out to say that the Litunga would see me in five minutes. After another half hour I was summoned within.

Inside the stockade I was met by two servants who led me slowly across the courtyard to the palace. Every few steps they dropped to their knees, bowed and clapped their hands; crept forward, knelt, bowed and clapped again. Solemnly I followed, keeping upright. At the porch I was abandoned, but rescued by a voice from the darkness: 'Come in, please, oh do come in.' He was a very tall gentleman in a grey suit, smiling shyly, with an ivory-handled fly whisk in his hand. Far above, as my eyes got used to the light, I could see the rafters and the thatch. It was like visiting a maharaja or a duke: everywhere these ancient chieftains, in these modern days, can only look at the glory of their ancestors and sigh. On the walls were photos of his father and grandfather and one of himself on a throne dressed like a Ruritanian admiral in a cocked hat with plumes. We sat on sofas among the coffee tables, wondering what to say.

The Litunga is nominal ruler of half a million people, though his authority is much reduced. He still goes down the Zambezi sometimes in a fleet of canoes, with drums beating to the rhythm of the paddles. ('They stand upright and keep the stroke with great precision,' Livingstone wrote. 'It was beautiful to see them skimming along so quickly, and keeping the time so well.') The people along the river love it, the Litunga told me, and build camps for him all the way to Sesheke. And every year, when the rains come and the island of Lealui is in danger of being flooded, he moves to his wet-weather palace at the edge of the Barotse Plain. The ceremonial procession, dragging the royal barge up a special canal to dry land, is called *kuomboka*. 'It means,' the Litunga said, 'coming out of the water. It might be out of your bath, or a swimming pool.' He is a sophisticated man.

From Mongu, I drove seventy miles south to Senanga through desiccated scrub – neither forest nor desert but a derelict zone of dry timber and brittle leaves with rare patches of maize or tapioca. A man stood in the shadows beside the road with a bow and arrow. A family of monkeys chattered in the branches. At Senanga the Zambezi comes swinging in from the Barotse Plain, bright blue and full of crocodiles. An Irish girl, wife of an engineer, said that four people had been eaten in the nine months since she had lived there, and a fifth was in hospital with terrible bites. She gave me a beer and asked me to lunch, but I had already ordered it in the rest house: a wodge of mealie porridge and some bits of meat, tough as crocodile. The trick is to roll a lump of porridge into a ball and dip it in the gravy.

For 200 miles below Senanga, the Zambezi flows through a 'restricted' area and the Zambia Government wouldn't let me in, arguing that a Land-Rover has no armour plating underneath. Within the Zambia frontier, close to the river, are SWAPO guerrilla camps which are sometimes raided by South African troops from the Caprivi Strip, the tongue of Namibia that separates Angola from Botswana. Roads are mined and not long ago a pontoon ferry was blown up. Another pontoon crosses at Kazungula, where I joined the river again. A fisherman mending his nets by the bank stood up and pointed to Namibia, Botswana and Zimbabwe over on the far bank, but it was hard to tell the difference: a sultry shore of reeds backed by thorn trees with the great tide rolling steadily in front. 'I do not know much about gods,' T. S. Eliot wrote, 'but I think that the river is a strong brown god – sullen, untamed and intractable.' The Zambezi is all of those, along this last stretch before it hurtles over the Victoria Falls. There is a metaphysical power, an infinite compulsion exerted by this colossal stream. A fisherman, like the poet, would know something about the river's relentless will.

Imperceptibly it widens, as if stretching its sinews for the tremendous plunge. Yet it remains placid, like the Thames below Oxford but on a giant's scale. You expect to see the chimneys of some stately English home and in fact there is, away above the trees on the Zimbabwe side, the pretentious pile of a country club. But this isn't Henley or Maidenhead, and those big animals grazing in the park, so cow-like in the distance, are rhinoceros. There are wild pigs and antelope, hippo pug marks on the banks, the great round plates of an elephant's footprint, and dung everywhere, freshly dropped. A hunter can put his finger into a heap of manure and tell by the temperature how far away the elephant has got. I didn't need to test it. A small herd was near the road – two large bulls, some cows and calves – and I left the car to walk towards them. At fifty yards I made them nervous; myself too. A cow kicked a calf and sent it packing. Then a bull turned towards me, his huge ears spread like square-rig sails, twitching at the edges. His trunk went up and he took two steps towards me, which was enough. The herd went crashing away in one direction, I in the other.

As the river becomes more boisterous and turbulent, dancing between islands and gathering speed, it spreads still wider till it is a mile across, racing to its climax, and you see ahead the pillars of spray rising from the falls. How many hippos and crocodiles – how many fishermen in their canoes – have been carried to the brink of the precipice and pitched into the gorge below? Years before he reached the falls in 1855, Livingstone had heard about *Mosi-oa-tunya*, 'the smoke that thunders', and had been asked if there were such things in his own country. He camped upstream and then, landing from his canoe on a small island at the lip of the falls, crept forward to the edge and looked over. The banks and islands bright with trees in blossom, the variety of form and colour, the tremendous cataract and plumes of vapour mingling with the clouds – he confessed it was the most wonderful sight he had witnessed in Africa. To him, the falling water was like a thick unbroken fleece and the whiteness reminded him of snow, which he hadn't seen for years. 'The whole scene was extremely beautiful,' he wrote when he got back to Britain and then, perhaps jogged by his publisher to put in something more lyrical, he added a famous sentence: 'It had never been seen before by European eyes; but scenes so lovely must have been gazed upon by angels in their flight.'

In the last few million years, there have been eight successive sites for the Victoria Falls as the Zambezi cuts its way back along faults of soft material in a vast block of basalt, 1,000 feet thick, that erupted and cooled and cracked at the beginning of the world. Eventually the river will wear through to the back of the block – it is already more than halfway there – and in a million years or so there will be no Victoria Falls left. The great river, for a few reckless seconds, loses control. It does it with sparks and rainbows and festoons of spray that rise and drift and fall across a forest of dripping evergreens. The first tourist, and all his successors, would have appreciated the American who cabled home: 'Have seen Victoria – sell Niagara.'

Awestruck by the rainbows and frightened of being sucked into the water, Livingstone's companions offered prayers and sacrifices to their gods, and were condemned by him for not feeling admiration in their hearts for the beauty of the place or recognising the true God's benevolence. Looking around, he noticed that the little island, watered by the spray, was covered with grass as green as an English lawn; on it grew trees whose seeds must have floated down from far upstream. He cleared a patch and planted 100 apricot and peach stones and some coffee beans, hoping that the hippos would let it grow into the first of many such gardens in Central Africa. (They didn't – and when he came back five years later he found his garden destroyed.) Then, forgetting himself – or remembering the small boy he had once been – he carved the date and his initials on a tree. It was the only time in his life that he indulged such vanity, and he regretted it immediately.

I crossed the river by the road-rail bridge, now nearly eighty years old, which Cecil Rhodes, founder of Rhodesia, decreed should be close enough to the falls for the passengers to feel the spray. Leaving Zambia on the north side was no trouble. Entering Zimbabwe on the south was no trouble either until, as I was being waved through the barrier, the customs officer saw on the back seat Anthony Burgess's great novel *Earthly Powers*. Quick as a crocodile he snatched it and carried it into the office, where he looked it up in a big album of illicit literature. Sure enough, among titles like *The Art of Spanking*, the works of Burgess were listed. It started a search which, from his portrait on the wall, the President of Zimbabwe, Rev Banana, seemed to think was funny. The car was stripped and my baggage put through a sieve of official fingers: socks unrolled, malaria pills counted and all books – mostly the works of D. Livingstone – referred to the album of shame. An hour later I was allowed to pass through the frontier into Zimbabwe, with only *Earthly Powers* confiscated. 'Why?' I enquired. 'Because we think it is dirty,' the crocodile said, and asked for a lift into town.

The Victoria Falls Hotel is one of those, like Raffles and Shepheards and other imperial pubs, that has acquired a touristic aura of its own. Coaches, striped like zebras, roll up to its canopied entrance and discharge their loads. A tame witch doctor is on hand, and tribal warriors dance every evening under the coloured lights, followed by a feast of barbecued T-bone steaks, charred or raw to suit your taste. In the foyer you can buy an ice bucket made from the scrotum of an elephant. In the bar a special cocktail is served, with white rum and ginger beer – the 'David Livingstone'. A fifteen-minute flight over the falls in a small aeroplane is advertised ('the flight of angels', naturally), or a visit to a crocodile farm. By day the distant thunder of the Zambezi is lost in the clatter of camera shutters and the zooming of the lenses. Only at night can you hear the river, when the warriors have gone home and the place settles down to another local ritual – honeymoons, for which Victoria Falls, like Niagara, is famous.

Something happens to the Zambezi's temper as it goes over the falls. It sheds its benignity for a darker mood, twisting down zigzag gorges before shouldering its way through thorny hills which, given vineyards and an olive grove, might be in Andalusia or Greece. Then, eighty miles downstream, it turns as if by magic – by a trick of modern engineering – into a beautiful lake, three times the length of Geneva, that Livingstone never dreamt of. When the Kariba Dam was built and the water rose, 50,000 Batonga tribesmen had to be resettled. But their snake-headed fish-tailed god, Nyami-nyami, stayed down in the flooded land below the surface where he still looks after his people. Never go fishing near a Batonga man, you are told: he pulls in the fish all day, while you catch nothing. Most of the commercial fishing is done at night, when the lamp-lit fleet shines like a floating village across the lake, and, though the fish were introduced by Zambia from one of the older natural lakes, most of the profits are made by Zimbabwean whites. I went down to the harbour at dawn, disturbing a herd of zebras on the way, to watch the boats bring in tons of tiny whitebait and a few boxes of bream. But the white company manager, stamping up and down the shore in the morning chill, was scornful of his fishermen. They had been steering into the harbour for years, he said, and still they couldn't get it right: 'Without us to keep an eye on them they'd be back where they began.' Back in the trees was the lethal insinuation.

A faintly malodorous whiff, not only from drying fish, hovers along the Zimbabwe shore of Lake Kariba. Perhaps political independence is too new for the sense of respect between blacks and whites that is so heartening to a visitor in Zambia. The years of fighting and acrimony have left a gap without any apparent purposefulness. It is an atmosphere of suspense, of wait-and-see, even of fear and hatred, pervading a stretch of coast which in other ways might be the Costa Brava or in the Caribbean. Yacht marinas, fishing trips, game-watching expeditions and, at the end of the sun-blistering day, drinks on the terrace and dinner by candlelight – all the signs of a playground are there, but sometimes it seems that the heart has gone out of the play. Many of the players, for one thing, have departed to countries where they feel more at ease, and many who are left are elderly and tired. They are 'staying on' without much enthusiasm: actors in a final scene, an epilogue of empire, which they never bargained for. Like actors, they have a touch of make-believe about them. In the bar of the Cutty Sark Hotel, with port and starboard lights and a model of the great clipper herself, two brave Africans slip into a corner with their beers to watch the performance. The white men, in shorts and stockings, are tanned and a little too handsome to be true. The women, in incredible coiffures, wear bright frocks or trouser suits, eccentric but perhaps fashionable in some unlikely past. There isn't much action. Somebody has a game of tennis, somebody else plays croquet by the swimming pool, others stare at the lake through binoculars or mutter over their gin about the sorry state of things. It is unreal, of course, but so is the lake itself – a figment of these people's vision, a superb monument to their ingenuity. And now the waters of another flood have risen round them and left them stranded. Nyami-nyami, the fish-tailed god of the Batonga, will hardly care what happens.

One morning I hired a speedboat and went ripping across the lake, past islands that once were hilltops and tell-tale trees still standing above the surface, to watch some elephants pulling up the grass. They too are 'staying on', with nowhere else to go. Antelopes gallop along the shore, buffaloes stand lowering at the edge of the bush. 'This is the real Kariba,' said a woman in the safari lodge on Fothergill Island where I stopped for coffee. 'Over at the Cutty Sark you might be in the city. But we've got a rhino on the island and last night we had ten lions coming through the huts – they're after our buffalo.'

That afternoon I returned to Zambia ('Welcome to the friendly country!' it says), driving across the Kariba Dam and stopping to look over the precipice, a smooth steep rock face curving over at the top. Were there no climbers clawing upwards? My driver wouldn't look down: he was afraid of jumping over. There are other temptations. Pull out the plug and let the water out! A dam can't last for ever. Surely one day the Zambezi will be back in its old bed down there, with the Cutty Sark high and dry on the hills. The last laugh, so the Batonga say, will be on Nyami-nyami.

Forty miles downstream is the bridge at Chirundu where the great north road, coming up the length of Africa from Cape Town, crosses the Zambezi, more than halfway to Nairobi. I stood in the middle of the bridge and watched a hippo lazily rising and sinking in the river, a great baby blowing bubbles. Below Chirundu the Zambezi is joined by a major river from the north, the Kafue, and after forming the frontier between Zambia and Zimbabwe for nearly 500 miles it enters Mozambique, with another 500 to the sea. From Feira, the last village in Zambia,

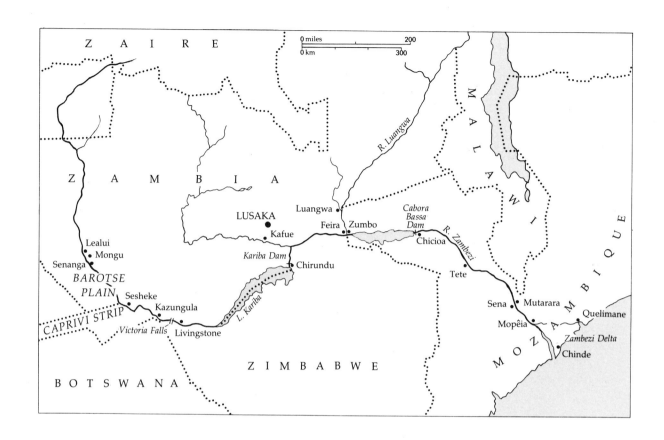

Captions for the following photographs:

1.   The Victoria Falls. Livingstone said it was the most wonderful sight he had witnessed in Africa. 'Scenes so lovely,' he wrote, 'must have been gazed upon by angels in their flight.'
2.   The river races away towards the Victoria Falls, once known by the natives as 'The Smoke That Thunders'. Ahead, the pillars of spray are visible, rising from the spot where the river plunges over its rocky precipice.
3.   The marshes of Mongu are like the Norfolk Broads on an African scale, complete with tropical exotica.

I crossed another tributary, the Luangwa, in a dug-out and walked a mile along the sandy shore to Zumbo, the first village in Mozambique. It appeared deserted. A few people vanished when they saw me, a few just stood and laughed. The huge stern faces of Marx, Engels, Lenin and the local president watched the empty football pitch. It was odd to think that the previous night in Lusaka I had had the Wembley Cup Final brought live to my sky-high hotel room with the compliments of Lonrho, proprietors of *The Observer*. This was a different Africa: a people's republic, given to wariness and silence. I know only a dozen words of Portuguese and nobody knew any more English. At sunset, when darkness quickly wipes out the day, a man called Hannibal agreed to give me supper and another called January said I could sleep in his house. I stayed three days in Zumbo and by the time I left the villagers had stopped running away at the sight of me and hardly bothered to laugh.

Zumbo, the deepest outpost of the Portuguese East African empire, was first colonised in the sixteenth century with a fort to defend it against the natives. Gold, ivory and slaves were the goods of trade and the place flourished, declined, flourished, was sacked, flourished and declined again. When Livingstone passed through, he admired the choice of site for commerce: 'The early traders, guided probably by Jesuit missionaries, must have been men of taste and sagacity. They selected for their village the most charmingly picturesque site in the country . . . The chapel, near which lies a broken church bell, commands a glorious view of the two noble rivers, the green fields, the undulating forest, the pleasant hills and the magnificent mountains in the distance.' But the broken bell wasn't the only sign of dereliction: 'It is an utter ruin now . . . The foul hyena has defiled the sanctuary and the midnight owl has perched on its crumbling walls, to disgorge the undigested remnant of its prey. One can scarcely look without feelings of sadness on the utter desolation of a place where men have met to worship the Supreme Being . . . Apart from the ruins there is nothing to remind one that a Christian power ever had traders here . . . Not a single art, save that of distilling spirits by means of a gun barrel, has ever been learnt from the strangers; and if all the progeny of the whites were at once to leave the country, their only memorial would be the ruins of a few stone and mud-built walls, and that blighting relic of the slave trade, the belief that man may sell his brother man.'

The whites have now left, though not with all their progeny, and those walls have fallen into further ruin. Hannibal – half Portuguese, a quarter Indian and a quarter African – apologised for the discomforts of his house. The water supply had broken down, the bathroom taps had been dry for years, the bidet was smashed, the toilet clogged. The only water came from an old paraffin tin brought up from the river on someone's head, and the house stank of sewage. Hannibal, who had been to Russia and East Germany, had seen better things (worse ones too – he had been taken to the death camp at Treblinka) and was embarrassed for my sake. There was no gas for the cooker and the village generator packed up during supper, so we finished by hurricane lamp while a rat knocked about inside the paraffin fridge, which wasn't working for lack of wicks. Somehow Hannibal produced a meal of fish and beans, with rice and pickle and some drops of Portuguese wine, before getting massively drunk on beer brought across the river by canoe from Zambia. Livingstone would have recognised the scene.

Hannibal, who once worked for the Party, wouldn't explain why he had come to live in this forsaken corner of Mozambique: banishment perhaps, or disenchantment. Either way, it is safer to keep quiet. Stories are whispered of remote camps where 'society's marginal elements' are kept indefinitely for re-education. Zumbo, too, may be remote, even marginal, but there is a way out.

Hannibal took me into the little shop he runs: bare shelves, except for a stock of oil lamps with no glass funnels for them, some packets of tea and a supply of remnants – shoes, trousers, T-shirts – too large or too small for anyone to want. And he spoke of the big mission up in the hills where priests and nuns used to have a school and hospital. It closed at the time of Independence in 1975 and now the orchards, where oranges and mangoes and grapes once grew, are smothered by the forest. In these parts you soon discover that there is no place for impatience or urgency, but when Africa reclaims her own it is swiftly done. The Zumbo airstrip has disappeared. There isn't a car that works. An old lorry cab, upside down between a disembowelled tractor and the shell of a Jeep, is the home of a goat. Though the guns that thundered over the Zambezi during the years of the Rhodesian war are silent, there are still windows broken by a Frelimo rocket in 1974 that haven't been mended. The potted household flowers, so Portuguese, are dead: only the plastic ones survive, with the weeds that saddened Livingstone. At night the throb of drums is real in Zumbo, unlike in Zambia: here there are no batteries left for radios.

Things were no better in January's house where I slept, though he is the local Party secretary. His trousers were sharply pressed and his office, where bureaucracy must be maintained, was busier than Hannibal's shop; but the drains of a commissar, when blocked, smell as bad as anyone else's, and the collected works of Lenin, even torn off page by page, are no substitute for toilet paper. Only from January's veranda, where a Portuguese colonial officer must once have sipped his sundown drink, could I appreciate Livingstone's rapture about the scene.

There are no clouds in Zambia, or not when I was there, but in Mozambique they sail in fleets like galleons. A bougainvillaea waves a carmine pennant, the flamboyant trees are sifted by a breeze, there is a flash of turquoise feathers in the branches. Women, with calabashes of water or loads of washing on their heads, file to and from the river. And the majestic stream down there, swollen by tributaries and stuffed with fish, continues on its way. The Zambezi brought the first traders to Zumbo 400 years ago and still provides such commerce as there is. Fish, scaled and split open, are smoked over charcoal pits, wafting a flavour of kippers and Bombay duck along the river bank. Baskets of them are ferried over to Zambia for the markets in Lusaka and the Copper Belt. Further profit is made, with less effort, from Zambian fishermen who come to poach in Mozambican waters and are charged commission. From Zumbo there is no way further into Mozambique except by slow canoe. Some people say the road is still mined, others that it has been flooded by the new lake, bigger than Kariba, formed by the dam in Cabora Bassa gorge. I had to go back into Zambia and make a long detour, driving 350 miles to reach the Zambezi again at Tete.

Africa reduces the biggest things to insignificance. I came over the hills and looked down at the Cabora Bassa Dam – a slender toenail curved across the bottom of the valley. Upstream a fjord winds back into an immense lake, stretching almost back to Zumbo. Downstream the Zambezi rumbles onwards, heading down the gorge for the coastal flatlands. In the middle, a tremendous gush bursts with astronomic force horizontally from the dam wall. Some toenail! In his own kind of gush, a Portuguese publicity man poured out the figures – the megatons and megawatts and cubic metric millions. Portuguese engineers had spent thirty years on its construction, he said, and now it is the sixth biggest hydroelectric works in the world. When I mentioned Kariba he spat contemptuously over the edge. Cabora Bassa, with the extra water of the Kafue and Luangwa rivers, is five times the size. I thought there must be something to dislodge this man's pride and asked about the cost in human life. Only 300 killed, he said, when they had allowed for 1,000.

'Now I will show you a scene for James Bond,' he announced theatrically, 'but this one isn't fiction.' We drove down a steep tunnel through the rock, curving back under the dam; past a ledge in the cliff overhanging the river, drenched in spray; then through a steel door into an underground chamber like a colossal sports hall, air conditioned, with a tiled floor and glimpses of rock beyond the gantries overhead. I could hear the distant hum of power, but there was nobody in sight. Then, far away, I saw a man alone at a desk, as if forgotten by the engineers who had gone back to Lisbon, leaving the computers in control. The Portuguese unhooked a telephone, spoke briefly and led me into a lift. Further down we came out into another chamber full of machinery, all with French or German labels, and entered the casing of one of the five huge turbines: roar and wind, and somewhere – above? below? all round me? – the Zambezi was rushing past. It was the water here in the Cabora Bassa gorge that wrecked Livingstone's hopes for God's Highway to the interior: 'Things look dark for our enterprise,' he wrote in his diary after seeing the terrible length of rapids and cataracts. Most of the energy from Cabora Bassa goes looping down pylons 1,000 miles to South Africa; so the Afrikaans housewife cooks dinner with electricity from her Marxist neighbour. But the dimensions of such power are inconceivable in terms of domestic switches and electric kettles. I couldn't believe in the remotest connection with the lovely dam, that night in the hotel at Tete, when the lights all fused.

From Tete I followed one of Africa's worst roads to Mutarara, 150 miles downstream, with poverty and malnutrition all the way: swollen stomachs, distended navels, matchstick limbs, shrivelled breasts. For lunch I bought some mealies from a half-clad woman with knobs on her knees like grapefruit, who was pounding flour in a wooden mortar. It was painful to remember my lunch the day before, of steak and wine in the works canteen at Cabora Bassa, and the crazy scene in the supermarket there, where workers scramble to buy custard powder, ketchup, coffee, washing powder, whisky – things unknown elsewhere in Mozambique. Even in Tete there are queues for bread, for fish, for cigarettes, and in the hotel there is no coffee for breakfast, or bread or butter or milk, or even spoons: just tea, for lack of tea cups, in a champagne glass.

At Mutarara, for the fourth and last time, the Zambezi – immensely wide and flowing between banks of high grass – is crossed by a bridge, a two-mile caterpillar of girders humping across to the town of Sena. But they say the railway lines are rusty and unsafe, and one of the two engines that pull trains across the bridge is out of action. I stayed the night in a house that had belonged to the Portuguese manager of a cotton estate, a pretentious villa full of tassels, pelmets and curtains. Three-piece suites and cocktail trolleys were disposed about the parquet floor. Mirrors duplicated the vulgarity. In the evening, the Party secretary with some of his officials – a 'delegation' – came to visit me. We sat on velvet sofas, drinking beer and exchanging platitudes. I was hungry, having eaten only the old woman's mealies that day, and suggested dinner. Someone was sent to kill a goat, but the cook in his custom-built kitchen, with fitted cupboards and an elaborate gas and electric stove, was in trouble: nothing worked. The delegates, full of beer, began to giggle. In the end the goat was stewed on a wood fire in the garden and we dined, towards midnight, under a chandelier. It was a pleasure to see how Mozambicans slip into the ways of a colonial household, though it was a pity to have no women with us: no earnest daughters of the revolution, still less any of those luscious *femmes fatales* from the casinos of Lusaka, in gimlet curls and tight-bottomed pants, tossing their chips across the green baize.

I asked the Party secretary about the local problems. 'We have no problems,' he replied, and over the bottles the others smiled. I suggested the poverty, malnutrition, scarcity of food. 'You see,' he said, 'we have very bad floods, and very bad droughts.' What about irrigation? This country might be ideal for growing rice. 'You see, our communications are not good.' But there's the Zambezi down there – just think what they would do in India or China with a waterway like that. 'You see, we have these bandits who blow up the roads and terrorise the villages and cut the power lines.' But that's what Frelimo used to do. 'You see, these are counter-revolutionaries, supplied by South Africa.' But South Africa buys the electricity – why should they cut the wires? 'You see, they take only a tenth of their supply from us, so they can afford to lose it if it suits their politics, and when it's cut off they can claim compensation.' That, everyone agreed, was a problem.

Either the floods or the drought or the roads or the ferries or the bandits, or all of them, prevented me going down to Mopêia Velha and on to Chinde, the little port in the centre of the Zambezi delta. Instead, I was allowed to fly to Quelimane at the mouth of the delta's northern branch. It is Mozambique's chief fishing port and I hoped to taste the famous prawns. It was at Quelimane that Vasco da Gama touched briefly on his voyage to India in 1497: the first contact between Europe and the Zambezi, and the beginning of colonialism in East Africa. And it was at Quelimane that Livingstone reached the sea in 1856, the first white man to cross Africa from coast to coast. He was exhausted with fever, he hadn't heard from his family for three years, and he decided it was a pestilential place, a verdict he didn't alter when he went back in 1862: 'Quelimane must have been built solely for the sake of carrying on the slave trade, for no man in his senses would ever have dreamed of placing a village on such a low, muddy, fever-haunted and mosquito-swarming site, had it not been for the facilities it afforded for slaving . . .'

The price of a slave was two pieces of calico, a bunch of beads and a necklace. Today, without the traffic in human flesh, the Quelimane market has little else. This should be a land of abundance, of fruits of the earth and sea, but there are only a few shreds of vegetables, marble-sized tomatoes, chillies and dried fish and ropes of plaited tobacco: not an ounce of meat in sight. 'The struggle continues!' as the banners say, and in the town each morning people gather on the verge of riot outside a shop that admits them, one or two at a time, to pick what they can from the daily consignment of cheap clothes. (Better things are available to the few who, with other privileges, aren't required to join the crowd.) The bookshop offers nothing but the literature of 'scientific socialism' and 'democratic centralism'. And in an empty motor showroom a man sits below a poster: 'One day you will own a Yamaha.' He doesn't look as if he ever will. Some people sit at the café tables, which at least is cheap: the waiter has nothing to bring them. Others go out to the airport and watch the daily plane flying away to somewhere else. There isn't much fun in Quelimane, it has been smothered by the rules. Driving past a school where the children were singing the national anthem, I had to stop and get out and stand to attention in the road till they had finished. I found the old church locked and the big new one empty, though at sunset the sugarcake mosque was full of the faithful, perhaps descendants of slave traders, bowing to Mecca. Allah anyway can bring consolation to this disconsolate town.

'Long live the First of June!' A fair was held, stalls were set up and loudspeakers hung in the trees. A boy flying a kite said that after dark there would be a film from Italy, and already a screen was propped against the church. Expectancy rose as the sun sank into Africa. A flock of Indian women passed through the crowd like gaudy birds, and a desultory trade began in plastic toys and coloured drinks. At last, as the Southern Cross came out, the projector flickered on, and flickered off again. In time, though they were used to waiting, the audience drifted back into the fair. The most popular attraction was a flutter on the revolving dartboard: anything for a thrill. Later, the stars were clouded over and a torrent of rain fell on Quelimane. The crowd scattered, shrieking, and the limp stalls were left in lakes of water.

'It is the people who suffer,' a young doctor from Geneva said. He had come on a two-year contract, at a minimum salary, but was breaking it after a year. There is one doctor for 40,000 inhabitants in Mozambique, yet this good man was unable to work, was disgusted with the disorganisation and incompetence and deviousness he found in hospitals, and was going home. It could be such a beautiful country, he thought, but the Portuguese had taken what they could and departed without leaving any basis for government. He was equally critical of their successors: 'They have a good time, they make a lot of money – they are exactly the same as the old ones.' They can be seen in the Quelimane Hotel, pecking at their tripe and potatoes: the Hungarians watching the Russians, the East Germans eyeing the North Koreans. Bearded Italians climb into their Land Cruisers and drive away in a cloud of importance. A single agitated Englishman, trying to clinch a contract but not yet adjusted to the system, complains that the telex hasn't worked since last year and a telegram takes eight days to the next town. And the prawns, the famous prawns: the whole catch is frozen for export – to Moscow and East Berlin, the doctor from Geneva sadly told me.

There is balm, however, in the patience, the sultriness, the moist and fragrant air of Quelimane. A hint of coconuts lingers in the streets, and a suspicion of the sea: out of sight beyond the mangroves is the Indian Ocean. And not far away, the reason for the town's existence, is the river. At the end of its run the great tired Zambezi, after carving its way through the land, is itself broken up by the land. The flow is dissipated, spent in the last miles to reach the sea, which comes up between the grey-green islands, through swamps and channels, to meet it. Gravity has brought it here, and there is none left. The sticks and dead leaves I threw in at the source, if they got to Quelimane, would have taken about three weeks. I took the same. The last word should go to David Livingstone who explored it and loved it, despite his disappointment, and called it simply 'a glorious river'.

THE GANGES

GEOFFREY MOORHOUSE

H oliness more than anything accounts for the imaginative grip the Ganges has held on ancients and moderns alike, celebrated by Virgil, Ovid and Dante, as well as by uncountable generations of Hindu faithful. Alexander the Great seems to have thought of her geographically as a boundary of the universe, and when Columbus reached Panama he thrilled and was wistful because he believed himself to be a mere day's march from her banks. Yet, except in the monsoon, the Ganges cannot be considered one of the mightiest torrents in a hydraulic or other physical sense, for there are twenty-eight rivers longer than this, with the Nile, the Amazon and the Mississippi-Missouri each running more than twice as far. Even on a local subcontinental reckoning, both the Brahmaputra and the Indus come off better for sheer size. What makes Ganges unique in her run of 1,678 miles from the source to the sea is the intensity of devotion – and the towering scale of devout humanity – to be found along her banks.

For once, the use of the feminine is not just sentimental fad. According to the myth, the female Ganga was brought down from heaven with the connivance of Lord Siva in order to purify the ashes of King Sagara's 60,000 sons, who had been incinerated by the wrath of a sage for overweening pride. A subsequent king, Bhagirathi, did penance for their offence high up in the mountains. When his propitiation was complete, and he began to descend, Lord Siva caught the falling Ganga in his matted hair, releasing her gently to follow Bhagirathi out of the Himalaya, through its foothills, across the northern plains, into the jungles of the east. Eventually, at the delta on the Bay of Bengal, the ashes of Sagara's sons were cleansed and those 60,000 souls attained paradise at last.

This story is the one constant that enthrals all who make for Ganges in an imperative second only to that which propels a Muslim to Mecca before he dies. Otherwise the variety of homage and belief exercised alongside and in this river simply reflects the baffling and sometimes paradoxical intricacies of Hinduism itself. People come here obsessed with their veneration of Kali, who was a murderous lady, while others are frantic in their submission to Durga, who is Kali's benevolent other self. They bring a personal addiction to Lord Vishnu the

142

Preserver, to Hanuman the monkey god, to jolly old Ganesh in his guise of elephant, and to hundreds more deities besides. But whatever the emphasis of his faith, each pilgrim believes that all sin is instantly wiped away by a ritual bath in Ganges; and if only death can happen here, with cremation on the banks and ashes cast upon the water, it will be the most blessed gift of all, the absolute assurance of entry into heaven.

A few miles below the ice cave source (which is called Gaumukh, the Cow's Mouth) stands the aspiration of millions, the small temple of Gangotri, where a silver image of Ganga is installed every spring, when at last pilgrims can reach the building after its seven-month fastness in the snows. Largely because the Indian army had strategic reasons for building a road in this region during the border dispute with China twenty years ago, it is now possible to achieve Gangotri in summer on wheels, provided a landslide or an avalanche hasn't wiped the route out. Before strategy came to his aid, the pilgrim had no alternative to walking for many weeks up through the foothills of Garhwal, and this is still the way many come who are too poor to pay for a ride.

The altitude near Gangotri isn't quite enough to be literally breathtaking, but the landscape is tremendous in every sense. The alpine peaks in the background are operatic in their grandeur and the infant Ganges tumbles boisterously down a ravine, whose sides are littered with boulders that from the mountain track above look deceptively small but which, after a moment's speculation, you realise are sometimes as huge as the Albert Hall's dome. Presently the pines and the deodars are enlivened by flaring masses of scarlet rhododendron, growing from the trunks of full-sized trees. Outside the pilgrim season it all looks utterly remote from the ways of mankind, except that here and there you come across tiny vestiges of his faith: three pink flags stuck into a hummock by the track, with a detritus of rancid bottles on the ground, left there as offering to Lord Vishnu, who notoriously dotes on milk.

The first villages appear where the ravine bearing Ganges broadens enough to sustain terraces on which wheat is grown in strips no more than a few feet wide, held in place on the steep hills by drystone walls that would be recognised as decent long and short work up in the Yorkshire Dales. The hillfolk are Bhotias, who look more Chinese than Indian, and the women must be among the most beautiful on earth, with faces so delicately made that you would wish to touch them only with fingertips. Their nose ornaments, sometimes a gold ring six inches across, are quite unnecessary to make you stop and gape. They are slim, too, even when they are short, doubtless from generations of being bred as the local beasts of burden. Almost always they are to be seen walking in files along the road, with a sickle in one hand while the other balances a load of grass on the head; or ascending a track from the river, their faces erect beneath brass vessels that glint from afar in the sun.

In spring the air is warm down here, not chill as it still is near the source. Vultures soar on thermals over the ridges as elegantly as eagles, quite unlike the repulsive creatures of the plains, which squat, sluggish with carrion, along the riverside. An immense variety of birds flourishes down the whole length of Ganges, much recovered from the days when the playful British shot everything in sight. Hoopoes potter for grubs now while green parakeets flash by, storks stand watchful for fish, tern scream and dive, drongos somersault everywhere.

The Ganges is, quite simply, idyllic up in those Garhwal hills, though it will be less so before long when the Maneri Hydro Project is complete and humanity pollutes it with commerce instead of merely touching it with faith. Already the clang of Uttarkashi's temple

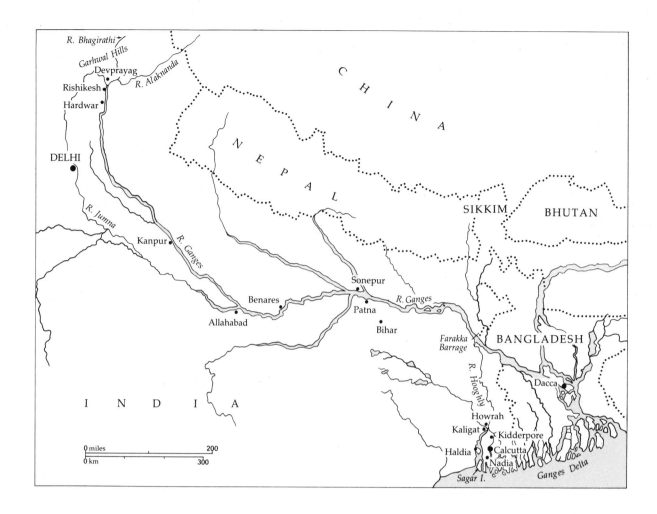

Captions for the following photographs:

1.   Devprayag, where the Bhagirathi and Alaknanda rivers join to form the Ganges proper. Monkeys patrol the cliffs and heavy chains hang from the riverside ghats for bathers to cling to. The racing current might otherwise sweep them away.
2.   The waterfront at Patna, chief city of Bihar, where the river runs wide and deep enough for these antique sternwheelers to run regular services.
3.   The Manikarnika burning ghat at Benares. The rich are cremated with sandalwood, the poor with neem.
4.   Allahabad, where the Ganges briefly meets and merges with the Jumna, another holy river.
5.   A Patna-based paddlesteamer belches smoke over the sand-banks as she makes upstream for Sonepur.
6.   At Calcutta boatmen use sweeps when the winds are light.
7.   There are two miles of ghats, or steps, lining the Benares waterfront. Each day thousands come here to bathe and pray. Buddha preached his first sermon on the town's outskirts.
8.   The dhobi wallahs, or laundrymen, are a commonplace sight along the river. Here the authorities have provided them with wooden platforms to beat their clothes against.

bells is counterpointed by the rumble of earth-moving equipment, and construction workers there live in rows of long huts as forbidding as barrack blocks anywhere. Tehri and its wild market place, where men stride now with antique flintlocks among jangling mule trains, is to vanish beneath a lake and soon outsiders (if no one else) will wish that the only industry in sight had remained a ramshackle shed housing the Himalayan Shuttle and Bobbin Udyog. Progress is moving apace and heavy Tata trucks, fringed with tinsel around the cab and inscribed with 'Horn Please' along the tailboard, are bearing it each day in the shape of steel girders as they come steaming and straining up that series of 1-in-10s. I just hope they leave Devprayag alone, quiet and unspoilt yet in its spectacular position at the junction of two ravines.

From one side the brown waters of the Bhagirathi pour past the town, from the other the blue of the Alaknanda, to go forth together in what even the cartographers at last recognise as the River Ganges. At this momentous point the Baba Mahant Vikram Geer has installed himself in a cave, where acolytes keep him well supplied with pan (which he stores in an old Capstan tin) to stimulate his juices and his seer-saying and his steadfast refusal to be photographed by anyone who isn't certifiably vegetarian and virgin both. Monkeys patrol the rocky banks at this point and people contemplate their destinies from two suspension bridges strung high in the air. Such is the tumult of water at this confluence that heavy chains trail down from the ghats [riverside steps] of Devprayag, so that bathers can hang on to them while they submerge themselves, to avoid being swept away downstream.

Another sage once set up shop where at last Ganges comes out of the hills, 200 miles from its Cow's Mouth. The Maharishi Mahesh Yogi is nowadays more likely to be found in Delhi, possibly because he decided that Westerners could be better canvassed in less primitive conditions, though their more recent infatuation deflected them to Poona, where the deodorised Rajneesh held court until he lit out one unsuspecting day for the richer blandishments of the United States. But a hoarding still invites all comers to enrol at the Maharishi's Institute of Meditation, situated across half a mile of river from the town of Rishikesh. There are many ashrams on that east bank, all bubbling with competitors of his, together with temples and a manifestly Victorian clock tower in cast iron, making the settlement look and feel something like a cross between Blackpool and Lourdes.

For the best part of one thousand miles now, Ganges makes her way across ground that is nearly pancake flat and in summer suffocatingly hot, those terrible northern plains which still sear the memory of old India hands in Dorset and Hants, who fled to the hills every year before May came round. It is here, too, that Ganges begins to succour and endow most magnificently the beguiling, maddening, attractive, repellent, exciting, soothing and always marvellous conglomeration of people that is India. And if anyone thinks that an adjectivally ridiculous sentiment, he should take himself to Hardwar, to Allahabad and to Benares, where this overwhelming phenomenon of contradictions, this pullulating dependence on the river is most clearly to be seen.

Hardwar, sixteen miles below the Maharishi's extravaganza, is where legend places Vishnu's footprint on the bank, which has drawn millions of people at a time into a town with a population of maybe fifty thousand. That is on the occasion of a Kumbh mela, an event which is astrologically scheduled for every twelfth year, but annually more than one hundred thousand turn up to celebrate Ganga's birth in spring. At any time of any year there will be at least hundreds performing their ablutions near the cluster of temples at Har-ki-Pairi, whose priests beckon the dutiful with gestures that brook no dissent. In aromas of jasmine and musk they mutter prayers, twist coloured threads around wrists, thrust grains of rice into palms, press gaudy powder on brows – and do not fail to indicate more than once the pile of rupees beneath the deity's image.

A little dazed by the intensity of it all, the pilgrims creep once more down the ghats and there launch upon the water small boats made of leaves, bearing marigold petals which are saturated with ghee and then lit. Long after nightfall these little craft are still despatched, their tiny flames bobbing and swaying down the river, past the stalls where pilgrim sticks and staves are sold, beyond the shadows of the police watch-towers which will be needed for the next mela's crowd control, on towards rougher water, where the last brave twinkling is doused. Then the pilgrims return to the railway station, to swarm aboard the Down 42 Express from Dehra Dun, with their plastic jerrycans, their plastic bottles, their any form of stoppered container which will bear some of the sacred water to the extremities of this land.

At Hardwar there is fervour, but Allahabad can offer religious hysteria to defeat the imagination. Many hold this to be the most numinous place of all along the Ganges, where briefly she meets and merges with another holy river, the Jumna, before they part and go their separate ways. People are regularly killed here by sheer weight of numbers when a mela is celebrated, and in 1954 there was a disaster that shook even this republic, which has always accepted human casualty as the luck of its draw.

Five million had turned up on the sand-banks at the confluence of the rivers for the famous procession of sadhus down to the water's edge. These holy men normally flaunt the austerities of their vocation by walking naked, their bodies smeared with mud and ash, but when they advance en masse at a Kumbh mela they transform themselves into a column the like of which nowhere else has seen for centuries. They are mounted on elephants and camels and horse-drawn chariots, each animal richly caparisoned with feathers, cloth and metal; or else they are borne by lesser men in palanquins, with equally vivid decoration. Buglers and pipers march with them in bands, while the sadhus – who are truculent as well as holy – brandish tridents and swords in the air.

It was this habit that started the 1954 catastrophe, when the procession found its way blocked by the congestion of the pilgrim crowds. The holy sadhus laid about them viciously with their ironwork, people panicked, animals began to run amok, and anyone who fell was a dead man that day. When the horror had subsided, the sand-banks were littered with trampled bodies and more corpses were floating in the two rivers. An official enquiry later estimated 500 dead and 2,000 hurt – but no one believes those figures told a quarter of the truth.

Even at calmer times, at no particularly auspicious moment of the year, the area at Sangam, the confluence on the outskirts of Allahabad, looks as if carnival has come. There are no temples here, but there are many flags marking the presence of pandas, a sect of debased Brahmins dedicated to plucking the faithful of every last rupee. Many of them have staked out little platforms in midstream where the waters may only be shin deep in summer. Boatmen bring the pilgrims out to them, and there is much shouting as each tries to entice a new boatload away from his rivals.

They are very shrewd judges of a customer's worth, and every ritual they offer has its correlated price – the crushing of grain, the arcane movements with stalks of corn, the pouring of milk, the immersion and the prayers. Quite openly, henchmen dredge up small coins from the riverbed in buckets while simple pilgrims are in the act of casting more money on the waters because they have been told that it is good for their souls. And the simplicities of faith know no bounds in this place. A boatload of super-jocks from Bombay is rowed out, each man stripping down to his Bermuda shorts or his Y-fronts before he bathes. For all his Old Harrovian loftiness, Jawaharlal Nehru willed that some of his ashes must be sprinkled here. In spite of the shabby commerce, there is something to lift the spirit at Sangam. A boatload of freshly bathed women glide back to the shore, their hands trailing dreamily in the water, their faces sublime. A youth sits passively with head bent, while a barber shaves his scalp except for one lock at the crown, which is left to show mourning for a father just dead. A figure in white robes picks his way quietly where the river runs just above the level of his feet, but because the sun has risen behind him and everything but his outline is dazzlingly indistinct, he seems to be walking on the water itself. Could this, perhaps, be the same trick of light that brought rumour of a miraculous Christ on the lake at Galilee?

The seething piety of Benares (a British corruption of the Mogul corruption of Varanasi, its old Hindu and now officially Indian name) has a longer history than that of anywhere else; indeed, there is some evidence for the local claim that this is the oldest city in the world, where faith flourished at least two thousand years before Christ. Buddha preached his first sermon on its outskirts, Islam still has a careful foothold here, but it is the myriad deities of the Hindus that make Benares feel like – even if statistically it is not – the most jam-packed city in India outside Calcutta.

There are forty thousand cycle rickshaws here, carrying the pilgrims and the tourists to the sacred areas and other sights. There is a university whose priceless deposit of Sanskrit texts was established by the British around a superheated Oxbridge quad. There is a maharajah's palace, whose collections of coaches and weaponry put both the royal stables at Buckingham Palace and the Tower armoury to shame. There is a distinguished seat of Indian musicology. There is a network of lanes in the bazaar, each scarcely wide enough for two people to pass, steaming with spices, discordant with shouts, dazzling with colour and mysterious with shadows, where, inspecting many purely Indian items of trade, I once picked up a very early and much mildewed edition of *Gulliver's Travels* – which seemed most appropriate, considering how far I had come.

And there is the waterfront, which must be the most romantic of all apart from those at Venice and Istanbul. Ganges runs here in a long crescent curve and Benares descends to the river from an escarpment down fifty-two separate ghats, each of which is a full cascade of steps. At the head of every ghat is a temple or a crumbling old palace, or some access to the city behind, where beggary lies in wait in leprous, mutilated or simply undernourished forms. Just before dawn, ghostly white shapes begin to steal down those ghats in ones and twos, early wakers wrapped in their sleeping sheets. There are scores at the water's edge before sunrise, hundreds by the time that fiery thing first lifts itself over the sand dunes on the opposite bank, thousands by eight o'clock, when it is already branding the world.

Along the whole curve of ghats, maybe two miles of them, men are standing in the river with their hands together in pre-Christian attitudes of prayer, women are doing modest wonders to themselves with soap and water beneath their flimsy clothes, and children are splashing and diving as though aquatics and not worship were the order of the day. Very old ladies gossip while, absent-mindedly, they bend double and purify brassware in rigmaroles of faith. Washermen flog garments clean against stone slabs, to the detriment of the cloth, then spread them to dry in gorgeous patchwork on the dusty slopes above. Wiry young men approach strangers and say, 'I give very good massage, O Babu, very nice,' not far from where glistening zealots higher up the steps are doing press-ups and wonderfully fluent kneebends. Everywhere walls are festooned with dung patties drying out for fuel. Some of the walls still bear the faded symbols of the birth-control programme that India launched long before Western ignoramuses believed everything they were told about the wickedness of Mrs Gandhi by self-interested people with political axes to grind.

The tourists direct their boatmen specifically towards the Manikarnika burning ghat, where relatives pray around stretchers bearing swaddled corpses awaiting their turn. Neat piles of logs stand criss-crossed ready for use, and workmen split tree trunks with axes and chisels, manufacturing more: sandalwood for the rich, neem for the poor, 440 kilograms for large people, 360 for somebody small, and about three hours for anyone to burn. The men who run the burning ghat belong to the distinctive caste of Doams, a rapacious crew whose chief has enriched himself enough to live in the grandest building along the river.

Some potential clients are too poor to pay for the wood, in which case the body is simply placed in the river, weighted with stones. It does not always decompose on the bottom: a long cloth-bound object floats out in midstream, with two vultures trying not to overbalance on top, while they peck through the bindings to get at the flesh. Rather a lot of disgusting things bobble about in the river here within inches of bathers who will assure you that some chemical property in this holy water does not allow germs to survive. And it is a fact that although all the great cholera epidemics of India, which have sometimes spread to Europe and North America, have started in Bengal and been borne up the Ganges by pilgrims, no form of sickness has yet been known to travel any distance downstream.

It is obviously possible to rationalise the veneration of this river and conclude that anything might be regarded with awe that is as much a matter of life and death to so many people as Ganges. In flowing through the three states of Uttar Pradesh, Bihar and Bengal, the river has a material bearing on one-third of India's entire population, many of whom would perish inside twelve months were it not for the moisture she provides. Those northern plains may be dreadful during the summer but at least they are viable because of the rich crops they bear in spring, over thousands of square miles that would be desert without the irrigation ditches and canals.

Captain Proby Cautley, of the Bengal Engineers, began to cut the main Ganges canal at Hardwar in 1842 and within half a century it had reached Allahabad, over 400 miles away. An unmitigated blessing in every sense, it has nonetheless had a dire effect upon the river's natural course by drawing off most of the water for controlled use. Even towards the end of April the canal still flows deeply while, a cockstride away, the true Ganges twists and turns miserably between ever-widening banks, a shallow mockery of her authentic self.

At that time of year there are places where the mainstream is a bare fifty feet across, the water nearly stagnant because its impetus has all but gone. At Kanpur, then, it is quite easy to wade from side to side, as people endlessly do, to reach their cultivations on the sand-banks. Ganges knows only two seasons of the year, the dry and the wet, and throughout the long months of the first she is steadily declining from the relatively brief but almighty inundation of the second.

The monsoon breaks about the beginning of June, and for four months after, the Cow That Gives Much Milk is transformed into a raging monster that sweeps everything out of its way. Villages are smashed in the tumult of brown water, crops are annihilated, and the loss of life in people and beasts is often very high. Landscapes that had glared with heat, in which the meagre thread of water was all but visibly evaporating day by day, are turned into gigantic inland seas several miles wide. So tremendously does the current flow that annually the Ganges alters her own water-course all over the place, leaving northern India with many strange loops and bends which she abandoned in headlong pursuit of short cuts to the east.

The rise in water-level during the rains is as devastating as the torrential flow. At Benares you can see the mark reached in 1978, when Ganges climbed fifty feet above her norm, submerging ghats and temples and flowing into the city itself, at a point where for several weeks she had become some ten miles wide. There is a railway bridge across the river near Patna, which needs ninety-three spans bearing two miles of track to ensure a safe passage during the monsoon months.

What with one thing and another, over most of her journey from the source to the sea, Ganges has an excellent claim to being the least navigable river of all. Above Allahabad, certainly, she either hasn't enough water to float a boat properly or she rushes so fiercely that no craft dares to put out. When Eric and Wanda Newby some years ago decided to make their way slowly down the Ganges, they spent the first few days pushing a punt from Hardwar through water rarely more than ankle deep and thereafter acknowledged that it was possible to boat only in fits and starts. A little later Sir Edmund Hillary came up from the sea in fine style with a jet-propelled craft that skimmed over all shallows, but this came to grief on the rocky riverbed somewhere below Devprayag.

Locals long ago learnt the limitations of navigation here. Up in the hills, just before Ganges flattens her descent to the plains, men sometimes ferry themselves across with the aid of an inflated buffalo skin, clasping the flatulent thing around its hindquarters and paddling for all they're worth. You see nothing else apart from the odd rowing boat until Allahabad, and not till Benares comes round the bend are cargo-carrying country boats a regular part of the river's life. They call them mahalia, and they have something to them of the Arab dhow, with prows closer to the water than the deck over the stern, rigged with lateens and a triangular rudder plunging straight down from the poop. So listless is the air over the Ganges Basin for much of the year that as often as not the sail is furled on its cross-jack, and the graceful black boat is moved very slowly along by men straining like galley slaves at heavy sweeps. They can take a full day to shift a few tons of grain no more than forty miles over the dry-season stillness of the Ganges' middle stretch.

Bursting with imperial energy, the British decided that this wasn't nearly good enough in their day, and in September 1828 despatched the brand-new steamboat *Hoogly* upstream from Calcutta to see how she would fare with her side-paddles and her thirty tons of fuel. She didn't do badly at all, reaching Allahabad in twenty-three days and coming back in fourteen, on a voyage of 787 miles each way. Within a few years improved versions of the *Hoogly* were running to a timetable between the two cities, enthusiastically backed by the Governor-General, Lord William Bentinck, but masterminded at East India House in London by the poet

Thomas Love Peacock, who earned his bread and butter as a Company official and became the resident expert on Ganges steam navigation.

Much of the cargo carried by the steamboats upstream consisted of wages for the imperial soldiery stationed along the river banks, or epaulettes for the 2nd Regiment at Ghazipur: coming downstream the steamers were likely to be loaded to the gunwales with more money, which in this case was the land revenue collected from subject Indians. But from time to time those high-minded Victorians, who believed bribery was wrong, would put aboard an outward-bound vessel things described on the bill of lading as 'valuable presents being returned to Nawab of Oudh'.

Ganges was always liable to interrupt the thrustful ways of the Raj, and groundings on any of the midstream sand-banks were a frequent occurrence. When one paddlesteamer went on the sand above Barh in 1838 it took over one thousand men to haul her off with hawsers. Yet it was another device introduced by the British, and not the river itself, which finished off the service. By 1859 the East India Railway from Calcutta had been flung as far as Cawnpore, and thereafter it was quicker to transport anything overland.

Today there is virtually no navigation with engines on the Ganges above Calcutta. The exception is at Patna, where even in summer the river runs wide and deep past the chief city of Bihar. There the sternwheelers *Hebe*, *Palta* and *Bhadra*, which may have seen better days on the Mississippi, belch smoke over the sand-banks as they trudge along with passengers making for Sonepur a few miles away on the farther shore.

Not long afterwards, Ganges moves to the south at last, as she passes into Bengal close to India's border with Bangladesh. The flatness of her surroundings doesn't alter much, but now the growth on either hand becomes lusher, with palm trees beginning to screen villages from the boatman's view until he is up to their banks. And on the very boundary of the two Indian states, at a point which is also but a stone's throw from Bangladesh, Ganges has once again been manipulated by engineers for a redistribution of her strength.

For 100 years or more, committees had intermittently considered how best she should be handled here, but it wasn't until 1962 that work began on the construction of the Farakka Barrage, not until 1975 that it was effectively complete. This had long been seen as desirable because of the river's own waywardness, which coincided with her second alteration of names. Hereabouts the word Ganges again disappears from the maps, while Bhagirathi is reinstated. Until the eighteenth century it was this Bhagirathi which carried the mainstream flow from Bihar towards the Bay of Bengal, past all the places thought most sacred by good Hindus. Then the river began to channel more and more of herself into what had hitherto been a sidestream, the Padma, which ran on to the east; and eventually the size of the two courses was almost exactly reversed.

The problem was that the British had by then established their seat of government in India at Calcutta, which duly became the biggest city in their whole empire after London. And as the great flow of water down the Bhagirathi (which later becomes the Hooghly) began to diminish, the British could see their capital and chief port one day being left high and dry. Hence the numerous discussions in committee, which outlasted the Raj, before anything was done. The irony is that it was independent Indians from Delhi who had to handle unforeseen political repercussions in the end, when Farakka was at last built. A number of formulae have been adopted to ensure that enough Ganges water proceeds along the Padma to satisfy

Bangladesh's needs until the river's individual identity is lost at its junctions with the Brahmaputra and the Meghna above the teeming watercourses of the Ganges delta, but the two nations still bicker about whether each is getting its fair share.

The Bhagirathi has been revived by Farakka's judicious intervention in the processes of nature; and so has the Hooghly lower down, which ten years ago was in danger of silting up completely. Small Bengali townships from which everything but the ancient piety seemed to have receded may yet have a new lease of life, and I am happy to report that Calcutta itself seems fractionally better off than when I wrote a book about it in 1971, with diesel-engined ferries across the river now and the makings of a second Hooghly bridge a mile below Howrah, as well as the tunnelling for an underground system and a fleet of mini-buses to reinforce those tormented doubledeckers which have been the best testimony of all to the durability of Leyland.

The city is signalled long before you get there by the appearance of chimneys belonging to the infamous jute mills of Bengal, which poke up out of modest jungle by the riverside. By and by, some old imperial silhouettes emerge from the sopping and blistering haze – the Victoria Memorial, the Writers' Building, the second biggest cricket ground in the world – and behind them is the most deprived but also the most vital community known to man, where death on the streets is a matter of course, where riots and tram-burning take place any day of the week. All this is dominated by the crushing mass of the Howrah Bridge, whose mesh of steelwork is habitually four feet longer by day than by night under the expansive summer sun.

Below that bridge the genuflections of faith are still profound; grisly at Kalighat, where a goat is beheaded each morning to appease Herself. But from now on the river accepts the nautical and commercial role that excited Conrad in 1885, when he sailed up the Hooghly as mate in the *Tilkhurst*, bound from Singapore to Dundee. Country boats lumber up and down, some carrying enormous cargoes of hay. Outriggers flick by, manned by fishermen hunting hilsa, which resembles the mackerel and is as rich in oil. And there are ocean-going vessels now, warping their way into Kidderpore Docks under flags of convenience and otherwise, owned by all the tramping companies that still send ships upon the seven seas. Since 1977 a new port at Haldia, fifty-six miles downstream and capable of handling almost anything afloat, has been functioning fully; but 1980 even so saw 700 vessels come all the way up to Kidderpore.

Only 126 miles of the river remain between those docks and the sea, and every inch is the especial province of a remarkable corps of men. It was Kipling who wrote that 'Almost any pilot will tell you that his work is more difficult than you imagine, but the pilots of the Hooghly know that they have the most difficult river on earth running through their hands; and they say nothing.' The difficulty is compounded of many things, the least of which is the occasional winter fog. Life on the bridge of a sixteen-thousand-ton tramp steamer can be nervous when one of the Hooghly's tidal bores rushes up from the sea, still six feet high when it reaches Calcutta, so that bathers have to be warned in advance to avoid being swept from the ghats.

It is the powerful current at any time, and its effect on the topography of the river, that makes the qualification of the Hooghly pilots such a long and thorough business; five years of training before a man is allowed to take any vessel out, the best part of twenty years before he is thought fit to con vessels with the deepest permissible draught. The current can run to eight knots at the ebb during the monsoon, and even during the dry season its force is sufficient to shift whole sand-banks from one position to another between tides. The worst of these, the Balari Bar just above Haldia, is four and a half miles long in midstream, and many vessels have foundered on that; soundings are taken twice every day with both Asdic and leadline. Another awkward customer is higher up at Hugli Point, where the channel turns through ninety degrees with a sidestream flowing in at right angles to the turn, so that your bows are often in slack water while your stern is in the tide. For all these hazards the pilots have a simple rule of the road: if your engines pack up, steer for the bank and put your nose ashore, where you'll be out of harm's way in a current that doesn't rush as fiercely as in midstream.

They are men with an old-fashioned taste for discipline (they ask politely what's become of it these days among the British who, they gather, don't much behave like their mentors of old). Their high skills are rewarded more handsomely than those of anyone in the republic with the exception of the other pilots belonging to Air India. Thus armed with the confidence of a recognised elite, they coolly bring the big vessels to and fro and praise God for the blessing bestowed by Farakka, which is beginning to flush the accumulated silt of two centuries from the Hooghly, already reducing the number of tidal bores from a peak of about 160 days in the year.

Down from Kidderpore go the ships, passing the Botanical Gardens to starboard and the Bata Shoe Factory to port, nosing through the river's treacherous eddies and swirls, anchoring three times until flood tides have turned, then cruising serenely on through proper Lord Jim jungle to the Bay of Bengal. After Haldia has fallen away astern, the pear-drop shape of Sagar Island comes out of the haze, the last place of pilgrimage on the river that has glorified them all, where the mythical king's sixty thousand sons were at last set free for paradise.

Sandheads lies just beyond, where the pilot vessel waits, and to the east stretches the vast swamp of the delta with its innumerable openings to the sea which the cartographers, abandoning their struggle for precision, simply term the Mouths of the Ganges. Thus the mother of the world gives herself to Neptune with an amplitude that, so the mariners say, stains the ocean 400 miles out into the Bay.

She has been all things to all men since she came out of her ice cave in the Himalaya – highway and sewer, irrigator and drinking fountain, burial ground and source of food, washtub and bath. But never for one moment has she been anything less than an inspiration to those millions ladling her sacred liquids over themselves; a promise of better things to come. What Ganges really means, above all else, is best described in the words of a witness during the enquiry into the disaster at Allahabad in 1954. 'People said beforehand, "If we are killed we shall attain salvation. If we escape death we shall go home. We shall be gainers in either case. Those who die at such a sacred spot, at such an auspicious moment, would be very lucky. We wish to have the good fortune." '

NOTES ON THE CONTRIBUTORS

Bruce Chatwin

Born in Sheffield in 1940. Was a director of Sotheby's before resigning to devote himself to writing. He is the author of three widely acclaimed books – *In Patagonia, The Viceroy of Ouidah* and *On the Black Hill*. Has spent many years studying nomads, and his own life is correspondingly peripatetic.

Ronald Fraser

Born in Hamburg in 1930. Fluent Spanish-speaker and author of *In Hiding* and *Blood of Spain*, a history of the Spanish Civil War. Was consultant on Granada TV's highly regarded Spanish Civil War series. Lives in London.

Alexander Frater

Born in Port Vila, Vanuatu, in the South West Pacific in 1937. He has contributed to many publications, including *Punch* and *The New Yorker*, and is at present deputy editor of *The Observer Magazine*. Author of *Stopping-Train Britain*. Lives in London.

Geoffrey Grigson

Born in Pelynt, Cornwall, in 1905. His many distinguished publications include two volumes of *Collected Poems* and *Notes from an Odd Country*, a book about France – where he lives for four months of the year. The rest of the time he is domiciled in Wiltshire.

Colin Jones

Born in London in 1936. Was a member of the Royal Ballet, a soldier and a farm labourer before becoming a full-time photographer in 1962. Has worked for *The Sunday Times* and *The Observer*, as well as many international magazines. Held a major exhibition – called 'The Black House' – at the Photographers' Gallery, and illustrated a book on Leningrad. Lives in London.

Norman Lewis

Born in Enfield. Educated at Enfield Grammar School and spent World War II serving with the Intelligence Corps. Has travelled widely and written extensively for *The Observer* and *The Sunday Times*. Author of numerous books, including *A Dragon Apparent, Golden Earth* and *Naples '44*. Lives in Essex.

Geoffrey Moorhouse

Born in Bolton, Lancashire, in 1931. Worked as a journalist – he was chief features writer of *The Guardian* for seven years – before becoming a full-time author. His many publications include *Calcutta* and, recently, *Lord's*, a profile of the famous cricket ground. Lives in Yorkshire.

Libby Purves

Born in London in 1950. The daughter of a diplomat, she was educated in Thailand, Israel,

France, South Africa, Tunbridge Wells and Oxford. Presented the *Today* programme on Radio 4 and *Choices* on BBC 1. Was editor of *The Tatler* for six months. She is author of *Britain at Play* and the editor of *Adventures Under Sail*.

Piers Paul Read

Born in Beaconsfield in 1941. Winner of numerous literary awards. His books include *The Junkers, Monk Dawson, The Professor's Daughter, The Train Robbers* (non-fiction) and *A Married Man*. Lives in Yorkshire.

Paul Theroux

Born in Medford, Massachusetts, in 1941. Taught at the University of Singapore. His novels include *Saint Jack, The Family Arsenal* and *The Mosquito Coast*, his travel books the classic *The Great Railway Bazaar* and, more recently, *The Kingdom by the Sea*. Lives in London.

Nicholas Wollaston

Born in Gloucestershire in 1926. Has written four novels, four travel books and a biography – the life of Augustin Courtauld, the Polar explorer. Has also written extensively for *The Observer, The Sunday Times* and *The Sunday Telegraph*. Lives in Suffolk.

INDEX

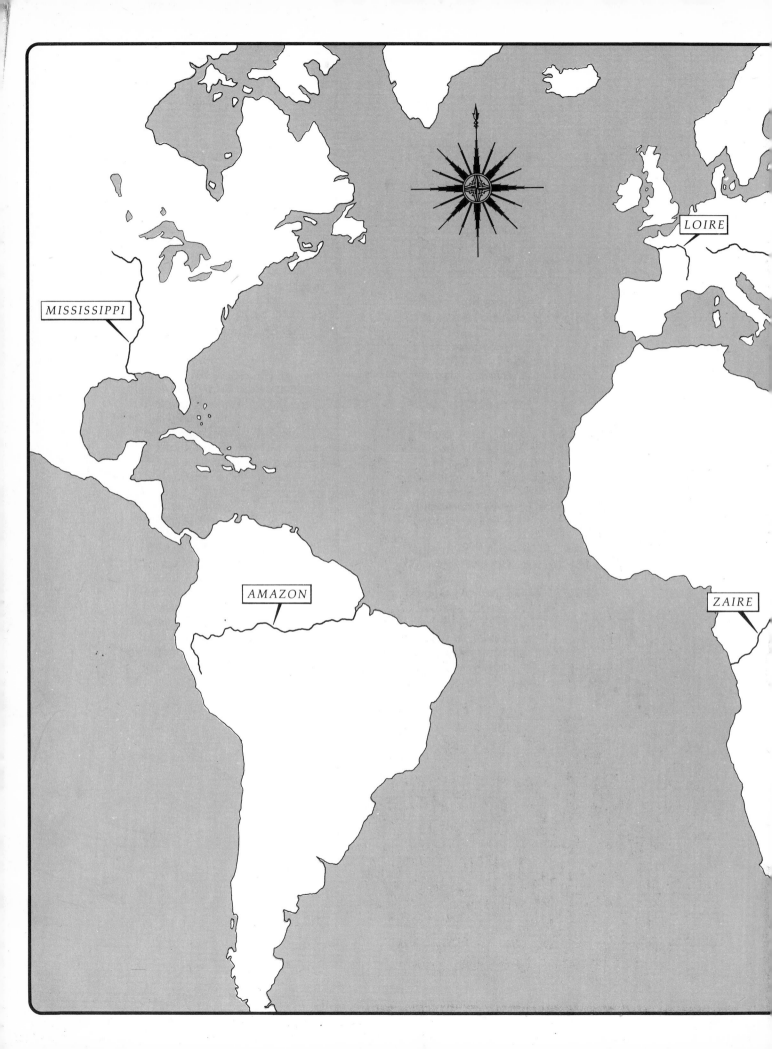